THE FLORIDA GUN OWNER'S Guide

Who
can bear arms?

❖

Where
are guns forbidden?

❖

When
can you shoot to kill?

by *Donna Lea Hawley*
and Alan Korwin

illustrations by Gregg Myers and Ralph Richardson

BLOOMFIELD PRESS

Phoenix, Arizona

BLOOMFIELD PRESS

12629 N. Tatum #440
Phoenix, AZ 85032
602-996-4020 Offices
602-494-0679 Fax
1-800-707-4020 Order Hotline
www.bloomfieldpress.com

ISBN: 1-889632-00-7
Library of Congress Catalog Card Number: 96-86454

ATTENTION

Firearms Training Instructors, Clubs, Organizations, Educators and all other interested parties: Call us for information on quantity discounts!

To Order: For single copies or for wholesale shipments, call 1-800-707-4020, or write to us at the address above.

FOR UPDATES: Send us a self-addressed stamped envelope or check our website. Was a new law passed yesterday? Call us at 1-800-707-4020

Every gun owner needs this book—
"It doesn't make sense to own a gun and not know the rules."

Printed and bound in the United States of America

10 9 8 7 6 5 4 3 2 1

TABLE OF CONTENTS

ILLUSTRATIONS

ACKNOWLEDGMENTS

This book is very much a result of the help we received, great and small, from the good people who provided their thoughts, answered our endless questions, and shared resources with us. Several individuals in government positions were very helpful, public servants in the true sense, but asked not to be credited directly, perhaps a telling commentary on the times. You know who you are, and thank you once again for all the information and your great cooperation.

Michael P. Anthony, Attorney

Bill Ashford, WOCA-AM Radio 1370

Charles S. Berrane, Firearm Training Counselor

Sandra Crouch

Candice M. DeBarr, Author

David B. Etherington, Attorney

Dr. Dave Gowan

Marion Hammer, President, United Sportsmen of Florida

Jim Hatfield, American Firearms Industry

Victor Heyes

Bob Hollingsworth

Lt. Col. Randy Hopkins, Fla. Game and Fresh Water Fish Comm.

Cheryl and Tyler Brittany Korwin

Irving and Shirley Korwin

Frank Kozlowski, South Florida Firearms Owners

Jordan Meschkow, Registered Patent Attorney

Becky Miller, Legislative Analyst, Florida Legislative Services Division

Andy Molchan, President, American Firearms Industry

Larry Tahler, Executive Director, American Self Defense Institute

Paul Updike

Albert Wehlberg, Past President, Florida Shooting Sports Association

Ian C. White, Legal Research

Preston T. Robertson, Fla. Game and Fresh Water Fish Comm.

Clark Vargas, President, Florida Shooting Sports Association

Michael Weissberg, Certified Firearms Trainer

David Witenstein, Certified Firearms Trainer

In preparing this book we were impressed with the meticulous and thorough job the Florida Dept. of State, Division of Licensing, is doing in administering the concealed weapons license requirements.

The publicly available information provided by the Florida Dept. of Law Enforcement was invaluable in producing this book.

Cover Design by Ralph Richardson

Illustrations by Gregg Myers and Ralph Richardson

Book design by Alan Korwin

PREFACE

Florida has strict gun laws. You have to obey the laws. There are serious penalties for breaking the rules.

Many gun owners don't know all the rules. Some have the wrong idea of what the rules are. It doesn't make sense to own a gun and not know the rules.

Here at last is a comprehensive book, in plain English, about the laws and regulations which control firearms in Florida.

This book is published under the full protection of the First Amendment with the expressed understanding that you, not we, are completely responsible for your own actions.

The One-Glaring-Error theory says there's at least one glaring error hidden in any complex piece of work. This book is no different. Watch out for it.

FOREWORD • WARNING! • DON'T MISS THIS!

This book is not a substitute for the law. You are fully accountable under the exact wording and current interpretations of all applicable laws and regulations when you deal with firearms under any circumstances.

Many people find laws hard to understand, and gathering all the relevant ones is a lot of work. This book helps you with these chores. Collected in one volume are the principal state laws controlling gun use in Florida.

In addition, the laws and other regulations are expressed in regular conversational terms for your convenience, and cross-referenced to the statutes. While great care has been taken to accomplish this with a high degree of accuracy, **no guarantee of accuracy is expressed or implied, and the explanatory sections of this book are not to be considered as legal advice or a restatement of law.** In explaining the general meanings of the laws, using plain English, differences inevitably arise, so **you must always check the actual laws.** The authors and publisher expressly disclaim any liability whatsoever arising out of reliance on information found in this book. New laws and regulations may be enacted at any time by the authorities. **The authors and publisher make no representation that this book includes all requirements and prohibitions which may exist. This book covers state laws—local laws are not covered.**

This book concerns the gun laws as they apply to law-abiding private residents in the state of Florida only. It is not intended to and does not describe most situations relating to licensed gun dealers, museums or educational institutions, local or federal military personnel, American Indians, foreign nationals, the police or other peace officers, any person summoned by a peace officer to help in the performance of official duties, persons with special licenses (including collectors), non-residents, persons with special permits or authorizations, bequests or intestate succession, anyone under indictment, felons, prisoners, escapees, dangerous or repetitive offenders, criminal street gang members, delinquent, incorrigible or unsupervised juveniles, government employees, or any other people restricted or prohibited from firearm possession.

While this book discusses possible criminal consequences of improper gun use, it avoids most issues related to deliberate gun crimes. This means that certain laws are excluded, or not explained in the text. Some examples are: criminally negligent homicide and capital murder; manslaughter; concealment of stolen firearms; enhanced penalties for commission of crimes with firearms, including armed robbery, burglary, theft, kidnapping, drug offenses and assault; smuggling firearms into public aircraft; taking a weapon from a peace officer; possession of contraband; possession of a firearm in a prison by a prisoner; false application for a firearm; removal of a body after a shooting; drive by shootings; and this is only a partial list.

The main relevant parts of Florida statutes that relate to private gun ownership and use are reproduced in Appendix D. These are formally known as *Florida Statutes.* Other state laws which may apply, such as Hunting Laws and official agency regulations, are discussed, but these laws are *not* reproduced. Key federal laws are discussed, but the laws themselves are *not* reproduced. Case law decisions, which affect the interpretation of the statutes, are generally *not* included.

FIREARMS LAWS ARE SUBJECT TO CHANGE WITHOUT NOTICE. You are strongly urged to consult with a qualified attorney and local authorities to determine the current status and applicability of the law to specific situations which you may encounter. The proper authorities are in Appendix C.

Guns are serious business and require the highest level of responsibility from you. **What the law says and what the authorities and courts do aren't always an exact match.** You must remember that each legal case is different and frequently lacks prior court precedents. A decision to prosecute a case and the charges brought may involve a degree of discretion from the authorities involved. Sometimes, there just isn't a plain, clear-cut answer you can rely upon. **ALWAYS ERR ON THE SIDE OF SAFETY.**

Note to this Historic First Edition

Never before have Florida's gun laws been released in a single edition. As the earliest existing compiled copy of state gun laws this is guaranteed to age from the moment of its release. When future generations look back at this first edition, it will represent "the way things used to be," as it seems quite likely that new laws and court cases will change the landscape in time to come.

That will make this edition quite a conversation piece and perhaps of collectible value, but it also brings out a dilemma you should not ignore. The accuracy of this book will diminish with time, and the historical value of its contents is not a substitute for current information about gun laws.

Keep in mind that first editions, by their very nature, may have errors which are only detected after their initial release. It is the book's readers who will eventually fine tune the contents, and we encourage you to notify us about anything you feel is inaccurate, incomplete or in need of attention in any way. Despite all our efforts at completeness and accuracy, we recognize that we aren't perfect and that corrections may be needed. You must recognize this too.

This book will be updated periodically, and news about updates is available from the publisher, Bloomfield Press. You are invited to send us an old-fashioned stamped self-addressed envelope which we will fill and return when news of updates is available.

If you believe you have found an error or item needing adjustment, notify the publisher. A free copy of this book will be provided to any reader whose comments are used in the next edition.

Special Note on Pending Legislation

Bills have been proposed by law makers nationally who would:

- Outlaw specific or classes of firearms by name, by operating characteristics, by price range or by appearance
- Restrict the amount of ammunition a gun can hold and the devices for feeding ammunition
- Restrict the number of firearms and the amount of ammunition a person may buy or own
- Require proficiency testing and periodic licensing
- Register firearms and owners nationally
- Use taxes to limit firearm and ammunition ownership
- Create new liabilities for firearm owners, manufacturers, dealers, parents and persons involved in firearms accidents
- Outlaw keeping firearms loaded or not locked away
- Censor classified ads for firearms, eliminate firearms publications and outlaw any dangerous speech or publication
- Melt down firearms that are confiscated by police
- Prohibit gun shows and abolish hunting
- Deny or criminalize civil rights for government-promised security
- Repeal the Second Amendment to the Constitution

In contrast, less attention has been paid to laws that would:

- Mandate school-based safety training
- Provide general self-defense awareness and training
- Encourage personal responsibility in resisting crime
- Protect citizens who stand up and act against crime
- Guarantee citizens' right to travel legally armed for personal safety
- Fix the conditions which generate hard-core criminals
- Assure sentencing of serious criminals, increase the percentage of sentences actually served, provide more prison space and permanently remove habitual criminals from society
- Improve rehabilitation and reduce repeat offenses
- Reduce plea bargaining and parole abuses
- Close legal loopholes and reform criminal justice malpractice
- Reform the juvenile justice system
- Improve law enforcement quality and efficiency
- Establish and strengthen victims' rights and protection
- Hold the rights of all American citizens in unassailable esteem
- Provide for the common defense and buttress the Constitution

Some experts have noted that easy-to-enact but ineffectual "feel good" laws are sometimes pursued instead of the much tougher course of laws and social changes that would reduce crime and its root causes. Many laws aim at disarming citizens while ignoring the fact that gun possession by criminals is already strictly illegal and largely unenforced. Increasing attacks on the Constitution and civil liberties are threatening freedoms Americans have always had. You are advised to become aware of any new laws which may be enacted. Contact your legislators to express your views on proposed legislation.

To all those who possess and use firearms
safely and legally

THE RIGHT TO BEAR ARMS 1

In the United States of America, people have always had the right to bear arms. The Second Amendment to the United States Constitution is the historic foundation of this right to have and use guns. The Second Amendment is entitled *The Right To Keep And Bear Arms*. This is what it says:

> "A well regulated Militia, being necessary to the security of a free State, the right of the people to keep and bear Arms, shall not be infringed."

The intentions of the revolutionaries who drafted the Constitution were clear at the time. It was this right to bear arms that allowed those people 200 years ago to break away from British rule. An armed populace was a precondition for independence and freedom from oppressive government. The founders of the United States of America were unambiguous and unequivocal in their intent:

No free man shall be debarred the use of arms.
–Thomas Jefferson

The Constitution shall never be construed to authorize Congress to prevent the people of the United States, who are peaceable citizens, from keeping their own arms.
–Samuel Adams

Little more can reasonably be aimed at with respect to the people at large than to have them properly armed.
–Alexander Hamilton

Americans have the right and advantage of being armed.
–James Madison

The great object is that every man be armed.
Everyone who is able may have a gun.
–Patrick Henry

Today the issue is controversial and emotionally charged. There are powerful and vocal groups on all sides of the topic of guns. Some people have taken to saying that the Second Amendment doesn't mean what it always used to mean, and there have been calls to repeal it. The Supreme Court has been mostly quiet on the subject, and its few pronouncements have been used to support all sides of the debate. Importantly, all 50 states recognize a person's right to act in self-defense, completely apart from firearms debates.

The Second Amendment of course means what it always used to mean, which explains the armed populace we observe today. This is also seen in the fact that most states have the right to keep and bear arms imbedded in their own Constitutions, often in terms more direct than the wording in the Bill of Rights itself. If our Second Amendment guarantee was ever torn asunder, the state constitutions would still be in place. This is what Florida has to say on the subject:

Florida State Constitution
ARTICLE 1, SECTION 8(a).
Right to bear arms

The right of the people to keep and bear arms in defense of themselves and of the lawful authority of the state shall not be infringed, except that the manner of bearing arms may be regulated by law.

Nothing in Florida law may conflict with our fundamental creed, the U.S. Constitution, and so the right to bear arms is passed down to Floridians, as it is to the people of all the states in the union. The states, however, have passed laws to regulate the arms that people bear within their boundaries. That's what this book is all about.

INTRODUCTION TO THE STATE GUN LAWS

The official, complete set of Florida's written statutes is called *Florida Statutes*. This is published in a set of five hardcover books. It is widely available in libraries.

Florida's statutes are arranged in *chapters*, with each chapter covering related points of law. The majority of Florida's "gun laws" (they are never actually called that) can be found in chapter 790 of *Florida Statutes*. In addition to chapter 790, Florida has gun laws in at least 41 other chapters of its state statutes.

Each chapter is divided into named and numbered *sections*. The legislature names the laws only for convenience, the names are not law, and as you'll notice, the names often do not reflect the meaning or content of a given section.

Each of the sections, abbreviated "*s.*" may be thought of as one law, although one section may control many things. The section number has three elements: the chapter number, a period, and the number for the particular law. One of the sections on self defense, for example, is s. 776.012. You say it like this, "Use of force in defense of person, section seven seventy six point oh one two," and you'll find it in Chapter 776. Some folks might say "point oh twelve." Being able to confidently say the section number of a law has a sort of ring to it, and carries a certain clout, which is part of its design. Some people find it intimidating to try at first, but being able to cite a law out loud has great power.

Sections may have layers of *subsections*, which are numbered with numerals and lower case letters in typical index fashion. Each subsection is listed in parenthesis, and you will find as many as three stacked after the basic section number.

As an example, the place that says you may take training with a state- or NRA-certified instructor as part of the qualifications for a concealed weapons license is s. 790.06(2)(h)(7). It's important to remember that *The Florida Gun Owner's Guide* makes its citations to the law's section number only, so that this example would appear in the text as s. 790.06. The actual subsection is easy to identify, listed in order, in Appendix D.

Copies of the law are available that include brief summaries of cases decided by Florida courts. These are called *Annotated Statutes*. Two publishers, Westlaw and The Harrison Co., have sets available with about 60 volumes each, and one or both sets are available in law libraries, at university law schools, court houses, and in larger public libraries. Law offices worth their salt keep a copy in the office. Full copies of the precedent-setting court decisions can generally be found in the set of books known as *Southern Reports*.

The decision to publish a case and thereby set precedent is not automatic, and only the officially published cases count for anything. It is a little known and rarely examined process, allowing politically charged decisions to take control, that may have as much effect as acts of the legislature.

In addition to *Annotated Statutes* there is a publication called *Florida Jurisprudence*. This is also a large multi-volume set that is available in libraries. It sets out in narrative form the various areas of law and is thoroughly footnoted to give you cross references to statutes and cases. If you like this sort of thing, it's a great read. Try it and see.

REASONS FOR FLORIDA'S GUN LAWS

Florida's legislature has declared that as a matter of public policy it is necessary to promote firearms safety and to curb and prevent the use of firearms in crime and by incompetent persons. This must be done without prohibiting the lawful use of firearms in defense of life, home, and property, and use for target practice, hunting and other lawful purposes. See s. 790.25 for the letter of the law.

Florida criminal law includes a list of reasons for its existence in s. 775.012, all of which have direct impact on gun ownership and use:

1–To prohibit conduct which might harm people;

2–To give fair warning of conduct which is against the law and the penalties involved;

3–To define the acts and intentions which are crimes;

4–To organize crimes by how bad they are, and to match the penalty to the crime;

5–To safeguard behavior that is legal and limit condemnation of behavior which isn't criminal;

6–To deter crime, and provide for rehabilitation and punishment as needed.

Florida Statutes Chapters That Contain Gun Laws:

Chapter   27   State Attorneys; Public Defenders; Related Offices

Chapter   39   Proceedings Relating to Juveniles

Chapter 112   Public Officers and Employees; General Provisions

Chapter 125   County Government

Chapter 166   Municipalities

Chapter 230   District School System

Chapter 240   Postsecondary Education

Chapter 242   Specialized State Educational Institutions

Chapter 252   Emergency Management

Chapter 258   State Parks and Preserves

Chapter 281   Safety and Security Services

Chapter 285   Indian Reservations and Affairs

Chapter 316   Motor Vehicles

Chapter 321   Highway Patrol

Chapter 354   Special Officers for Carriers

Chapter 370   Saltwater Fisheries

Chapter 372   Wildlife

Chapter 493   Private Investigative, Private Security, and Repossession Services

Chapter 552   Manufacture, Distribution, and Use of Explosives
Chapter 626   Insurance Field Representatives and Operations
Chapter 705   Lost or Abandoned Property
Chapter 713   Liens
Chapter 772   Civil Remedies for Criminal Practices
Chapter 775   Crimes Definitions; General Penalties; Registration of Criminals
Chapter 776   Justifiable Use of Force
Chapter 784   Assault; Battery; Culpable Negligence
Chapter 790   Weapons and Firearms
Chapter 810   Burglary and Trespass
Chapter 812   Theft, Robbery, and Related Crimes
Chapter 828   Animals: Cruelty; Sales; Animal Enterprise Protection
Chapter 843   Obstructing Justice
Chapter 860   Offenses Concerning Aircraft, Motor Vehicles, Vessels, and Railroads
Chapter 870   Affrays; Riots; Routs; Unlawful Assemblies
Chapter 895   Offenses Concerning Racketeering and Illegal Debts
Chapter 901   Arrests
Chapter 916   Mentally Deficient and Mentally Ill Defendants
Chapter 933   Search and Inspection Warrants
Chapter 943   Department of Law Enforcement
Chapter 944   State Correctional System
Chapter 947   Parole Commission
Chapter 948   Probation and Community Control
Chapter 951   County and Municipal Prisoners
Chapter 985   Delinquency; Interstate Compact on Juveniles

The main relevant sections of all these laws, and related cross-referenced sections, are printed in this book in Appendix D. In addition, remember that "the law" includes many things that are not statutes passed by the legislature, and may not be covered in detail in this book, including court decisions, official regulations, common law, policies and more. Guns have become so well regulated in America that it strains the ability of anyone to know all the requirements.

A Word About Federal Law

The Florida Gun Owner's Guide covers federal laws that are directly related to your right to keep and bear arms. This is only a small portion of all federal gun laws.

Federal law generally does not control the day-to-day details of how you can carry a firearm in any given state, or the rules for self defense and crime resistance, or where you can go for target practice. The individual states control these things. Federal law focuses on the commercial aspects, interstate transportation, certain prohibited weapons, prohibited possessors, arming the proper authorities, crimes against the nation and other specifically defined areas.

Many people think that federal laws are "higher" than state laws, or that they somehow come first. Federal and state laws control different things. Lawyers would say they have differing jurisdictions. The states and the feds each have control over their respective areas. They may also disagree on exactly where those lines are drawn.

WHAT IS A FIREARM?

Florida gun law sets out key definitions in s. 790.001. A *firearm* is defined as:

> "any weapon (including a starter gun) which will, is designed to, or may readily be converted to expel a projectile by the action of an explosive; the frame or receiver of any such weapon; a firearm muffler or firearm silencer; any destructive device; or any machine gun. The term "firearm" does not include an antique firearm unless the antique firearm is used in the commission of a crime."

Weapon is defined as any:

> "dirk, metallic knuckles, slungshot, billie, tear gas gun, chemical weapon or device, or other deadly weapon except a firearm or a common pocketknife."

In this book, the words *gun, firearm* and *arms* are used interchangeably to refer to all handguns and long guns. When you see the terms *handgun, rifle, shotgun, long gun, machine gun, muzzleloader, semiautomatic pistol* or *semiauto,* or *revolver,* the reference is to that specific type of firearm only. The word *weapon* is used in the common sense to include guns, unless the non-gun category of weapons is the subject, which will be made apparent in the text.

A *destructive device* is basically an explosive, incendiary or poison gas device, or a firearm with a bore greater than .50 caliber (one-half inch), but does not include shotguns, ammunition or ammunition components. (See the full technical descriptions in Chapter 3, which includes federal details.).

An *antique firearm* is

1–one made before 1919 (including any matchlock, flintlock, percussion cap, or similar early type of ignition system);

2–a replica of such a firearm regardless of the date of manufacture; or

3–any firearm manufactured before 1919 using fixed ammunition, for which ammunition is no longer manufactured or readily available in the U.S.

A *machine gun* is any firearm which can shoot more than one shot automatically, without manually reloading, by a single function of the trigger.

WHO CAN BEAR ARMS IN FLORIDA?

An adult in Florida may have a gun except:

1–It is unlawful under state law for any of the following categories of people to own or have in their control any firearm or electric weapon, or to carry a concealed weapon (including a tear gas gun or chemical weapon as defined by law):

- Anyone who has committed a felony, or anyone who has committed a delinquent act that would be a felony for an adult (s. 790.23);

- Anyone who has committed a felony against the United States (s. 790.23);

- Anyone who has committed a delinquent act in another state, territory, or country that would be a felony if committed by an adult, and which was punishable by more than one year in prison (s. 790.23);

- Anyone who has committed a felony in another state, territory, or country which was punishable by more than one year in prison (s. 790.23);

- Anyone who is a career criminal as defined in s. 775.084 (s. 790.235);

  Note that the prohibition in the five categories above do not apply if you have had your civil rights properly restored, as covered in s. 790.23;

- Anyone who is on probation, unless authorized by the court with the consent of the probation officer (s. 948.03);

- A person who has been judged mentally incompetent, who is addicted to the use of narcotics or any similar drug, or who is a habitual or chronic alcoholic (s. 790.25);
- Any patient of any hospital providing mental health services (s. 394.458);
- *Vagrants* and other *undesirable persons* as defined in s. 856.02, (s. 790.25);
- A person in or around a *place of nuisance* as defined in s. 823.05, which includes a place of prostitution or a place where illegal gambling is held, unless you are there for law enforcement or some other lawful purpose (s. 790.25)
- Minors under 18 (s. 790.22, many special conditions apply, see the special section on juveniles);
- Anyone who is impaired by alcohol (.10 blood alcohol level) or by drugs may not shoot a firearm or hold a loaded firearm in their hand (s. 790.151).
- New for 1998, a person under a current, final injunction restraining acts of domestic violence may not have custody, care, possession or control of a firearm or ammunition (a class 1 misdemeanor under s. 790.233, making you subject to arrest under s. 901.15). However, the injunction must, on its face, indicate the firearm and ammunition restriction and penalty (s. 741.30). The law states that, in order to remain in step with federal policy, this law does not apply to the proper authorities, while performing official duties.

The Federal Prohibited Possessors List

You may be also be prohibited from having a gun under federal laws designed to keep weapons out of the hands of criminals. These overriding restrictions are listed in Section 8 of the Firearms Transaction Record, Form 4473, which must be completed when you buy a gun from a federally licensed dealer. It is commonly referred to as the *prohibited possessors list.* Federal law prohibits having, shipping, transporting or receiving a gun by anyone who:

- Is charged with or has been convicted of a crime which carries more than a one-year sentence (except two-year state misdemeanors);
- Is a fugitive from justice;
- Unlawfully uses or is addicted to marijuana, a depressant, a stimulant or a narcotic drug;
- Is mentally defective;
- Is mentally incompetent;
- Is committed to a mental institution;
- Has been dishonorably discharged from the armed forces;
- Has renounced U.S. citizenship;
- Is an illegal alien;
- Is under a court order restraining harassment, stalking or threatening of an intimate partner or partner's child;
- Has been convicted of a misdemeanor domestic-violence offense as described by federal law (for more on this new addition to federal law see Chapter 7; see also s. 741.28 for the state description).

In filling out a Firearm Transaction Record form you state that you are not in any of these categories. It's a five-year federal felony to make false statements on a Firearms Transaction Record form, and it's illegal to knowingly provide a firearm to a prohibited possessor.

The Proper Authorities

In addition to their right to bear arms as private individuals, the following people may have authority to bear arms at times or in ways which other people could not. For the letter of the law see s. 790.25.

1–Members of the Militia, National Guard, Florida State Defense Force, Army, Navy, Air Force, Marine Corps, Coast Guard, organized reserves, and other armed forces of the state and of the United States, when on duty, when training or preparing themselves for military duty, or while subject to recall or mobilization;

2–Citizens of this state subject to duty in the Armed Forces under s. 2, Art. X of the State Constitution, under *Florida Statutes* chapters 250 and 251, and under federal laws, when on duty or when training or preparing themselves for military duty;

3– Persons carrying out or training for emergency management duties under chapter 252;

4– Sheriffs, marshals, prison or jail wardens, policemen, Florida highway patrolmen, wildlife officers, revenue officers, forest officials, special officers appointed under the provisions of *Florida Statutes* chapter 354, and other peace and law enforcement officers and their deputies and assistants and full-time paid peace officers of other states, and agents of the federal government who are carrying out official duties while in this state;

5–Officers or employees of the state or United States duly authorized to carry a concealed weapon;

6–Guards or messengers of common carriers, express companies, armored-car carriers, mail carriers, banks and other financial institutions while actually employed in and about the shipment, transportation, or delivery of any money, treasure, bullion, bonds, or other thing of value within this state;

7–Investigators employed by the public defenders of the state, while actually carrying out official duties, provided such investigators:

    (a) Are employed full time,

    (b) Meet the official training standards for firearms established by the Criminal Justice Standards and Training Commission as provided in s. 943.12 and the requirements of ss. 493.6108 and 943.13, and

    (c) Are individually designated by a proper affidavit;

8–Investigators employed by the capital collateral representative, while actually carrying out the official duties. (applies to security and bank guards, etc.).

Law Enforcement Officers

Florida law specifies which law enforcement officers may carry firearms, what training is required, and certain restrictions on when officers may carry while they are off duty. Those officers who may carry firearms when on duty include:

- Common carrier special officers (s. 354.02);
- Community college police officers (s. 240.38);
- Division of Capitol Police (ss. 281.02 and 281.20);
- Division of Insurance Fraud investigators (s. 626.989);
- Florida Game and Fresh Water Fish Commission Wildlife Officers (s. 372.07);
- Florida Highway Patrol auxiliary officers (s. 321.24);
- Florida Highway Patrol officers (s. 321.05);
- Florida Marine Patrol officers (s. 370.02;
- Florida School for the Deaf and the Blind campus police officers(s. 242.343);
- Private correction officers (s. 944.105);
- Public defender investigators (s. 27.53);
- School safety officers (s. 230.23175);
- State attorney investigators (s. 27.255);
- Tribal council peace officers (s. 285.18);
- University police officers (s. 240.268).

Officers who may not bear arms while on duty include:

- State toll enforcement officers, (s. 316.640);
- County parking enforcement specialists, (s. 316.640);
- Municipal parking enforcement specialists, (s. 316.640);
- Animal control officers (chemical device OK), (s. 828.27);
- Institutional security personnel (except for a chemical device), (s. 916.19).

It's interesting to observe, that by virtue of selecting a certain job position, some people are obliged to forego their right to bear arms, raising a fundamental constitutional question.

JUVENILES

The law for a law-abiding parent to remember nowadays is that, any time your child goes shooting with you or without you, your kid needs to carry written permission from you—even if you're with your child—to legally receive or have a gun or go shooting. That's the net effect of a recent federal gun law.

The law divides juveniles (called *minors* in the law) into those under 18 years of age and those under 16 years of age. Some provisions affect everyone under 18 years while other special provisions allow those who are 16 and 17 years of age to possess and use firearms for specific purposes.

It is a third degree felony, under s. 790.17, to knowingly or willfully sell or transfer a firearm to a person under 18 years of age unless you have permission of the minor's parent or guardian. Transferring any other weapon is a misdemeanor, with the exception of an ordinary pocketknife.

If a firearms dealer sells a firearm to a minor it is a second degree felony, under s. 790.18. While a minor may legally own firearms (this could occur as gifts, or inheritance), the parent or guardian must maintain possession except when the minor is lawfully hunting, or at a shooting competition or target practice.

A minor under 18 years old generally may not possess a firearm, other than an unloaded firearm at home. There are some exceptions to this, under s. 790.22:

1–Lawful hunting by a minor 16 or older, or if under 16, when supervised by an adult (see Chapter 6 regarding hunting regulations);

2–A minor 16 or older may engage in lawful marksmanship competition or practice, or lawful recreational shooting, or if under 16, when supervised by an adult with the consent of the minor's parent or guardian;

3–A minor may transport unloaded firearms directly to or from hunting or lawful recreational shooting, competition or practice.

It is a first degree misdemeanor to violate these requirements, and in addition to any other penalty imposed the minor is required to perform 100 hours of community service. The driver's license of a minor caught with a firearm will be revoked (or issuance withheld) for up to one year for a first offense, and two years for a subsequent offense.

BB Guns

There are special rules for BB guns, pellet guns, and electric weapons (which are not included in the official definition of a firearm). Although not .categorized as firearms, unsafe use of these could lead to a variety of charges for any user.

Minors under 16 years of age may use BB guns, air- or gas-operated guns, or electric weapons only when they are under the supervision and in the presence of an adult who is acting with the consent of the minor's parent. It is a second degree misdemeanor for an adult who is responsible for the welfare of a minor under 16 years old to knowingly allow the child to use or possess a BB gun, air- or gas-operated gun, electric weapon, or a firearm, under s. 790.22. There is no age restriction on 16 and 17 year olds using BB guns, pellet guns, or electric weapons.

Child Safe-Storage Requirements

Florida law attempts to balance the need to keep children safe from firearm accidents and the right to bear arms for personal safety and all other lawful purposes. Section 790.173 expresses this concern:

> "(1) The Legislature finds that a tragically large number of Florida children have been accidentally killed or seriously injured by negligently stored firearms; that placing firearms within the reach or easy access of children is irresponsible, encourages such accidents, and should be prohibited; and that legislative action is necessary to protect the safety of our children.

(2) It is the intent of the Legislature that adult citizens of the state retain their constitutional right to keep and bear firearms for hunting and sporting activities and for defense of self, family, home, and business and as collectibles. Nothing in this act shall be construed to reduce or limit any existing right to purchase and own firearms, or to provide authority to any state or local agency to infringe upon the privacy of any family, home, or business except by lawful warrant."

If you know that a person under 16 years of age is likely to have access to your firearms, it is a second degree misdemeanor to store or leave a loaded firearm on your premises where the youngster may get it, under s. 790.174. You must keep the gun in a securely locked box or container, or secured with a trigger lock, or in a location that you believe is secure, except when you carry the firearm on your self or in such close proximity that you can retrieve and use it as easily and quickly as if you carried it. If you don't have children or expect no minors to visit you, you don't have to lock up your firearms.

It is a third degree felony to store or leave a loaded firearm within the reach or easy access of a person under 16 if the person obtains the firearm and uses it to injure someone, under s. 790.174. It is a second degree misdemeanor to store or leave a loaded firearm within the reach or easy access of a person under 16 if the person obtains the firearm and has or exhibits it, without proper supervision, in a public place or in a rude, careless, angry, or threatening manner, under s. 790.174.

If you are charged with a violation of the safe-storage rules you can claim as your defense that:

1– the firearm was stored or left in a securely locked box or container, or with a secure trigger lock, or in a reasonably secure place;

2– the minor obtained the firearm from an unlawful entry;

3– the occurrence involved an injury in a target or sport shooting accident or a hunting accident;

4– the violation occurred during the official duties of a member of the Armed Forces, National Guard, State Militia, or law enforcement officers.

Firearms dealers must provide warnings about safe storage requirements. It is a second degree misdemeanor if a dealer does not provide warning signs and notices as required by s. 790.175. Dealers must conspicuously post signs in block letters at least one inch high that say:

> "IT IS UNLAWFUL TO STORE OR LEAVE A FIREARM IN ANY PLACE WITHIN THE REACH OR EASY ACCESS OF A MINOR UNDER 18 YEARS OF AGE OR TO KNOWINGLY SELL OR OTHERWISE TRANSFER OWNERSHIP OR POSSESSION OF A FIREARM TO A MINOR OR A PERSON OF UNSOUND MIND."

In addition to posting signs, dealers must give purchasers written notice in block letters at least 1/4 inch in height, saying:

> "IT IS UNLAWFUL, AND PUNISHABLE BY IMPRISONMENT AND FINE, FOR ANY ADULT TO STORE OR LEAVE A FIREARM IN ANY PLACE WITHIN THE REACH OR EASY ACCESS OF A MINOR UNDER 18 YEARS OF AGE OR TO KNOWINGLY SELL OR OTHERWISE TRANSFER OWNERSHIP OR POSSESSION OF A FIREARM TO A MINOR OR A PERSON OF UNSOUND MIND."

Federal Regulation of Juveniles

Federal law generally prohibits people under 18 from possessing handguns or matching ammunition, or providing these to juveniles, unless they meet the following additional requirements. While carrying written consent from a parent or guardian (who must not be prohibited from possessing a firearm themselves), a minor may have a handgun:

1–in the course of employment;

2–in legitimate ranching or farming;

3–for target practice;

4–for hunting;

5–for a class in the safe and lawful use of a handgun;

6–for transport, unloaded in a locked case, directly to and from such activities.

To comply with the new federal rule, you should make sure your minor children have a written note from you, that they must carry with them anytime they are involved in the shooting sports, even if they are accompanied by you.

Also excluded is a minor who uses a handgun against an intruder, at home or in another home where the minor is an invited guest. If a handgun or ammunition is legally transferred to a minor, who then commits an offense with the firearm, the firearm must be returned to its lawful owner after due process. Minors may inherit title (but not possession) of a handgun. Violation of this law carries fines and a one-year jail term.

Because the federal and state laws for minors are different, it is possible to comply with one rule while at the same time violating another. The most prudent course is to follow the more restrictive of both requirements, to avoid violations that can lead to serious legal troubles. Another possibility is to work to fix the entire system.

HOW DO YOU OBTAIN FIREARMS?

Guns and ammunition may be bought or sold between private residents of this state under the same conditions as any other private sale of merchandise, provided you comply with all other laws (you can't sell prohibited weapons or knowingly sell to prohibited persons or to minors, etc.).

Sale *and delivery* of firearms by a private resident to any non-resident is prohibited by federal law. Such sales are allowed, but delivery must take place through licensed dealers in the two people's states—it's a violation to transport the firearm interstate yourself. Details are in this chapter under *Transport and Shipping* and *Out of State Purchases*.

As long as all other laws are complied with, federal law allows a non-resident to temporarily borrow or rent a firearm for any lawful sporting purpose from a dealer or resident. You may own any number of firearms and any amount of ammunition.

If you are going to deal in guns (or for that matter, import, manufacture or ship firearms in interstate or foreign commerce), you need a license from the Bureau of Alcohol, Tobacco and Firearms. Federal and state authorities may exercise a degree of judgment in determining when multiple firearm sales by a private individual constitute "dealing" in firearms, which is a felony without a license. Federal regulations provide some guidance on the matter. A dealer is:

"a person who devotes time, attention, and labor to dealing in firearms as a regular course of trade or business with the principle objective of livelihood and profit through the repetitive purchase and resale of firearms, but such a term shall not include a person who makes occasional sales, exchanges, or purchases of firearms for the enhancement of a personal collection or for a hobby, or who sells all or part of his personal collection of firearms." (27 CFR §178.11)

In-State Purchase

Federally licensed dealers of firearms and ammunition are spread across the state. Residents need no special license or permit to walk in and buy a regular firearm from a regular dealer. Firearms may be paid for in the same ways as any other retail merchandise. You may sell a gun you own to any dealer in the state willing to buy it from you.

To purchase a handgun and matching ammunition you must be at least 21 years old. When you request the purchase of a handgun from a dealer, the dealer must conduct an instant criminal-history background check, and a 3-day waiting period usually applies. Both of these are described in detail below.

To buy a rifle or shotgun and matching ammunition you must be at least 18 years old. The Florida instant background check, described below, is required for long guns, but there is no waiting period as there is with handguns.

Some ammunition may be used in either a handgun or a rifle. This type of ammo can be sold to a person between the ages of 18 and 21 only if the dealer is satisfied it will be used in a rifle and not a handgun.

When you buy firearms from a licensed dealer you must fill out a federal Firearms Transaction Record, form 4473. There are no duplicate copies made of this form and the dealers file the originals on their premises. When a dealer goes out of business, the records are sent to a federal repository. The form requires personal identification information, identification of the gun and its serial number, and your signature. By signing the form you are stating that you are not ineligible to obtain firearms under federal law. Licensed dealers keep copies of this form available.

When you buy a firearm from a Florida dealer the federal 4473 form is used to record the approval number from the state instant check, which is typically obtained by telephone. A driver's license or state identification card is the usual form of identification required by dealers. You cannot use a concealed weapons license for identification to purchase a firearm.

The Florida Instant Criminal-History Check

In 1989 Florida authorized a criminal background checking system to help determine the legal eligibility of retail firearms buyers. An instant-check system was developed to avoid delays often associated with background checks, and it has become a model that other states follow.

When you purchase any firearm from a licensed dealer, the dealer phones a toll-free number to an office at the Florida Dept. of Law Enforcement (FDLE) in Tallahassee. The dealer is charged a search tax of $8 for making the call, whether or not a sale is made, and so dealers frequently collect a non-refundable instant-check fee from you before making the call.

The office is open from 9 a.m. to 9 p.m. Eastern time, seven days a week (except Christmas Day and New Year's Day). It is a typical office with people wearing telephone headsets, in cubes, facing a terminal, who type in your data and wait while the computer searches local and national databases, looking for matches. The search typically completes in mere seconds.

The criminal history check system may only be used for proper firearms-purchase checks. It is a third degree felony for a licensed dealer to request criminal-history record information under false pretenses, or for FDLE staff to give out any details about criminal records.

Because mismatches occur due to name similarities, entry errors and other factors, there is no assurance that a "fiend" identified by the computer is the same person standing in front of the dealer while the call is made. In most cases, the "probable cause" is considered insufficient to dispatch a police unit, although it's enough to stop the sale. This is supported by the fact that many initial denials are later reversed on simple non-criminal grounds. Dealers only learn if the sale is approved, denied or conditional, and may give the results only to the customer.

If you are not disqualified, the department provides a unique *approval number* to the dealer, usually during the call or shortly after by a return call. This is noted on the federal 4473 form dealers are required to use for all sales. At the outside, the department must make a determination within 24 working hours (8 a.m. to 5 p.m., Mon. to Fri., not including holidays).

If no determination has been made in that time, a *conditional approval number* is issued. If the department subsequently finds that you are prohibited they will revoke the conditional approval number and notify local law enforcement. Of course, any time anyone is subsequently found to be or becomes prohibited, all approvals are removed.

The department issues a *non-approval number* if you appear to be prohibited from possessing a firearm. This occurs if:

1–You have been indicted or have had an information filed against you for an offense that is a felony under either state or federal law;

2–You have an injunction for protection against domestic violence entered against you under s. 741.30 or s. 784.047;

3–You are prohibited from buying a gun due to a conviction for misdemeanor domestic violence;

4–You have had either a suspended sentence or a judgment of guilt withheld, for any felony or for a domestic violence misdemeanor, until 3 years after your probation or other court conditions expire, or unless the case has been expunged;

5–You have been arrested for a dangerous crime as specified in s. 907.041 or for any of the following felonies:

- Criminal anarchy under s. 876.01 and s. 876.02;
- Extortion under s. 836.05;
- Explosives violations under s. 552.22;
- Controlled substances violations under chapter 893;
- Resisting an officer with violence under s. 843.01;
- Weapons and firearms violations under chapter 790;
- Treason under s. 876.32;

- Assisting suicide under s. 782.08;
- Sabotage under s. 876.38;

6–An error occurs.

If it appears you're ineligible but some question persists, FDLE can issue a *conditional non-approval number*. If further information clarifies the search and shows you are eligible, this becomes an approval number (saving an additional tax fee).

Approval numbers expire when you make the purchase, or after four working days (8 a.m. – 5 p.m., Mon. - Fri., excluding legal holidays). You may purchase as many firearms as you wish with an approval number, but each subsequent sale requires a new background check, fee and approval number.

If you are denied the right to purchase a firearm by the criminal-history check you may request a criminal history records review and correction, under s. 790.065. Sometimes, an informal review or a second instant check can clarify minor problems such as spelling errors. Dealers keep official appeals forms handy, which require your fingerprints for a more thorough background check. If your appeal is successful, the letter FDLE sends to notify you becomes your approval to buy.

Under s. 790.065 it is a third degree felony for:

- a buyer to provide false information or fraudulent ID to a licensed dealer;
- to buy a firearm for a person who is prohibited by law from possessing or receiving a firearm, a so-called "straw purchase"; or
- for a dealer to fail to receive an approval if one is required by law, before transferring a firearm.

A criminal history record check is not currently required for firearms transfers to:

- Holders of a valid Florida concealed weapons license;
- Law enforcement officers certified by the Florida Criminal Justice Standards and Training Commission;
- Federally licensed dealers when dealing among themselves;
- A pawn or sale on consignment picked up within 90 days by

the person who brought it in;

- A warranty replacement or repair picked up by the person who brought it in; or

- A firearm rented for one purpose and used where it is rented (for example, skeet range, plantation hunting, etc.).

No background check is required on the sale of antique firearms, as defined by state law, which includes modern replicas of antiques. A check is required when you trade in another firearm (though the waiting period, described below, is waived).

A licensed dealer is not required to conduct a criminal history check if there is a loss of telephone service in the region of the licensed premises because of telephone equipment failure, tornado, flood, natural disaster, force majeure, war, invasion, insurrection, riot, other bona fide emergency or other reason beyond the control of the dealer (s. 790.065).

The check is also not required if the Dept. of Law Enforcement fails to comply with the requirements of providing the criminal-history check service. The operational effect of the National Instant Check System, scheduled to begin when Part 2 of the Brady law takes effect in late 1998, will not be known for some time. See Chapter 7 for further details.

Florida's system of background checks, like that of 31 other states, makes it exempt from the federal Brady law delays and paperwork. The media-circulated notion that the Brady law requires a five-day waiting period for a background check has never been true.

Three-Day State Waiting Period

Florida's Constitution was amended in 1990 to require a three-day waiting period between the purchase and delivery of a handgun from any retailer (longer if weekends or legal holidays intervene). *Purchase* is defined as the transfer of money or other valuable consideration to the retailer. The only exceptions allowed in the amendment are for holders of a valid Florida concealed weapons license, and for the trade in of another handgun. In 1991, s. 790.0655 became effective, to implement the new amendment.

It is a third degree felony for any licensed dealer or employee to deliver a handgun before the three working days have elapsed. It is also a third degree felony to obtain a handgun by fraud, false pretense, or false representation.

The new amendment and statute superseded the waiting period conditions described in s. 790.33, but that law was not repealed since it forms the basis of the state's preemption requirements. Its well-known exceptions for waiting periods are *no longer valid* (though perhaps very well remembered by many people, and missed by some—such as law enforcement officers who now must wait out the three days, along with customers the retailer has previously sold to, anyone with a receipt from a former purchase, and individuals who have reported a serious physical threat against themselves to the authorities; these people must wait along with the rest of us, in the name of stopping crime).

It's interesting to note that the three-day wait and the four-day window on an instant check approval do not have to run at the same time. In fact, if a customer pays for a handgun (which starts the clock on the waiting period) but intends to pick it up a week later, the dealer needs to delay the background check, so the approval number will still be valid when the customer returns, days after the three-day wait has expired.

Out-of-State Purchases
Residents and businesses in Florida are specifically granted permission in the state statutes, under s. 790.28, to buy and take delivery of long guns from licensed dealers in states that are "contiguous to" (adjoining) Florida. Licensed dealers, collectors, importers and manufacturers may also sell long guns under this law to residents of states adjoining Florida. Such purchases must conform to the local laws of both states and

federal laws. Buying and then taking possession of handguns out of your home state is prohibited by federal law. Such handguns must be shipped to a dealer in your home state for delivery to you.

The adjoining-states language is left over from a former federal "contiguous states" rule that used to limit interstate sales to states that shared borders. That was replaced at the federal level with language allowing you to buy and take possession in any state, as long as the sale involves a rifle or shotgun, takes place face-to-face with a licensed dealer, and, once again, if it complies with both states' laws. In such a sale, the long gun can be shipped directly to your home.

Since an out-of-state dealer may not be able to access the Florida instant background check system, you may find that the system in the dealer's state, or some other procedure, will be used. Determining whether a Floridian meets both state's intricate eligibility requirements may be difficult for an out-of-state dealer. Some dealers, concerned with overlapping and often conflicting state and federal gun laws, and reluctant to jeopardize their licenses, have been known to refuse sales to residents of other states, even when those sales would be perfectly legal.

In any case, to purchase a firearm from an out-of-state dealer, you can always have that dealer transfer the firearm (handgun or long gun) to a Florida dealer, from whom you can legally make the purchase and take possession with few concerns about the perplexing proprieties of interstate purchases.

Gun Shows

Gun shows are periodically sponsored by national, state and local organizations devoted to the collection, competitive use or other sporting use of firearms. Show promoters must comply with business license requirements in the municipality or county of the show.

You may purchase firearms from an in-state dealer at a gun show the same as you could on their regular retail premises. Out-of-state dealers can display their wares and take orders, but cannot make deliveries at the show. Purchases made from an out-of-state dealer must be shipped to a licensee within this state, from the out-of-state dealer's licensed premises.

Transport and Shipping

You may ship and transport firearms around the country, but it's illegal to use the U.S. Postal Service to ship handguns, under one of the oldest federal firearms statutes on the books, dating from Feb. 8, 1927. (The oldest federal law still in effect—except for Constitutional provisions—appears to be a firearm forfeiture law for illegal hunting in Yellowstone National Park, passed on May 7, 1894. It's interesting to note that no federal gun laws from the country's first 128 years are still on the books. The very first federal gun laws, in the late 1700s, actually *required* gun possession.) The Post Office says to use registered mail and not identify the package as containing a firearm (long gun). Check with your local Post Office yourself before shipping a firearm.

You may have a weapon shipped to a licensed dealer, manufacturer or repair shop and back. However, depending upon the reason for the shipment and the shipper being used, the weapon may have to be shipped from and back to someone with a federal firearms license. You should check with the intended recipient and you must inform the shipping agent in writing before shipping firearms or ammunition.

Any handgun obtained outside Florida, if shipped to you in Florida, must go from a licensed dealer where you bought it to a licensed dealer here. Many dealers in the state will act as a "receiving station" for a weapon you buy elsewhere, sometimes for a fee. Taking *any* gun with you from a *private transfer out of state,* if it's coming back to your home state, is generally prohibited by federal law, and must be transferred between licensed dealers

The only times when you may directly receive an interstate shipment of a gun are:

1–the return of a gun that you sent for repairs, modification or replacement to a licensee in another state; and

2–a long gun legally obtained in person from an out-of-state dealer.

Interstate Travel

Personal possession of firearms in other states is subject to the laws of each state you are in. The authorities have been known to hassle, detain or arrest people who are legally traveling with weapons, due to confusion, ignorance, personal bias and for other reasons, even when those reasons are strictly illegal.

Federal law guarantees the right to transport (not the same as carry) a gun in a private vehicle, if you are entitled to have the gun in your home state and at your destination. The gun must be unloaded and locked in the trunk, or in a locked compartment other than the glove compartment or the console, if the vehicle has no trunk. Some states have openly challenged or defied this law, creating a degree of risk for anyone transporting a firearm interstate. Carrying a firearm (armed and ready) is practically impossible unless you're willing to face misdemeanor or felony criminal charges as you pass through each state.

Article IV of the U.S. Constitution requires the states to respect the laws of all other states. In addition, the 14th Amendment to the Constitution forbids the states from denying any rights that you have as an American citizen. These fundamental requirements are unfortunately frequently ignored by some states. Your Constitutional guarantees may be little comfort when a state trooper has you spread eagled for possession of a firearm that was perfectly legal when you were at home.

The bottom line is that the civil right and historical record of law-abiding American citizens traveling with firearms for their own safety has evaporated due to laws and policies at the state level. People often have no idea what the gun laws are in any state but their own (and rarely enough that), a complete set of the relevant laws is hard to get, understanding the statutes ranges from difficult to nearly impossible, and you can be arrested for making a simple mistake.

The legal risk created by our own government for a family traveling interstate with a personal firearm may be greater than the actual risk of a criminal confrontation. Because of this, the days of traveling armed and being responsible for your own safety and protection have all but ended for people who leave their home state. The proper authorities are generally exempt from these restrictions.

The chilling conclusion is that the Constitution no longer constrains law making as it used to, and the government has rights to travel that the people do not.

Countless people have asked Bloomfield Press for a book that would cover all 50 states, to resolve the problem. This is an appealing idea, but: having such a book won't save you from arrest as you leave one state where, say, a loaded gun in the glove box is perfectly all right (Arizona for example), to another state where such a gun counts for two crimes (loaded gun, accessible gun) as in California; the amount of labor needed for such a work is formidable to say the least; it would take time and resources on a national scale to accomplish the task; keeping the information current in such a book would require a team of full-time specialists with a satellite link to your home; and using a book fifty times the size of this one is, well, a joke.

The main fault with the "just write a book" fix is that it's the wrong approach. You don't fix a major national problem like this by writing a book—even though those books would be enormously valuable and ought to exist. You fix it by restoring the Lost National Right to Carry, also known as the Second Amendment, to the position it always held in America until the last few decades, during which its erosion has been nearly total for interstate travelers.

Those readers who purchased this book hoping it would somehow enable or empower them to legally travel interstate with a loaded personal firearm must contact their elected representatives and begin to ask about The Lost National Right to Carry. It has quietly disappeared through incremental attrition at the local level.

Reciprocity

A national movement is afoot to ease the stranglehold that state laws have placed on law-abiding travelers. Introduced at state and federal levels, *reciprocity laws* seek to guarantee that people who may legally carry in their home states cannot be held in violation when in another state. It seems that the Second Amendment is providing no protection for travelers, and a legislative solution is being sought.

Your home state's rules would not apply when you go "abroad." You would be subject to the laws, regulations and customs of the state you are in at the time.

Most proposals seek to obtain this relief only for individuals with government-issued permits. Supporters typically cite the portion of Article IV of the Constitution, known as the *full faith and credit clause*, which says in pertinent part, "Full Faith and Credit shall be given in each State to the public Acts, Records, and judicial Proceedings of every other state;". This sets a model similar to marriage and driver licenses.

Other attempts seek to allow any person who is not acting criminally to be free from harassment or arrest for simple possession of a legally owned firearm, independent of the state involved. This would emulate the way people are basically free to speak their minds regardless of their location (and no license to exercise the First Amendment is available at this time, except that broadcasts are forbidden without a government license).

Some states take the approach that, if your permit is similar to ours, and your state formally honors ours, then we will honor yours. A method is then set up to determine if the two state's requirements are a rough match. Such comparisons are problematic because they once again subject your rights to bureaucratic review, as in the days before "shall issue" permits, and indeed, states have already experienced difficulty in agreeing if their "standards" are a match. When the officials decide there is no match, they remove the right to carry between those states. To link all 50 states to each other and thus restore rights to properly government-licensed individuals would require 1,225 pacts.

Each state's requirements are of course different. Studying the laws of your home state (a common requirement) hardly prepares you and is certainly not a match for the laws in any other state. Florida requires no shooting test for its permit, Virginia asks for proof of demonstrated competence with a gun but does not define it further, Texas requires 50 shots at three distances with all shots timed, Arizona requires seven hits out of ten, and so it goes, state to state.

Some states are considering honoring anyone who has a state-issued permit. Some will issue a license to anyone qualified, resident or not, getting around the problem in yet another way. This is the approach taken by Florida and indeed, many residents of other states carry a Florida license in addition to one for their home state. (Interestingly, such double ID is generally not allowed with drivers' licenses). Florida currently has no provision for recognizing CCW licenses from other states.

A handful of states have no permit system, presumably leaving them out of the picture when their residents are on the road, or for you when you visit. A few have introduced laws that would allow you to drive through their states on a "continuous journey," or to enter the state but only for a competition or designated event.

A federal bill seeks to require all states to honor the permits of all other states. Residents in Vermont are excluded because they need no permit to carry in the first place. The 98% of Americans who bear arms but have refused to sign up for a government carry-rights permit are also left out of these plans.

Rumors are swirling about which state has adopted what policy, and relying on a rumor where no rule exists can get you arrested. Viewing the printed statute yourself is a good way to help avoid rumors. Laws may offer less protection when new, before on-the-street police policy is established and well known throughout the law enforcement community. _Do not assume from the information provided below that reciprocity exists, only that the states are looking into the possibilities, and you might want to too._

It would be nice if there was a rock-solid reliable place to call to find out exactly where reciprocity exists, but there is none at the present time. Besides, a complete answer with precisely all the do's and don'ts is more than you can possibly get over the phone. The job of telling you is not the role of the police, the sheriff, the DA, the AG, the library or anyone else. Why, you'd need a book the size of this one for every state you visited.

One solution that addresses these problems is the proposed American Historical Rights Protection Act. This basically says that if a person has a gun, the person isn't a criminal, and the gun isn't illegal, then that is not a crime, based on the 14th Amendment. For a copy of this draft statute contact Bloomfield Press or visit our website.

The Reciprocity List

Expect the information that follows to change rapidly. Four states currently have some form of recognition for out-of-state permit holders—check with them for details: Idaho, Indiana, Michigan and Wyoming.

These states have passed laws that would allow some bureau within the state (indicated in parenthesis) to cut deals with a bureau in another state, or they have set up other conditions that might lead them to recognize each other's permits— check with them for details: Arizona (Dept. of Public Safety), Arkansas (State Police), Connecticut (Commissioner of State Police), Georgia (County Probate Judge), Kentucky (Sheriff), Louisiana (Deputy Secretary of Public Safety Services), Massachusetts (Chief of Police), Mississippi (Dept. of Public Safety), Missouri (residents currently prohibited from concealed carry), Montana (Governor), New Hampshire (Chief of Police), North Dakota (Chief of the Bureau of Criminal Investigation), Oklahoma (State Bureau of Investigation), Pennsylvania (Attorney General), Rhode Island (Attorney General), South Carolina (Law Enforcement Division), Texas (Dept. of Public Safety), Utah (Dept. of Public Safety), Virginia (Circuit Court), West Virginia (Sheriff).

The different authorities named in this list are a measure of the consistency of the laws from state to state.

A number of states will issue firearms permits to non-residents if you meet their requirements—check with them for details: Florida, Iowa, Maine, New Hampshire, Pennsylvania, Rhode Island, New Jersey, Utah, Washington and Wyoming.

If, after reading these lists, you get the sense that reciprocity schemes don't solve the problem and unshackle honest citizens, well, you're not alone.

Common or Contract Carriers

You may transport firearms and ammunition interstate by "common carriers" (scheduled and chartered airlines, buses, trains, ships, etc.), but you must notify them and comply with their requirements. Note that it must also be legal for you to possess the firearms and ammunition at your destination.

Although federal law requires written notice from you and a signed receipt from the carrier when you pick up the firearm, verbal communication is often accepted. Call in advance and get precise details and the names of the people you speak with—you wouldn't be the first traveler to miss a departure because of unforeseen technicalities and bureaucratic run-arounds.

For air travel, firearms must be unloaded, cased in a manner that the airline deems appropriate, and may not be possessed by or accessible to you in the "sterile" area anywhere on the gate side of the passenger security checkpoint, including on the aircraft. You may ship your firearms as baggage, and it is also legal to give custody of them to the pilot, captain, conductor or operator for the duration of the trip (though they're not required to take custody).

Airlines must comply with firearms rules found primarily in the Code of Federal Regulations, Title 14, Sections 107 and 108, and other laws. A little-known provision of the Brady law prohibits carriers from identifying the outside of your baggage to indicate that it contains a firearm, a prime cause for theft in the past.

Local Ordinances and Preemption

Florida's intent is to provide uniform firearms laws in the state and this is set out in s. 790.33. To accomplish this the statute declares all ordinances and regulations null and void if they were enacted by any jurisdiction other than state or federal, to regulate firearms, ammunition or components. The state prohibits enactment of any further ordinances or regulations relating to firearms, ammunition or components unless specifically authorized by state law. Local jurisdictions are required to enforce state firearms laws.

No county government or municipality may adopt any ordinance relating to the sale or possession of ammunition and any such ordinance that was in effect on June 24, 1983 is void under s. 125.0107 and s. 166.044.

To accomplish this the legislature declares in s. 790.33 that it is occupying the whole field of regulation of firearms and ammunition, including the purchase, sale, transfer, taxation, manufacture, ownership, possession, and transportation of firearms. Any county, city, town, or municipal ordinances or regulations in this regard are null and void and these jurisdictions are prohibited from enacting any such ordinances.

This preemption does not affect zoning ordinances which encompass firearms businesses along with other businesses. However, zoning ordinances that are designed for the purpose of restricting or prohibiting the sale, purchase, transfer, or manufacture of firearms or ammunition, as a method of regulating firearms or ammunition, are strictly prohibited.

Some cities and counties have tried to restrict gun shows by not allowing them to be held in public buildings such as those at fairgrounds. Although this is apparently illegal, generally, gun show promoters have gone to private buildings, finding that bringing a lawsuit to enforce the preemption law is too expensive and time consuming.

LOSS OF RIGHTS

The right to bear arms is not absolute. Gun control—in the true sense—means disarming criminals and is a good idea, a point on which everyone but the criminals agree. The list of people who may not bear arms at all appears earlier in this chapter. A person whose rights are whole may lose those rights, mainly for conviction of a felony.

Conviction of any felony removes your civil right to bear firearms under state and federal law. The right to bear arms is forbidden to anyone who is or becomes a prohibited possessor under federal law, as described earlier.

A law enforcement officer is empowered to disarm an individual during an arrest, under s. 790.08.

Illegal Training
Training with the intention to use firearms illegally or for a civil disorder is a third degree felony, under s. 790.29.

It is a second degree misdemeanor, under s. 870.06, for a group of people to associate together as a military organization for drill or parade with firearms, without special licenses from the Governor and local officials.

Restoration of Rights
A person with a truly compelling reason, and sufficient time, money and luck, can conceivably pursue a relief from federal firearms prohibition through the federal courts. Successful examples of this are few. Federal law (18 USC §925) also provides a method for restoring a person's right to bear arms if it has been lost. This has been useful to some people who are responsible community members and whose restrictions were based on decades-old convictions of youth, or other circumstances that pose little threat. The Treasury Dept., responsible for implementing this law, has claimed for several

years that they have no budget with which to accomplish this work, and the federal restoration of rights process has effectively ground to a halt for anyone whose disability is based on federal charges.

WHAT DOES IT ALL MEAN?

WHAT DOES IT ALL MEAN

Florida law divides crimes into two categories to help match the punishment to the crime. Felonies are extremely serious; misdemeanors are less serious.

Felonies are divided into *degrees,* starting with the most serious, first degree to the less serious third degree. The most serious crimes are in their own categories, called capital and life felonies. Generally, a felony conviction revokes your civil rights, including your right to bear arms, to hold public office and your right to vote, and may include limits on your right to travel, associate with certain people and other conditions at court discretion.

Misdemeanors are also grouped into degrees, with a first degree misdemeanor being the more serious charge, and second degree being the lesser.

Punishments are matched to the seriousness of the crime. This runs from a capital felony, which can be punishable by death (Florida uses the electric chair), to any prison term up to life imprisonment. A "noncriminal violation" carries a fine or civil penalty only (no jail sentence). The way a particular crime is committed, known as aggravating or mitigating circumstances, can increase or decrease the penalty. See the Crime and Punishment Chart in Appendix B for the basic penalties for each type of crime.

Florida statutes refer to a *felony of the third degree* but in common usage, people say *third degree felony*. The same is true of a *misdemeanor of the second degree* which is commonly referred to as a *second degree misdemeanor*. This book uses the common language style.

WHAT DO YOU NEED TO GET A FIREARM?

WHAT DO YOU NEED TO BUY A FIREARM FROM A FEDERALLY LICENSED DEALER?

- You must be at least 18 years old for a long gun, 21 years old for a handgun, and not be a "prohibited possessor" under state or federal law;

- You need a government-issued photo ID which establishes your name, address, date of birth and signature;

- You must file a federal form 4473 with the dealer and pass an instant background check for any disqualifying factors before taking delivery of a firearm;

- You must wait for three business days after buying a handgun to take delivery unless you are exempt (have a valid Florida concealed weapons license, or trade in another handgun);

- If you are not a Florida resident:

    –It must be legal to have the weapon in your home state;

    –The transaction must comply with your state's laws;

    –You may take possession of a long gun over the counter if you could in your home state;

    –You may not purchase and take possession of a handgun out of your home state (federal law) but you may have a licensed dealer ship a handgun to your home state for purchase there, if dealers in both states are willing to arrange such a transaction; and

- You must be able to pay for your purchase.

Certain changes may take place if and when the federal Instant Background Check takes effect, as early as Nov. 1998. Visit our website (listed on pg. 2) for up to the minute details.

CARRYING FIREARMS 2

In order to understand the carry laws in this state, you must first understand a number of words and phrases that have specific meaning for carrying firearms in Florida. These are found in s. 790.001 and include the following terms.

A *concealed firearm* is any firearm carried on or about you that is concealed "from the ordinary sight of another person." Not included are antique firearms or replicas of antiques unless they are used in a crime.

A *concealed weapon* includes any firearm (including antiques), or any dirk, metallic knuckles, slungshot, billie, tear gas gun, chemical weapon or device, or other deadly weapon, carried on or about you and concealed from ordinary sight. A self-defense chemical spray that has up to two ounces of chemical is not included. Also, a nonlethal stun gun or remote stun gun is not included.

In general, a firearm that is *securely encased* is one that is in a vehicle and is:

1–In a glove compartment, whether or not locked;

2–Snapped in a holster;

3–In a gun case, whether or not locked;

4–In a zippered gun case; or

5–In a closed box or container which requires a lid or cover to be opened for access.

The courts have made some inconsistent judgments regarding what *securely encased* means, and you may find differences between court districts. Rather than become a test case to see if a snapped holster includes Velcro, it's probably best to meet or exceed the definitions. When a statute says securely encased *or* not readily accessible, you may be at less risk to meet both conditions simultaneously.

A firearm or other weapon is *readily accessible for immediate use* when you carry it on yourself, or if it is close enough and in a way that you can get and use it as easily and quickly as if you carried it on yourself.

An *electric weapon or device* is any device that uses electric current for offensive or defensive purposes, destroying life, or inflicting injury.

For the purpose of the concealed weapon law (s. 790.06), a *concealed weapon or firearm* is a handgun, electronic weapon or device, tear gas gun, knife or billie, and specifically does *not* include a machine gun.

The expression *open carry* is not defined in the statutes, but is commonly used to refer to a firearm which is in plain sight. As examples this would include a firearm worn in a holster, a long gun in a scabbard on horseback, a firearm you are actually holding or carrying, a firearm that is resting out in the open in a vehicle or at a given location, and more.

A *conveyance*, not defined (but used) in the statutes, is a vehicle, and has two forms—private vehicles such as cars and trucks, and public vehicles such as buses, trains and airplanes. One part of the carry statute is limited to "within the interior of a private conveyance" while another part simply refers to "traveling by private conveyance." This casts some shadow on the proper method for carry while on a bicycle, motorcycle or other conveyance that has no interior.

The battery of laws that describe the rules for carrying firearms:

s. 790.001   Definitions

s. 790.01   Concealed carry is a first degree misdemeanor

s. 790.053   Open carry is a second degree misdemeanor

s. 790.06   The concealed weapons license law, it overrides
             s. 790.01 for licensees

s. 790.11   National Forest limitation

s. 790.25   Open carry is allowed only as defined

Open Carry

Although the statutory language in s. 790.25 appears to allow open carry of firearms under some situations, open carry is practically non-existent in Florida. An examination of this statute shows that what the law says and what the authorities do isn't always an exact match. As a law-abiding adult in Florida you may openly carry firearms:

1– In your own home;

2–At your place of business;

3– While firing guns in a safe and secure indoor range for testing and target practice;

4– During testing or target practice under safe conditions and in a safe place not prohibited by law, (the statute's phrase 'or going to or from such place' cannot be relied upon for open carry to and from target practice);

5– While you are legally hunting, or going to or returning from lawful hunting, (the statute's phrase 'or going to or from such place' cannot be relied upon for open carry to and from hunting except, perhaps, in direct proximity to the field, and certainly does not include in a vehicle; the protection mentioned about 'to, from or during fishing and camping' in this well-known clause is not always honored by the authorities);

6–While carrying a pistol unloaded and in a secure wrapper, concealed or not, to or from either a place of purchase or a place of repair, and your home or place of business; secure wrapper, though not defined by law, is generally taken to imply packaging sufficient to prevent the gun from being noticed (the phrase originated in the 1920s when guns were bought at general stores, and wrapped in brown paper with a piece of string); because the gun is not visible most people wouldn't think of this as open carry even though the law covers it as if it were;

7– While making, fixing, or dealing in firearms, while you are engaged in the lawful course of such business.

Open carry under other circumstances is a second degree misdemeanor, under s. 790.053. Special rules apply to state-certified security guards, the military, the proper authorities, and in designated areas, listed under *Prohibited Places,* later in this chapter.

The authorities may tend to lean toward a narrow view of what constitutes your home or business, so be cautious about presuming that surrounding land or features actually count as "home base" for protection under this law.

Because guns may attract attention, and knowing that some people react negatively to the presence of firearms, it may be prudent to be discreet when legally carrying firearms.

In addition to the items described above, s. 790.25 describes many aspects of possession and use of firearms, including the following lawful pursuits:

1–Lawful defense of life, home and property (though defense of home or property with deadly force, if no risk to life exists, may not be justifiable);

2–Being on public transportation, if the firearm is securely encased and not in your personal possession (enables travel using common carriers, by placing the firearm in the operator's possession for the duration);

3–Own, possess and lawfully use firearms, other weapons, ammunition and supplies if you are a regularly enrolled member of any organization authorized for or organized to:
  • Purchase or receive weapons from the United States or from this state (would include anyone involved in the federal Civilian Marksmanship Program, available to most law-abiding citizens, discussed in Chapter 7);

- Conduct target, skeet, or trap shooting, while you are at or going to or from shooting practice;
- Collect modern or antique firearms, while you are at or going to or from your gun shows, conventions, or exhibits.

Open carry of a self-defense chemical spray, a nonlethal stun gun or a remote stun gun is allowed under s. 790.053.

Concealed Carry

Under most conditions, carrying a concealed firearm without a concealed weapons license is a third degree felony (s. 790.01). It is a first degree misdemeanor to carry a concealed non-firearm weapon or electric weapon (but a self-defense chemical spray, nonlethal stun gun or a remote stun gun, as defined by law, are allowed).

Handguns in cars must be securely encased or not readily accessible for immediate use, as discussed in detail under *Carrying in Vehicles*, below, and may only be carried under the specified conditions.

Court precedent generally provides for concealed carry in your home, as seen in French v. State, 1973. Your surrounding property such as a privately owned yard or driveway is included (Collins v. State, 1925) and it has included a bench on store property where a person worked and lived (Peoples v. State, 1973).

Home includes your room while you are registered at a hotel or motel, but this does not apply to guests who are visiting you, who would be in violation of carrying a concealed firearm if they don't have a concealed weapons license (Cockin v. State, 1984). Only your room is your private dwelling and you will be in violation of carrying a concealed weapon if you are in the hallway or other public area (Brant v. State, 1977). This allows you to have your firearm in your room for self protection, but provides no way to carry it to your room without a license.

In Sherrod v. State, 1986, the court decided that *home* does not include the parking lot of a multiple unit apartment dwelling, and Facion v. State, 1974, excluded the common area of an apartment building as well.

This leads to the quite unusual situation many Floridians have noticed. Concealed carry is basically illegal, and the open carry provisions of s. 790.25 fail to include a way to walk with a firearm between places. It has been described as everything from sloppy legal work to unabashed infringement. You can properly carry in your car and you can carry in your home but, unless you're in one of the special cases or you get the government-issued concealed weapons license, there's no way to go from one to the other legally. (The special cases include on private property, and going to or coming from fishing, camping, hunting, target practice, a gun store or a repair shop. Remarkably, carrying for personal safety or any other reason is not allowed under the present statutes.)

Carrying a concealed weapon illegally in Florida is deemed a breach of the peace. A law enforcement officer may arrest you on the spot if the officer has reasonable grounds or probable cause to believe you are illegally carrying a concealed weapon (s. 790.02). This implies giving the officer a reason to act, from carelessly letting a concealed weapon "print" through your clothes or otherwise show, to attracting too much attention for any reason. People who have been convicted of illegal carry while going from home to car, or in other public areas, have generally brought the charges on by doing something foolish instead of behaving demurely.

The bottom line is that, in modern-day Florida, the only practical way to legally carry a handgun is with a government license.

Carrying in Vehicles

The law prohibiting concealed carry of firearms (s. 790.01) does not apply to possession of a concealed firearm or other weapon for a lawful purpose, in the interior of a private conveyance, if the person is at least 18 years old and the weapon is securely encased or not readily accessible for immediate use.

What this means is that a law-abiding individual at least 18 years old may carry a loaded handgun in a car or other private vehicle if the gun is in the glovebox, a snapped holster, a locked or unlocked gun case, a zippered gun case or a closed box or container which requires a lid or cover to be opened for access. For an extra margin of protection, you should also ensure that the gun is not readily accessible.

Section 790.025 sets out these allowances for lawfully carrying a firearm in a private vehicle. Note that a concealed weapon cannot be carried directly on yourself in these situations, without a concealed weapons license. A long gun may be carried anywhere in a vehicle, as long as it is carried for a lawful purpose.

Some law enforcement officers believe there is a "two-step rule," meaning it must take two separate actions to access a gun, for it to be legally carried in a vehicle. No such rule exists, and the law covering guns in cars states that it must be construed liberally in favor of the lawful use, ownership and possession of firearms, including self defense.

A loaded gun in an unlocked glovebox meets the requirements of the statute, though it may not be greeted kindly by some officials. If you carry a firearm in the glovebox, as many people prefer to do, there is value in carrying your registration and other papers in another location to help avoid any incidents.

There have been many cases of people convicted for illegally carrying a concealed weapon in a vehicle, a third degree felony under s. 790.01. The cases usually involve some other traffic or criminal violation that caused officers to search the vehicle, in addition to the concealed firearm that was not securely encased or was readily accessible. A handgun in plain sight is a first degree misdemeanor under s. 790.053.

To minimize the risks, you may want to carry firearms in the trunk of your vehicle, which clearly eliminates the readily accessible aspects, and if unloaded, is also protected under federal law.

THE CONCEALED WEAPONS LICENSE

Carrying a concealed weapon is an awesome responsibility. The legislative battles to establish the concealed weapons license law were long and hard-fought, and the law is not perfect. It is now up to the people to demonstrate intelligent use of this law, to exhibit restraint in all but the most life-threatening situations, and to work hard to make Florida a better place to live.

Obtaining a license to carry a concealed weapon used to involve the often arbitrary decisions of government workers in individual counties, who required you to prove a need for the license. Personal safety, crime deterrence and Constitutional guarantees were not enough and many people were denied licenses.

Now, any person who meets basic standards will qualify and receive a license. Where the previous law called for a discretionary *proven need*, the law now says the government *shall issue* a license to any qualified applicant. Section 790.06, which is known as the "Jack Hagler Self Defense Act," sets out the procedures regarding concealed weapons licenses. The legislature made a uniform system for issuing licenses that is not arbitrary or subject to "who you know" limitations.

Having a concealed weapons license reduces or eliminates many of the hassles and legal intricacies of carrying a firearm around the state. In some situations, it provides the only legal means of getting a firearm from one place to another. The protection the license offers from unwanted harassment by the authorities is quite broad, and has motivated many people to obtain one.

A license to carry a concealed weapon in Florida is sometimes incorrectly referred to as a *permit,* because under the old law counties issued permits to carry a concealed weapon. While some people think the use of a word is a trivial matter the correct word is very important.

A *permit* is granted to allow you to do something for a short period of time or in a limited geographic area. For example, you get a permit to hold a parade during certain hours on certain streets. A *license* is issued to allow you to do something for a longer period of time and in a larger geographic area. For example, you get a driver's license to drive almost any type of private passenger vehicle, for a number of years, anywhere in the world.

The technical phrase in Florida law is *concealed weapon or firearm license*, to make clear that legal non-firearm weapons may be carried. Because a firearm is defined as a weapon under state law, and in keeping with common usage, this book uniformly refers to it as a *concealed weapons license*.

While the procedure takes a lengthy three months, and the license fee is fairly expensive (presently $117 for five years), it does allow everyone who qualifies to obtain a license.

Qualifications for a Concealed Weapons License

The Dept. of State is required by s. 790.06 to issue your concealed weapons license if you:

1–Are a resident of the United States;

2–Are 21 years of age or older;

3–Do not suffer from a physical infirmity which prevents the safe handling of a weapon or firearm;

4–Are not ineligible to possess a firearm under s. 790.23 (for a felony conviction);

5–Have not been committed for the abuse of illegal drugs or been found guilty of a drug-related crime within a three-year period immediately preceding the date on which your application is submitted;

6–Do not chronically and habitually use alcoholic beverages or other substances to the extent that your normal faculties are impaired. It is presumed that you are a chronic and habitual alcohol or substance user if you have been committed under chapter 397; convicted of a firearms offense involving alcohol; deemed a habitual offender; or have had two or more convictions for impaired driving within the three-year period immediately preceding your application date;

7–Desire a legal means to carry a concealed weapon for lawful self defense;

8–Demonstrate competence with a firearm by any one of the following:

   a–Completion of any National Rifle Association firearms safety or training course;

   b–Completion of any hunter education or hunter safety course approved by the Game and Fresh Water Fish Commission or a similar agency of another state;

   c–Completion of any firearms safety or training course available to the general public offered by a law enforcement, junior college, college, or private or public institution or organization or firearms training school, using instructors certified by the National Rifle Association, Criminal Justice Standards and Training Commission, or the Florida Dept. of State;

   d–Completion of any law enforcement firearms safety or training course offered for security guards, investigators, special deputies, or any division or subdivision of law enforcement or security enforcement;

   e–Presentation of evidence of equivalent experience with a firearm through participation in organized shooting competition or military service;

   f–Are licensed or have been licensed to carry a firearm in this state or a county or municipality of this state, unless such license has been revoked for cause; or

   g–Completion of any firearm training or safety course conducted by a state-certified or National Rifle Association certified firearms instructor.

   Remember that you must be able to provide a photocopy of your course certificate or an affidavit from the instructor or an official of the organization that provided the training to obtain a license.

NOTE: In 1998 the legislature added a shooting requirement for anyone who seeks to qualify by taking a public training program. The trainer who certifies that you completed the course must keep records saying that you were observed safely handling and shooting a firearm. This means that classes must now include a live fire shooting-range segment. Classroom-only training will be insufficient to qualify.

Florida, like some states (Virginia is an example) doesn't set conditions for the shooting "test." Other states are more specific. Arizona for example requires seven hits out of ten on a large silhouette target. Texas requires fifty shots, at distances of 3, 7 and 15 yards, with all shots timed and a minimum score of 175 (225 for instructors) out of a possible 250 to qualify. Florida instructors will set their own course of fire, and an increase in training prices is likely.

9–Have not been adjudicated an incapacitated person, unless five years have elapsed since your restoration to capacity by court order;

10–Have not been committed to a mental institution, unless you produce a certificate from a licensed psychiatrist that you have not suffered from disability for at least five years prior to the date of your application; and

11–Have not had adjudication of guilt withheld or imposition of sentence suspended on any felony, or domestic violence misdemeanor, within three years since your probation, or your record has been sealed or expunged.

12–You are not under a current injunction restraining you from committing domestic violence or repeat violence.

Even if you meet all of these requirements the Dept. may deny your license if you were convicted of one or more misdemeanors involving violence and it is less than three years since you completed probation or other conditions set by the court. This also applies if you've had a suspended sentence or judgment of guilt withheld for a misdemeanor crime of violence, until three years have elapsed following any court conditions, or the case has been sealed or expunged.

Any resident of the United States who meets these qualifications can obtain a Florida concealed weapons license. The license is presently only valid in Florida, but this allows "snowbirds" who spend the winter in Florida, and other law-abiding individuals, to be licensed to carry a weapon while they are in the state.

Unlike some other states, there is no requirement that training courses be of any particular length or contain any particular content, but as of 1998, your instructor must watch you safely fire a firearm. Many people take the free Hunter Safety Course offered by the Florida Game and Fresh Water Fish Commission. Others get a letter from the president of their shooting club stating that they participate in shooting competitions and can safely handle a firearm.

Those with military service can use a copy of their discharge papers even if they were in a branch of the service that doesn't train in or require the use of firearms by personnel. There are a great variety of private classes available, each with content decided upon by the instructor. All of these meet the requirements of the law. Considering the awesome responsibility involved, it makes sense to get the best training you can.

Application and Approval Procedure

To apply for a concealed weapons license you must obtain an application package from the Dept. of State, Division of Licensing. You can phone the department at 850-488-5381 and they will mail you an application package. The package includes complete instructions on how to apply, a one-page application form, fingerprint card, a copy of Florida Statutes chapter 790 (firearms and weapons law), and a return envelope.

The application form requires your name, address, date and place of birth, sex, race, occupation, and Social Security or Alien Registration Number. You then check yes or no to 12 questions that cover the qualifications and disqualifications for a license.

The application form contains the statement that you desire a legal means to carry a concealed weapon or firearm for self defense. You don't have to explain any more than that printed reason why you want to carry. The affidavit also contains the statement, "I have been furnished a copy of Chapter 790, Florida Statutes, relating to weapons and firearms and I am knowledgeable of its provisions." You should read that chapter, because you have sworn (or affirmed) that you know the gun laws in Florida. Ignorance of the law is not an excuse for doing something wrong.

Giving any false information on the application is a second degree misdemeanor, under s. 837.06. You must sign the form with a notary public as a witness.

You must get your fingerprints taken at a law enforcement office (county sheriffs are a common choice, police depts. may do this as well) and they may charge you a fee of up to $5 (reportedly, some authorities charge more than the limit). You can only use the fingerprint card that comes with your application. Type or print the information on the top of the card in black ink, but *don't sign it* until you are with the person who takes your prints. Leave blank the part of the fingerprint card that says "Employer and Address." This is for the law enforcement agency that takes your prints. Use the codes listed in the instructions that come with your application for completing the information on the card. If you make any mistakes or leave any information out your application will be rejected.

You must include a recent color photograph. Any place that does instant passport photos will be able to take this for you. You should bring along the instructions from the application package, however, since the technical specs are different from those required for a passport photo. (Basically, you need an unmounted correctly exposed full-color unretouched glossy frontal portrait with no hat or sunglasses, against a plain light-colored background, in good, clean and flat condition, larger than 1-1/4 x 1-3/8 inches, with a portrait that fits inside an oval template on the application form.)

The picture must be taken within 30 days of your application, so do this last, especially if you haven't yet taken a firearms course.

You must be able to show that you took a firearms safety course or have other acceptable evidence of firearms training. Make sure you receive a certificate of training with the instructor's name and number on it. Don't send in the original certificate because you won't get it back, so make a photocopy of the certificate to send with your application, and store your original in a safe place.

The complete license application includes:

1–The completed and notarized application form;

2–The license fee of $117 ($75 license fee plus $42 fingerprint card processing fee). The license fee is non-refundable. Personal checks are not acceptable;

3–A color photo of yourself that meets the state's requirements;

4–The official fingerprint card;

5–Evidence of firearms safety training.

Deliver all of this to the Dept. of State in Tallahassee in the envelope provided in the application package. You may want to send it by certified mail with return receipt requested so you know that they received it and the date they received it.

When the Dept. of State receives your application they send your fingerprint card to the Florida Dept. of Law Enforcement for state and federal processing for any criminal record. Within 90 days of receiving your application the department must:

1–Issue your license, which they send by mail, or

2–Deny your application. They can only deny it if you fail to qualify under the grounds listed above. If your application is denied the department must give you the reasons in writing and advise you of your right to a hearing; or

3–Suspend the time limit if they don't get a final disposition on any criminal history information you may have. The time limit can be suspended until they receive a final disposition or proof of restoration of your civil and firearms rights.

If the fingerprints submitted are not legible, the Dept. of State will request that you submit another fingerprint card. If after your second set of fingerprints the department or FBI still find them unreadable, they must determine your eligibility based on a name check for a criminal history.

The total cost you can expect to pay for the five-year license is $117 to the Dept. of State, up to $5 for having your fingerprints taken, about $10 for a photo, about $4 for certified mail, and whatever you pay for your training (which is usually between $25 and $50).

Changing or Replacing Your License

If you move and change your address you must notify the Dept. of State within 30 days. If you don't it is a noncriminal violation with a penalty of $25. A letter addressed to the Division of Licensing at the department should be sufficient since there is no form for making a change of address.

If you lose your license or if it is destroyed you must notify the Dept. of State within 30 days. If you don't it is a noncriminal violation with a penalty of $25. If your license is lost or destroyed it is automatically invalid. You can get a duplicate license if you pay a $15 fee to the Dept. of State and provide a notarized statement that the license was lost or destroyed. You will also need to send a new photograph for the license (until the Dept. switches over to scannable photographs, expected soon).

What Your License Allows You to Do

A Florida concealed weapons license allows you to carry throughout the state (except in restricted places noted in this chapter), as long as it is completely concealed from plain sight:

1–a handgun;

2–an electronic weapon;

3–a tear gas gun;

4–a knife;

5–a billie.

The license specifically prohibits the concealed carry of a machine gun. If you let your concealed handgun show, you are in violation of s. 790.053, the open-carry prohibition, a second degree misdemeanor.

You must carry your concealed weapons license and other valid identification whenever you have a concealed weapon with you. You must show the license and your other identification to any law enforcement officer who asks to see it. If you don't carry both your license and other valid identification while you are carrying a concealed weapon it is a noncriminal violation with a $25 penalty.

Revocation or Suspension

A valid concealed weapons license may be suspended or revoked if you are later found to be ineligible to hold a license, under s. 790.06, due to:

1–You have become ineligible under the qualification criteria for the license;

2–You develop or sustain a physical infirmity which prevents the safe handling of a weapon or firearm;

3–You are convicted of a felony which would make you ineligible to possess a firearm;

4–You are found guilty of a crime relating to illegal drugs;

5–You are committed as a substance abuser;

6– You are deemed a habitual offender;

7–You are convicted for a second time of impaired driving in Florida or in another state, within three years of a previous conviction. This applies even if your first violation occurred prior to the date on which you applied for your concealed weapons license;

8–You are adjudicated an incapacitated person;

9–You are committed to a mental institution;

10–You have had a suspended sentence or judgment of guilt withheld, for one or more crimes of violence, within the past three years.

Also, if the Dept. of State is notified that you have been arrested or formally charged with a crime that would disqualify you from holding a license, your license will be suspended until the final disposition of your case, under s. 790.06. Suspension also occurs if an injunction is issued restraining you from committing domestic violence or repeated acts of violence.

If after you have received your license the department finds that you have committed a felony or any of the other disqualifications, it will suspend or revoke your license. The Dept. of State can also revoke a license for an adjudication withheld or if you had a court plea of *nolo contendere* (no contest) accepted to an offense that would disqualify you for a license, two years before the new license law was in effect and before you applied for your license. The court said, "Here, the public interest in strict regulation of carrying concealed weapons is very great in comparison with the withdrawal of that privilege, for a three-year period, for anyone who has had a felony disposition." (Crane v. Dept. of State, 1989)

Renewal

The license was originally issued for a three-year period, but this was increased to five years in 1998, under s. 790.06. At least 90 days before the expiration date of your license the Dept. of State is required to mail you a written notice of the expiration with a renewal form. To remain valid you must renew your license on or before its expiration date. To do this you complete the renewal form, which states that you are still qualified to possess a license, and have it notarized. You send the renewal form, a new color photograph, and the renewal fee of $65 to the department. Out-of-state license holders must also send in a new fingerprint card and the fingerprint processing fee of $42.

If your renewal form doesn't arrive at the Dept. of State by the expiration date of your license you must include a late fee of $15 in addition to the renewal fee. If you wait for six months after your license has expired it can't be renewed. You will have to apply for a new license the same way you did the first time including submitting a new fingerprint card, paying the higher fee, having a new background check, providing proof of training and enduring the processing delays.

The Dept. of State is required by law to process your renewal form and send your new license to you in the mail. If there is a time between the expiration date of your existing license and when you get your renewal license in the mail, you may not carry a concealed weapon or firearm during this time. If you do, you may be committing a felony since your government approval to carry it is in lapse. If it has been issued and hasn't gotten to you in the mail yet you may be committing the noncriminal violation of not carrying your license with you while armed.

Special Licenses

Judges are not required to comply with all the application procedures in order to obtain a concealed weapons license, except they must demonstrate competence in the use of firearms by any of the training methods required for other license applicants, under s. 790.06.

Consular security officials of foreign governments who want a concealed weapons license must comply with all the regular application procedures, except the fee for such a license is $300 and it is valid for only one year. The Dept. of State must issue such a license within 20 days after receiving the application package, under s. 790.06. The foreign government must be one that maintains diplomatic relations and treaties of commerce, friendship, and navigation with the United States, and the individual must be certified by the foreign government and by the appropriate embassy in this country.

Private investigators and private security guards are subject to the special requirements found primarily in Chapter 493 of the Florida statutes.

Records of License Holders

The Dept. of State by law maintains an automated registry of license holders along with other information it determines pertinent. This information is available on-line at all times to law enforcement agencies that request it through the Florida Crime Information Center. The chilling effect of being cataloged in the state crime computer, for obtaining a government-authorized license to bear arms, has deterred many gun-owning residents from applying for the license. Approximately 1-1/2% of the population has been licensed, with the program now entering its second decade. In contrast, it is estimated that half of all homes in Florida have at least one firearm.

The department is also required to maintain statistical information on the number of licenses issued, revoked, suspended, and denied. Florida is an open-records state and you can request and receive this very interesting data from the department.

A WORD TO THE WISE

Changes may be made to the laws concerning concealed weapons licenses. Sometimes these changes are administrative, sometimes they affect how you carry, and they can make what once was legal illegal. You need to be aware of these changes and ensure that you comply with all the current rules and regulations to avoid even innocent violations.

Officials may not agree on everything, and how individual law enforcement officers interpret the law may be different from how an attorney interprets it and how you understand it from your own study and training. Unfortunately, the law is not always black and white. The statutes may appear to clearly say one thing but an officer on the scene or a court may interpret it very differently when it addresses the facts of a particular case or when it applies past court precedents.

The **elements of this book will undoubtedly change**. Remember that you may face serious repercussions for what may be seemingly minor infractions. _The Florida Gun Owner's Guide is just one tool for helping you on a long road to knowledge, and the road is not perfect._ That road has many turns and pitfalls—you should not rely on a single vehicle for such a complicated route, and be extremely cautious as you travel its course. Take steps to stay current.

Bloomfield Press will be preparing **updates** periodically. To receive free news about updates send us a stamped, self-addressed envelope, or visit our website. The addresses are on page two.

PROHIBITED PLACES

In days long gone people would check their firearms before entering where guns were traditionally not allowed, such as a bar or a courthouse.

Today, prohibited places make it necessary to leave your firearm in your car, as risky as that might be, or at home, which also carries some risk. The list has grown with the passage of time, giving rise to the phrase "infringement creep."

Although your concealed weapons license allows you to carry a concealed weapon throughout Florida, there are some places where you may not carry weapons even with a license. Many of these places are listed in s. 790.06, and others can be found throughout the statutes and in certain agency regulations (especially hunting regulations, outlined in Chapter 6).

Even if a place is prohibited without proper authority, or prohibited without proper notice to you, or if you feel it illegally compromises your rights, a violation can have the most serious effects on you, including arrest, confiscation of the weapons involved, and loss of the right to hold a license or even to bear arms altogether. You may win in court at a later date but you have to ask yourself if the hassle is worth the trouble. Use caution, common sense and good judgment to help minimize the legal risks you face.

Keep in mind that this list may change, officials may prohibit new places with or without the apparent authority to do so, places may be posted by people whose authority to do so is unknown, and the following list may not be comprehensive.

1–Any place of nuisance (generally defined as a house of prostitution or a place where illegal gambling is held);

2–Any police, sheriff, or highway patrol station;

3–Any detention facility, prison, or jail;

4–Any courthouse;

5–Any courtroom, but this does not prevent a judge from carrying a concealed weapon and a judge may decide who will carry a concealed weapon in the courtroom;

6–Any polling place;

7–Any meeting of the governing body of a county, public school district, municipality, or special district;

8–Any meeting of the legislature or its committees;

9–School zones (defined in its own section below)

10–Any school, college, or professional athletic event that is not related to firearms;

11–Any school administration building;

12– Bars, meaning any portion of an establishment licensed and primarily devoted to dispense alcoholic beverages for consumption on the premises; it does not include liquor stores or other places that sell packaged alcohol, and does not include restaurants that serve alcohol in the restaurant area;

13–Any elementary or secondary school facility;

14–Any technical center;

15–Any college or university facility. There is an exception to this that allows a licensee who is a registered student, employee or faculty member of a college or university to carry only a stun gun or nonlethal electric weapon designed solely for defensive purposes. The weapon must not be able to fire a dart or projectile. Notice that this exception only applies to colleges and universities and not to other types of schools;

16–Inside the passenger terminal and sterile area of any airport. You may take any legal firearm that is properly encased for shipment into the terminal so you can check the firearm as baggage. The sterile area of an airport is the area beyond the inspection and metal detector devices, and includes the aircraft itself;

17–Any place where the carrying of firearms is prohibited by federal law. Guns are generally prohibited in federal facilities. Knowingly having a gun or other dangerous weapon (except a pocket knife with a blade under 2-1/2 inches) in a federal facility is punishable by a fine and imprisonment. Exceptions include authorities performing their duties, possession while hunting, and possession for other lawful purpose. You cannot be convicted of this offense unless notice of the law is posted at each public entrance or if you had actual notice of the law (which, it could be argued, you now do). A federal facility is a building (or part), federally leased or owned, where federal employees regularly work. The exception for "other lawful purpose" may seem to include proper licensed carry, but this is an unsettled point of law, and may subject you to severe legal risks. See Chapter 7 for additional information on federal requirements.

18–Where prohibited by hunting regulations, although the authority of wildlife managers to restrict concealed-carry licensees or others is unclear. See Chapter 6 for additional details on this unsettled area of law, and some of the places involved.

Willfully carrying a concealed weapon into any of the places listed in s. 790.06, even if you have a license, is a second degree misdemeanor.

In addition to the places which are specifically prohibited for those with a concealed weapons license, there are other places where privately held weapons are forbidden altogether:

1–Any state correctional institution (s. 944.47);

2–Any county detention facility (s. 951.22);

3–Any forensic facility (s. 916.178);

4–Any hospital providing mental health services (s. 394.458);

5–The Savannas State Reserve (s. 258.157);

6–National Forests, under s. 790.11 unless you have a permit under s. 790.12, during hunting season, or unless you are on a state road within the National Forest and the firearm is securely locked within a vehicle. (It's interesting to note that nothing at the federal level prohibits possession of firearms in National Forests, and discharge may only be restricted under narrow conditions—in fact, the forests are one of the primary remaining public lands where people may use firearms (Bureau of Land Management lands is another). The authority of the state to regulate federal land, as it does to the National Forests in these statutes, is not entirely clear);

7–Wildlife management areas, under FL regulations (F.A.C. 15.004 and 16.004);

8– A pharmacy as defined in chapter 465, unless you have a concealed weapons license (s. 790.145);

9–State parks, under Florida regulations;

10–Schools as defined under s. 790.115 and federal law, with exceptions and special conditions noted above, and in Chapters 1 and 7.

It seems likely that a person with a concealed weapons license is prohibited from carrying in these places even though they are not listed in s. 790.06. The section that prohibits carrying a firearm into a pharmacy excludes those with a concealed weapons license. None of these other sections prohibiting firearms makes the same exclusion for license holders and so they appear to apply to everyone.

The prohibited places listed may not apply to the proper authorities in the performance of their duties—peace officers, licensed security guards, licensed bodyguards, members of the military, prison guards, special exempt agents of the government and many more. The federal list alone includes more than 50 different statutes that exempt special people from gun laws. For more on this subject see *Gun Laws of America*, also published by Bloomfield Press.

Gun-Free School Zones Laws

Like most states, Florida has strict prohibitions about guns and schools. For federal school zones laws, see Chapter 7.

Every code of student conduct for elementary and secondary schools must contain a provision that the possession of a firearm, knife, or weapon by a student on school property or at a school function is grounds for disciplinary action and possible criminal prosecution (s. 230.23).

State law makes it a third degree felony to possess a firearm on any school property, school bus, or school bus stop (s. 790.115). There is no exception for holders of a concealed weapons license and s. 790.06 specifically prohibits license holders from carrying a concealed firearm to any elementary or secondary school, vocational technical center, college or university facility, school administration building, school or college athletic event not related to firearms, or to any meeting of a public school district.

However, under s. 790.115 you may possess a firearm at a school, school bus, school bus stop or in public within 1,000 feet of a school if:

1– It is for a firearms program, class or function and you have the prior approval of the principal or chief administrative officer of the school;

2– The school has a firearms training range;

3– You are lawfully carrying a firearm in your vehicle under s. 970.25;

4– You are a law enforcement officer.

It is a third degree felony to exhibit a firearm to anyone in a rude, careless, angry, or threatening manner, unless in lawful self defense, on the grounds or facilities of any school, school bus, school bus stop, or within 1,000 feet of the real property that comprises a public or private elementary, middle, or secondary school. This applies during school hours or during the time of a sanctioned school activity, under s. 790.115. This does not apply if the firearm is on private real property within 1,000 feet of a school, if you are the owner or a lawful visitor on the private property.

It is a second degree felony to discharge any firearm on any school property, school bus, or school bus stop, unless in lawful self defense, under s. 790.115. See Chapter 7 for extensive federal school zone requirements.

Emergencies

The Governor or a public official who legally declares a state of emergency may suspend or limit the sale of firearms or ammunition in the state, or restrict the possession of firearms in public places, under ss. 252.36 and 870.044.

Trespass

Some places, such as pawn shops, may display signs that say "No Firearms," even though many of them buy and sell firearms. How does this affect you if you are licensed and legally carrying a concealed firearm? Under the law there are two ways to legally enter private property:

1–If you are invited (called an "invitee"). An invitation may be specific ("come to my house for dinner") or general (a store "invites" potential customers by going into business and unlocking its door).

2–If you are licensed (called a "licensee"). You have a license to enter private property for lawful purposes such as asking for directions, to sell things if you are a sales person, or to undertake any other lawful activity.

Trespass is an unlawful entry onto property (s. 810.09). A trespasser is someone who enters private property after being warned not to enter, and it includes a person who, though lawfully on the property, is told to leave, and refuses or fails to leave. The warning may be explicit (a sign or a verbal refusal to allow entry), or implicit (you know you're not allowed in a place that's closed or fenced off). Simple trespass is a first degree misdemeanor.

However, if you are armed with a firearm or other dangerous weapon, trespass in a structure or vehicle is a third degree felony. Trespass on property other than a structure or vehicle, if notice against entering or remaining is given (either directly to you or by posting, fencing, or cultivating the land) while you're armed with a firearm or other dangerous weapon, is a third degree felony.

In the first instance, if you see a sign on a building that says "No Firearms" and you enter, you may be charged with committing armed trespass, a felony. The legality of discriminating against a person for bearing arms in a public place is an untested point of law, one that would be quite expensive to pursue.

The second instance of trespass on other property mostly affects hunters. If you are lawfully hunting and shoot an animal that jumps across a fence with a properly posted No Trespassing sign, you can't legally enter to retrieve the animal. You must get specific permission from the land owner to enter the posted property. Without that permission, you are trespassing, and if you carry your firearm while you do you are committing felony armed trespass.

HOW CAN YOU CARRY A GUN?

Can you tell which people are "legal?"

HOW CAN YOU CARRY A GUN?

How you carry depends on where you are, what you are doing, and if you have a concealed weapons license or not. The list of prohibited places (in this chapter) comes first in determining if a particular manner of carry is legal.

The top two pictures are only legal if you have a concealed weapons license, or if you are at home or your place of business. Rules established by the owner of the business would affect whether employees could carry without risking their jobs or criminal charges.

The man drinking the unidentified beverage would be legal at home or at work. If the drink is alcoholic, the man would be in violation if he becomes drunk, though drinking per se is not prohibited. If he is hunting, fishing or camping, he might technically be legal but still face harassment or even charges for open carry, by the authorities. At a gun show, for an enrolled club member, the shoulder holster would probably be acceptable. Wearing the gun in a bar, even with a concealed weapons license, would be a violation.

The man walking is likely illegal in this state, since he appears to be openly carrying on a public street. Appearances can be deceiving, however, and if he is lawfully hunting with a handgun, or at his home or business, he may be OK.

As you can see, the right to keep and bear arms has been significantly (infringed, restricted, encumbered, limited, hampered, diminished, gray, outlawed, pick one) under state law. Many small laws have combined to supplant the original intention and operation of the Second Amendment in modern-day Florida.

Much of this has been done in the name of stopping crime. Other efforts appear aimed at disarming the public. While efforts at stopping crime have had questionable results, the effect of gun laws on the law abiding in the state has become acute. The concealed weapons license law has eased the restrictions somewhat, but more than 98% of Floridians have been unwilling to register with the government for a license.

WHEN CAN YOU CONCEAL A FIREARM?

If you have a concealed weapons license you may carry a concealed firearm at any place that is not prohibited by law (see the *Prohibited Places* list in this chapter).

Without a concealed weapons license:

- You may carry a concealed firearm in your own home. Your home includes the *curtilage*, or area immediately surrounding your home. Your home also includes a hotel or motel room where you are a registered guest. Home does not include the public areas and hallways outside your room or apartment, or any land you have beyond your house.

- You may carry a concealed firearm in your place of business. However, if you're an employee, this will depend on the rules the boss establishes.

- A firearm may be concealed in a private vehicle by complying with the law that says a gun in a conveyance may be kept in the glovebox, a snapped holster, a locked or unlocked gun case, a zippered gun case, or a closed box or container which requires a lid or cover to be opened for access, as long as the gun is not carried on you personally, or is otherwise not readily accessible for immediate use. Because the authorities may interpret statutes in unexpected or unusual ways, it's often best to remain as discrete as possible when traveling legally with firearms.

TYPES OF WEAPONS 3

There are weapons and there are weapons. Guns are only one kind of weapon. If a gun is modified in certain ways, it may become a prohibited weapon, which may make it a crime to own or possess. Certain weapons, defined by name or by operating characteristics and appearance, may only be owned if they were made before Sept. 13, 1994.

A responsible gun owner needs an understanding of the different types of firearms, their methods of operation, selections for personal defense, holstering options, ammunition types, loading and unloading, cleaning and maintenance, accessories, safe storage and more. Many fine books cover these areas. This chapter of *The Florida Gun Owner's Guide* only covers weapons from the standpoint of those which are illegal, restricted or otherwise specially regulated.

Firearms vs. Weapons

Florida law sometimes makes a distinction between the words *weapon* and *firearm*, so it can refer to a class of weapons that are not firearms. When used in the law this way, the term *weapon* refers to a dirk, metallic knuckles, slungshot, billie, tear gas gun, chemical weapon, or any other deadly weapon *except* a firearm or a common pocketknife.

However, the term *firearm* is itself defined by law as a *weapon*, and this has caused confusion for many years. It's common practice to refer to a firearm as a weapon, the military rarely calls your weapon a firearm, the carry license is a concealed weapons license, and federal law often refers to firearms as deadly weapons. In order to communicate in plain English, which is one goal of this book, *The Florida Gun Owner's Guide* uses the word *weapon* to include firearms. When *weapon* means only non-firearm-type weapons as defined by Florida law, we make that clear in the text.

Plain English definitions of the various weapons mentioned in Florida law are found in Appendix A, the statutory definitions are in Appendix D.

PROHIBITED WEAPONS

In 1934, responding to mob violence spawned by Prohibition, Congress passed The National Firearms Act (NFA), the first major federal law concerning guns since the Constitution. This was an attempt to control what Congress called "gangster-type weapons." Items like machine guns, silencers, short rifles and sawed-off shotguns were put under strict government control and registration. These became known as "NFA weapons."

This gave authorities an edge in the fight against crime. Criminals never registered their weapons, and now simple possession of an unregistered "gangster gun" was a federal offense. Failure to pay the required transfer tax on the weapon compounded the charge. Other types of personal firearms were completely unaffected.

Political assassinations in the 1960s led to a public outcry for greater gun controls. In 1968, the federal Gun Control Act was passed, which absorbed the provisions of earlier statutes and added bombs and other destructive devices to the list of strictly controlled weapons. It is generally illegal to make, have, transport, sell or transfer any prohibited weapon without prior government approval and registration. Violation of this is a second degree felony under s. 790.221, and carries federal penalties of up to 10 years in jail and up to a $10,000 fine.

Defaced Deadly Weapons

Removing, altering or destroying the manufacturer's serial number on a gun is a federal felony. Knowingly having a defaced gun is a federal felony.

It is also a third degree state felony, under s. 790.27, to alter or remove the manufacturer's or importer's serial number from a firearm. If you sell, deliver, or possess any firearm that has the serial number illegally altered or removed it is a first degree misdemeanor. These requirements do not apply to antique firearms.

Plastic firearms

Firearms designed to evade detection by X-ray machines and metal detectors are prohibited by federal law. If a firearm does not contain at least 3.7 ounces of metal, it is generally illegal to handle it in any way. The lightweight Austrian-made Glock, with its polymer frame, created the commotion that lead to passage of this law. A model 21 (.45 cal) Glock uses about 18 ounces of metal, or nearly five times more than is required.

State Prohibited Weapons

It is a second degree felony, under s. 790.221, to own or have in your care, custody, possession, or control any *short-barreled rifle, short-barreled shotgun,* or a *machine gun* which is or may be readily made operable. This prohibition does not apply to firearms that are lawfully owned and possessed under federal law, or antique firearms as defined in Florida.

A knife that propels a knifelike blade projectile by means of a coil spring, elastic material, or compressed gas is known as a *self-propelled knife* under state law. It is a first degree misdemeanor to manufacture, display, sell, own, possess, or use such a knife. This does not include any device that propels an arrow, bolt, or dart, such as a common bow, compound bow, crossbow, or underwater spear gun. A self-propelled knife is a dangerous or deadly weapon and is subject to seizure and disposal, under s. 790.225.

A *slungshot* is a small mass of metal, stone, sand or similar material on a flexible handle or strap and used as a weapon (sometimes known as a blackjack). Under s. 790.09 there is no prohibition against possession of this, or of metallic knuckles, but it is a second degree misdemeanor to manufacture, sell, or have for sale either one.

It is a third degree felony to unlawfully make, possess, throw, project, place or discharge a *destructive device*. These are defined by s. 790.001 to include any bomb, grenade, mine, rocket, missile, pipebomb or similar device containing an explosive, incendiary or poison gas, and are also defined in federal law (outlined in this chapter). The state includes Molotov cocktails in this category, and possession of the parts to make a destructive device counts as having one. See the statutes for the complete technical descriptions.

Firearms with a bore of more than one-half inch in diameter (i.e., greater than .50 caliber) are generally considered destructive devices, but shotguns or big game non-autoloading hunting rifles are typically not included, and an exception exists for line-throwing, signaling and safety devices.

State Prohibited Ammunition
Florida law prohibits making, selling, offering to sell or delivering certain types of ammunition. As listed below, it is a crime to knowingly have the prohibited types of bullet loaded in a handgun (or the prohibited shells in a firearm), even if you don't intend to commit a crime. It is a more serious offense if such ammunition is used in a crime. Though illegal for civilians,

the following ammunition is generally not prohibited for the proper authorities. See s. 790.31 for the letter of the law on these types of specialty ammunition.

An a *rmor-piercing* bullet is a handgun bullet that has a steel or hard core and truncated cone that is designed as an armor-piercing or metal-piercing bullet.

An *exploding bullet* is one that is designed to detonate or forcibly break up from an explosive contained in the bullet.

A *dragon's breath shotgun shell* is one that contains exothermic pyrophoric misch metal (heat emitting, self-igniting rare-earth metal alloy typically used in tracers) as the projectile and is designed for the sole purpose of throwing a flame or fireball to simulate a flamethrower.

A *bolo shell* is a cartridge that expels two or more metal balls that are connected by solid metal wire.

A *flechette shell* is one that expels two or more pieces of fin-stabilized solid metal wire or dart-type projectiles.

It is a third degree felony to manufacture, sell, offer for sale, or deliver any of the ammunition described above.

It is a third degree felony to possess an armor-piercing bullet or exploding bullet in a handgun, or to possess a dragon's breath shotgun shell, bolo shell, or flechette shell loaded in a firearm, if you know of the ammunition's capabilities.

It is a second degree felony to possess an armor-piercing bullet or exploding bullet, dragon's breath shotgun shell, bolo shell, or flechette shell, with the intent to use them in a crime.

ILLEGAL GUNS

(Sometimes also referred to as NFA weapons,
prohibited weapons or destructive devices)

Frequently but inaccurately termed illegal, these firearms and destructive devices are among those that are legal only if they are pre-registered with the Bureau of Alcohol, Tobacco and Firearms.

1–A rifle with a barrel less than 16 inches long;

2–A shotgun with a barrel less than 18 inches long;

3–A modified rifle or shotgun less than 26 inches overall;

4–Machine guns;

5–Silencers of any kind;

6–Firearms over .50 caliber;

7–Street Sweeper, Striker-12 and USAS-12 shotguns.

As of Mar. 1, 1994, Street Sweeper, Striker-12 and USAS-12 shotguns are classified as destructive devices, subject to NFA regulations (similar to machine guns), and *must now be registered*. The tax is waived for all such weapons that were owned before the effective date. If you own and do not wish to register such a weapon, or wish to transfer ownership without filing federal transfer papers, you may transfer the weapon to a properly qualified dealer, manufacturer or importer (with their permission), or to a law enforcement agency.

Guns other than regular shotguns with a bore of greater than one-half inch (.50 caliber) are technically known as destructive devices. Some antique and black powder firearms have such large bores but are not prohibited, as determined on a case-by-case basis by the Bureau of Alcohol, Tobacco and Firearms. Also excluded federally are safety and pyrotechnic devices. Federal law includes rockets as destructive devices if they have more than a four-ounce propellant charge, and missiles with greater than a quarter-ounce explosive or incendiary charge.

AFFECTED WEAPONS

The federal Public Safety and Recreational Firearms Use Protection Act (sometimes called the Crime Bill or the assault-weapons ban, set to expire on Sept. 13, 2004), allows possession of certain firearms and accessories only if they were made before Sep. 13, 1994. New products must have a date stamp and are off-limits for the public. If you have an affected weapon or accessory (referred to as *assault weapons* by the news media) that has no date stamp, there is a legal presumption that the item is not affected (that is, it is a pre-crime-bill version) and is OK. Affected weapons (there are about 200) include all firearms, copies or duplicates, in any caliber, known as:

Norinco, Mitchell, and Poly Technologies (Avtomat Kalashnikovs, all models); Action Arms Israeli Military Industries Uzi and Galil; Beretta AR-70 (SC-70); Colt AR-15; Fabrique National FN/FAL, FN/LAR, and FNC; SWD M-10, -11, -11/9, and -12; Steyr AUG; Intratec TEC-9, -DC9, and -22; and revolving cylinder shotguns, such as (or similar to) the Street Sweeper and Striker 12, and, any **rifle** that can accept a detachable magazine and has at least 2 of these features: a folding or telescoping stock; a pistol grip that protrudes conspicuously beneath the action; a bayonet mount; a flash suppresser or threaded barrel for one; and a grenade launcher, and, any semiautomatic **pistol** that can accept a detachable magazine and has at least 2 of these features: a magazine that attaches outside of the pistol grip; a threaded barrel that can accept a barrel extender, flash suppresser, forward handgrip, or silencer; a shroud that is attached to, or partially or completely encircles, the barrel and permits the shooter to hold the firearm with the non-trigger hand without being burned; a manufactured weight of 50 ounces (3-1/8 lbs.) or more when unloaded; and a semiautomatic version of an automatic firearm, and, any semiautomatic **shotgun** that has at least 2 of these features: a folding or telescoping stock; a pistol grip that protrudes conspicuously beneath the action; a fixed magazine capacity in excess of 5 rounds; and an ability to accept a detachable magazine, and, any **magazines**, belts, drums, feed strips and similar devices if they can accept more than 10 rounds of ammunition (fixed tubular devices for .22 caliber rim fire ammo are not included).

MACHINE GUNS

Under strictly regulated conditions, federal law allows private individuals to have weapons that would otherwise be prohibited. An example is the machine gun.

Unlike normal firearm possession, the cloak of privacy afforded gun ownership is removed in the case of so-called "NFA weapons"—those which were originally restricted by the National Firearms Act of 1934. The list has grown since that time, through subsequent legislation. The most recent additions are Striker-12 type shotguns seen frequently in Hollywood films. As a law-abiding private individual, if you want to have an NFA weapon you must meet special federal conditions. These requirements are designed to keep the weapons out of criminal hands or to prosecute criminals for possession.

1–You must register the weapon itself in the National Firearms Registry and Transfer Records of the Treasury Dept. This list of arms includes about 193,000 machine guns.

2–You must obtain permission in advance to transfer the weapon by filing "ATF Form 4 (5320.4)" available from the Bureau of Alcohol, Tobacco and Firearms.

3–An FBI check of your background is performed to locate any criminal record that would disqualify you from possessing the weapon. This is done with the help of a recent 2" x 2" photograph of yourself and your fingerprints on an FBI form FD-258 Fingerprint Card, which must be submitted with the application.

4–The transfer of the weapon from its lawful owner to you must be federally registered. In other words, a central record is kept of every NFA weapon and its current owner.

5–You must pay a $200 transfer tax. For some NFA weapons, the transfer tax is $5.

A properly licensed dealer can sell a registered machine gun to a qualified private buyer, and help you through the federal and state procedures.

You may apply for approval to make NFA weapons, such as short rifles or sawed-off shotguns. The application process is similar to the process for buying such weapons. Unregistered NFA weapons are contraband and are subject to seizure. Having the unassembled parts needed to make an NFA weapon counts as having one.

The authorities are generally exempt from these provisions.

The official trade in machine guns is specifically prohibited from becoming a source of commercial supply. Only those machine guns (and other NFA weapons) which were in the National Firearms Registry and Transfer Records as of May 19, 1986, may be privately held. The number available nationally will likely drop, since no new full-autos are being added to the registry, and the existing supply will decrease through attrition.

State Controls on Machine Guns

Anyone who has a machine gun that is registered under the provisions of the federal law is specifically allowed under state law (s. 790.221) to possess such a machine gun. Some restrictions on shooting machine guns apply.

It is a first degree felony to shoot a machine gun upon, across, or along any road, street, or highway or upon or across any public park, or in, upon, or across any indoor or outdoor public place, with intent to injure someone or damage property, under s. 790.16. However, those who have federally registered machine guns are allowed to shoot them at ranges that permit such firearms and many clubs have special days or events for machine gun enthusiasts.

This exception has been upheld in court, allowing Florida residents to own federally licensed machine guns (Rinzler v. Carson, 1972).

CURIOS, RELICS AND ANTIQUES

Curios and relics are guns that have special value as antiquities, for historical purposes, or other reasons that make it unlikely they will be used currently as weapons. The Curio and Relic List is a 60-page document available from the Bureau of Alcohol, Tobacco and Firearms. They can also tell you how to apply to obtain curio or relic status for a particular weapon.

Antique firearms, defined in federal law as firearms with matchlock, flintlock, percussion cap or similar ignition systems, manufactured in or before 1898, and replicas meeting specific guidelines are exempt from certain federal laws. For complete details contact the Bureau of Alcohol, Tobacco and Firearms.

Under s. 790.27 of state law, the term *firearm* does not generally include antique firearms, and so the instant background check and 3-day waiting period do not apply to the purchase of an antique firearm, which includes a modern muzzleloader.

The exclusion of antique firearms and modern muzzleloaders from the term *firearm* creates some potentially gray areas in the law. Felons and violent career criminals are prohibited from possessing or owning firearms, under s. 790.23 and s. 790.235. However, because the state definition of a firearm excludes an antique firearm—unless it is used in the commission of a crime—it might be argued that felons or other criminals who own or possess muzzleloaders in Florida do not violate state law for mere ownership or possession (although they would apparently be in violation of federal law). This situation has apparently not been the subject of any court cases.

This same unusual reasoning might be applied to exclude muzzleloaders from the state prohibitions against taking firearms onto school property or selling firearms to minors. Again, there is a probable violation of federal law, and it is advisable to treat muzzleloaders and antiques as regular firearms when dealing with schools and minors.

New Legislation

Congress and state legislatures nationwide have been considering a variety of selective and categorical firearms bans. Everyone is advised to follow developments and remain keenly aware of any firearms or accessories that were formerly legal and then declared illegal or subject to new requirements. One such example is the Striker-12 shotgun, described earlier. Bloomfield Press posts updates on its web page when they are available. The address is found on page two.

WHAT'S WRONG WITH THIS PICTURE?

WHAT'S WRONG WITH THIS PICTURE?

WHAT'S WRONG WITH THIS PICTURE?

It is a federal felony to have these weapons and destructive devices unless they are pre-registered with the Bureau of Alcohol, Tobacco and Firearms.

- A rifle with a barrel less than 16 inches long
- A shotgun with a barrel less than 18 inches long
- A modified rifle or shotgun less than 26 inches overall
- Street Sweeper, Striker-12 or USAS-12 shotguns
- Fully automatic firearms (machine guns)
- Silencers of any kind
- Firearms using fixed ammunition over .50 caliber
- Armor-piercing ammunition
- Explosive, incendiary or poison gas bombs
- Explosive, incendiary or poison gas grenades
- Explosive, incendiary or poison gas mines
- Explosive, incendiary or poison gas rockets with more than 4 ounces of propellant (includes bazooka)
- Missiles with an explosive or incendiary charge greater than 1/4 ounce
- Mortars

Keep in mind that additional weapons may be added to this list in the future.

WHERE CAN YOU SHOOT 4

Once you own a gun, it's natural to want to go out and fire it. In fact, it makes good sense. If you've decided to keep a gun, you should learn how it works and be able to handle it with confidence.

Most hunting and outdoor shooting in Florida takes place on private land. Shooting is not prohibited on private land provided the shots pose no risk to life or property, and the location is sufficiently remote to avoid complaints about noise.

There are a number of public ranges operated by the Game and Freshwater Fish Commission and some public gun clubs have access to ranges operated by the Department of Law Enforcement. Commercial ranges that are open to the public, whether indoor or outdoor, generally provide an excellent and safe shooting opportunity. A U.S. Army facility near you may have range time available for the public through the Civilian Marksmanship Program, which is listed in Appendix C.

In order to understand where you may shoot outdoors in this state, you must first know where you may not shoot. The restrictions come first when determining if shooting in an area is permissible.

Certain legal justifications may allow shooting, even if it would otherwise be illegal. An example is self defense. This chapter notes these exceptions.

Local police or the sheriff's dept. are often the first place a person contacts for gun-law information. However, the police are generally not legal experts, and you have no way to evaluate the quality and correctness of the information you receive—which may depend entirely upon who answers the phone. Most important, if you inadvertently violate a law, "the police told me I could do it," may not be much of a defense.

Private Land

You can shoot on your own land as long as you and your gun are in compliance with the law. That means you need enough land to shoot safely, on land that's not open to the public, with legally possessed arms, without disturbing the peace, and so forth.

Land owners may grant permission for others to shoot on their land and may allow access to the public. Permission can be withdrawn at will. To prohibit shooting or hunting on private land, the landowner must put up plainly legible signs, as described later under *Posted Land*.

Shooting in Public

It is a first degree misdemeanor, under s. 790.15, to knowingly shoot:

1–In a public place, which is a place the public generally has a right to go to;

2–On or over the right-of-way of a paved public road;

3–Over any occupied premises;

4–From inside a vehicle, willfully, within 1,000 feet of a person (this violation is a second degree felony). Directing someone else to shoot from your vehicle is a third degree felony.

The law makes exceptions to the first three prohibitions if you are legally shooting in defense of life or property, or if the road or property is approved for hunting by the proper authorities. There are also allowances for proper shooting ranges.

It is possible (though perhaps unlikely) that if you are charged with a homicide, assault with a deadly weapon, or some other offense for shooting a criminal who has attacked you in your home or car, that you may also be charged under s. 790.15 as well, unless it is determined that the shooting was legally justified. Presumably, this could occur even if the assault charges are dropped.

Shooting at Buildings and Vehicles

It is a second degree felony, under s. 790.19, to wantonly or maliciously shoot into, at, or within:

1–a public or private building whether occupied or not;

2–any public or private vehicle of any kind that has someone in it;

3–a boat on water;

4–an airplane that is flying;

5–a train or railway car (under s. 860.121).

Any person who is lawfully shooting would never be shooting in these places because of the likelihood of injuring someone.

If you shoot in self defense in one of these places, and it is clear to the authorities that you were justified, it seems unlikely that you would be charged with a shooting offense. However, since an exemption for shooting in self defense is not written into these requirements (as it is in s. 790.15, for example) a shooting charge is not impossible. It is one of those awkward cases where using a gun to save a life is legal but shooting it is not. No one ever said that all these laws make sense, just that they are the laws.

Shooting into a building is a "flagrant disregard for the safety of others" and this is taken into consideration by a court if you are convicted of this offense (Cleveland v. State, 1996).

If you shoot at someone in or near a building, you may be convicted of shooting at or into a building (Skinner v. State, 1984). You may be convicted of this offense if the court finds that you were not shooting in lawful self defense. If the situation shows that you were legally entitled to shoot in self defense, however, it seems unlikely that you would be charged with shooting at or into a building.

A burglar who shot at a dog in a house was convicted of shooting within a building (Smith v. State, 1985)

Shooting on School Property

It is generally illegal to carry a firearm onto school property, under s. 790.115. Even a concealed weapons license doesn't allow you to carry on school property. Illegal carry of a firearm on school property is a third degree felony as well as a federal violation. Three exceptions include:

1–teaching an approved firearms class,

2–approved use of a school shooting range,

3–lawfully carrying firearms in your car (see Chapter 7 for special federal requirements).

It is also a separate and more serious charge, a second degree felony, if you are illegally carrying a firearm on school property and shoot it, under s. 790.115. However, an exception exists if you shoot for lawful self defense or for another lawful purpose. The way the law is worded, it is illegal to carry a firearm onto school property, but if you end up using it in legitimate self defense no charges may be brought.

National Forests

You may have firearms in the National Forests as allowed by law during hunting season. You may also have a firearm in the forests if it is securely locked in a vehicle on a state road. To otherwise carry a firearm on this federal land, you must first get a permit from the county commissioners where the forest is located. No federal permit is needed to carry or shoot on this land, but if you can't get a state permit to carry a firearm there, you can't shoot there.

Some people have questioned the state's authority to prohibit the bearing of arms on federal public lands such as this. The rules controlling the National Forests are in a book called *Code of Federal Regulations, Title 36,* available at larger libraries. These federal rules prohibit shooting:

• Within 150 yards of a residence, building, campsite, developed recreation site or occupied area;

• Across or on a Forest Development road;

- Across or on a body of water adjacent to a Forest Development road;
- In any way which puts people at risk of injury or puts property at risk of damage;
- Which kills or injures any timber, tree or forest product;
- Which makes unreasonable noise;
- Which damages any natural feature or property of the United States.

Violation of these restrictions carries a possible $5,000 fine and a maximum prison sentence of 6 months under federal law.

See Florida Statutes s. 790.11 and 790.12 for the letter of state law. The issue of prohibiting bearing arms on hunting lands is discussed in more detail in Chapter 6.

Posted Land

Private land may be posted by the owner or lawful occupant of the land to prohibit hunting and shooting. Under s. 810.011 signs must use the words "No Trespassing" in letters at least two inches high and include the owner or occupant's name.

It is advisable to avoid land with any type of "No Trespassing" sign, even if it doesn't meet the exact legal requirements, because although you may not be criminally liable, the land owner can still sue you for civil trespass. Don't forget that, from the landowner's perspective, the presence of an armed intruder may be a very serious thing.

State and federal lands may have signs or laws that prohibit firearms or shooting in certain locations or during certain time periods. It may be difficult to know just exactly what prohibitions exist because there aren't always signs, and the rules may be in a statute or regulation that you have never seen. Always check with the proper authorities, many of whom are listed in Appendix C, before venturing into the field to go shooting.

State and Federal Military Land

The land reserved for military use, whether under the jurisdiction of the National Guard or a branch of the federal armed forces such as the Army or the Air Force, is controlled by a military commander. What a commander says, goes. As a practical matter, possession or use of firearms on a military base is subject to control by the commanding officer, though no statute specifically prohibits private arms.

You can't do much of anything on military land without prior approval. In general, military shooting ranges are not available for public use, though exceptions may apply, and Army bases are required to comply with the Civilian Marksmanship Program (described in detail in Chapter 7). If limited hunting privileges are available, they are subject to the regulations of the Florida Game and Fresh Water Fish Commission *and* the base commander. Anyone on military land is subject to a search. For details concerning a specific military installation, contact the base provost marshal or the base commander's office.

Carrying firearms while traveling on a public road which passes through military land is subject to standard state regulations.

Shooting Machine Guns

It is illegal to shoot a machine gun, under s. 790.16:

1–across or down a road,

2–in a public park,

3–in a public place (defined above).

Nothing prohibits shooting a lawfully owned machine gun at shooting ranges that allow such firearms, or at a private place with the permission of the land owner, as long as the neighbors don't complain about the noise and no risk to life or limb is created.

Hunters

Many hunters station themselves along unpaved roadways to shoot at game flushed out of wooded areas by their dogs. This can be a very unsafe practice. In some places, a hunting area containing unpaved roads borders upon paved county or state roads. Authorities may have declared or posted no shooting zones along the paved roads. It may also be illegal to carry a hunting firearm along these right-of-ways while retrieving your hunting dogs who stray out into these no hunting areas. See the chapter on hunting for details.

Shooting and Alcohol

Not only is it unsafe to use firearms when drinking, it is illegal to get intoxicated. In Florida it is a second degree misdemeanor to shoot or have a loaded firearm in your hand while under the influence of alcohol or an illegal or controlled drug, under s. 790.151. There is an exception if you are shooting or using the gun for self defense.

If you are arrested for using a firearm while impaired you will be required to take a breath or urine test. If you refuse, your refusal can be used as evidence in a criminal trial. If it appears that someone was killed or seriously injured, an officer may use reasonable force to make you submit to a blood test.

You may also request a test, if you think it will show you aren't using alcohol or drugs, and the officer must administer it.

Medical records obtained from blood or urine testing are not confidential and must be released to the proper authorities. However, if such a test shows that you were using an illegal drug, this information cannot be used to charge you with a crime for illegal drug use. This was done to "encourage" people to submit to the test, knowing that other charges won't result. There are no medical records for breath tests since the police administer these, and the results are treated as required by law.

A blood alcohol level of less than 0.05 means that you weren't under the influence of alcohol. If your blood alcohol is between 0.05 and 0.10 the court will allow other evidence to show whether or not you were impaired. If your blood alcohol is 0.10 or more, you were legally impaired.

Shooting Ranges

Public or commercially operated ranges may be the best place to learn and practice shooting skills. The availability of shooting ranges varies widely in Florida. Some cities and counties have an abundance of ranges, while others have very few.

You can find commercial ranges in the yellow pages. Local law enforcement agencies may be able to provide you with information about local ranges.

You can also contact firearms or shooting organizations such as the National Rifle Association, the Florida Shooting Sports Association, the United States Practical Shooting Association, or one of the several shotgun associations. The Florida Game and Fresh Water Fish Commission has ranges throughout the state that are open to the public, and their list is free on request. The phone numbers you need are in Appendix C.

Anyone who keeps a gun for personal safety would be wise to visit a range regularly and practice. Get off your duff, call a friend, and go out target shooting before next month.

WHAT'S WRONG WITH THIS PICTURE?

WHAT'S WRONG WITH THIS PICTURE?

WHAT'S WRONG WITH THIS PICTURE?

1–Shooting within city limits is normally prohibited. Florida actually restricts shooting in *public places,* which covers much more than just cities.

2–It's illegal to deface signs.

3–Trespassing is illegal. Armed trespass is a more serious charge.

4–You shouldn't use targets that leave debris.

5–Shooting at wildlife generally requires a permit or license.

6–The target doesn't have a backstop. The shooter is not controlling the entire trajectory of the bullet.

7–If the shot crosses the road it is illegal.

8–The shooter isn't wearing eye or ear protection.

9–Saguaro cacti don't grow in Florida.

THERE'S NOTHING WRONG WITH THIS PICTURE!

THERE'S NOTHING WRONG WITH THIS PICTURE!

Practicing the shooting sports outdoors is a natural and wholesome pursuit as long as you comply with the laws.

• The shooters are at a remote location, on private land with the landowner's permission, or at an established shooting range.

• The remote location is not a public place as defined by law, and does not create a noise problem for neighbors.

• The target has a backstop which prevents bullets from causing a potential hazard.

• No wildlife or protected plants are in the line of fire.

• The shooters are using eye and ear protection.

DEADLY FORCE and SELF DEFENSE 5

**"I got my questionnaire baby,
You know I'm headed off for war,
Well now I'm gonna kill somebody
Don't have to break no kind of law."**

–from a traditional blues song

There are times when you may shoot and kill another person and be guilty of no crime under Florida law. The law calls this justification, and says justification is a complete defense against any criminal charges (see Appendix D for the letter of the law). The specific circumstances of a shooting determine whether the shooting is justified, and if not, which crime has been committed.

Whenever a shooting occurs, a crime has been committed. Either the shooting is justified as a legal defense against a crime or attempted crime, or else the shooting is not justified, in which case the shooting itself is the crime.

Your civil liability (getting sued) in an unjustified shooting case may be a greater risk than the criminal charges which this book covers. You can be charged with both, and your legal protections are less vigorous in civil cases than in criminal ones. With very narrow exceptions, overcoming criminal charges does not protect you from a civil lawsuit—you can be tried more than once.

Two chapters of *Florida Statutes* provide for self defense: chapter 782, Homicide, and chapter 776, Justifiable Use of Force, which includes when you may use non-deadly and deadly force. In addition to these chapters, a number of other sections that define crimes include an exception for cases of self defense.

USE OF DEADLY FORCE

A reasonable person hopes it will never be necessary to raise a weapon in self defense. It's smart to always avoid such confrontations. In the unlikely event that you must resort to force to defend yourself, **you are generally required to use as little force as necessary to control a situation. Deadly force may only be used in the most narrowly defined circumstances, and it is highly unlikely that you will ever encounter such circumstances in your life.** You have probably never been near such an event in your life so far. Your own life is permanently changed if you ever kill a person, intentionally or otherwise.

When can you "shoot to kill" and not be convicted of a crime? When the authorities or a jury, after the fact, determine that your actions were justifiable. *You never know beforehand.* And as a strategic matter, experts teach students to "shoot to stop" or "shoot to control or neutralize the threat," never shoot to kill. In a true self-defense case, your goal—your intention and mental state—is not to kill, but to protect.

No matter how well you understand the law, or how justified you may feel you are in a shooting incident, your fate will probably be determined much later, in a court of law. Establishing all the facts precisely is basically an impossible task and adds to your legal risks.

What were the exact circumstances during the moments of greatest stress, as best you remember them? Were there witnesses, who are they, what will they remember and what will they say to the authorities—each time they're asked—and in a courtroom? What was your relationship to the deceased person? How did you feel at the moment you fired? Did you have any options besides pulling the trigger? Can you look at it differently after the fact? Has there been even one case recently affecting how the law is now interpreted? Was a new law put into place yesterday? How good is your lawyer? How tough is the prosecutor? How convincing are you? Are the police on your side? Does the judge like your face? What will the jury think?

Be smart and never shoot at anyone if there is any way at all to avoid it. Avoiding the use of deadly force is usually a much safer course of action, at least from a legal point of view. You could be on much safer ground if you use a gun to protect yourself *without* actually firing a shot. Even though it's highly unlikely you'll ever need to draw a gun in self defense, the number of crimes prevented by the presence of a civilian's gun—*that isn't fired*—are estimated to be in the millions. And yet, just pulling a gun may subject you to serious penalties. Think of it in reverse—if someone pulled a gun on you, would you want to press charges because they threatened you and put your life in danger? You must be careful about opening yourself up to such charges.

Still, the law recognizes your right to protect yourself, your loved ones and other people from certain severe criminal acts. In the most extreme incident you may decide it is immediately necessary to use lethal force to survive and deal with the repercussions later.   Shooting at another human being is a last resort, reserved for only if and when innocent life truly depends on it. If it doesn't, don't shoot. If it does, don't miss.

You are urged to get and read some of the cases cited in this book to get a deeper understanding of the ramifications of using deadly force—and dealing with the legal system after the fact.

The Florida Gun Owner's Guide **is intended to help you on a long journey to competence. Do not rely solely on the information in this book or on any other single source, and recognize that by deciding to prepare to use deadly physical force if it ever becomes necessary you are accepting substantial degrees of risk.**

Even with a good understanding of the rules, there may be more to it than meets the eye. As an example, shooting a criminal who is fleeing a crime is very different than shooting a criminal who's committing a crime. You may be justified in shooting at someone in a specific situation, and you might miss and only wound, but if you ever shoot to intentionally wound you may have an uphill battle in court. The law is strict, complex and not something to take chances with in the heat of the moment if you don't have to.

It's natural to want to know, beforehand, just when it's OK to shoot and be able to claim self defense later. Unfortunately, you will never know for sure until *after* a situation arises. You make your moves whatever they are, and the authorities or a jury decides. The laws and legal precedents don't physically control what you can or can't do—they give the authorities guidelines on how to evaluate what you did after it occurs. **There are extreme legal risks when you choose to use force of any kind.** Using lethal force is so risky legally it is yet another reason to avoid it if at all possible—*for your own safety.*

Because cases of murder outnumber cases of justifiable homicide, the authorities have a distinct tendency to think of the person holding a smoking gun as the perpetrator, later as the suspect, and finally as the defendant, while the person who gets shot, or was merely threatened with a gun, is the victim and in need of protection. If you ever come close to pulling the trigger, remember there is a possibility you will face a murder charge when it's all over. The effects of the shot last long after the ringing in your ears stops.

DEADLY FORCE LAWS

Precedents

The statutes set out only the bare bones of self-defense law. To get the full picture you need to look at the court cases, called *precedents*, that have dealt with this issue. The legal principles governing self defense and use of deadly force have been developed in common law from court cases for hundreds of years. Setting this law down in statutes has only happened relatively recently.

The history of case precedents is often followed by the courts to interpret and expand the wording of the statutes. Sometimes, the courts' use of precedents seems to change the law from how it is set out in the statutes.

Florida is divided into five judicial districts and the courts in each district may interpret the law slightly differently by relying on precedents set in their own district more than cases from another district. In addition, precedents are often restricted to a specific set of facts. A court may find that in one situation a defendant was justified in using deadly force while another court may find, in a very similar situation, another defendant was not justified. This may result from relying on different precedents, subtle differences in the fact situations, or from the type of evidence presented by the attorneys.

Whatever the cause, the result is that two cases that appear to be similar may have opposite outcomes. This means that precedents are valuable for a general understanding of the law, but you cannot rely on any case or even group of cases as an infallible example of when you may or may not use deadly force.

In addition to the direct effects of the statutes and precedents, an attack survivor gets a crash course in how authorities on the scene behave, the role of prosecutors and grand juries, and how judges and trial juries think and react. As the American Self Defense Institute has observed, if you are criminally attacked and survive, in this day and age, one of the first things you need is a good attorney with experience in self-defense cases. A good attorney will have a private investigator on the scene as soon as possible to observe, collect witness lists and statements, and generally act to support your position in court should that become necessary.

This chapter discusses how the statutes and courts have described the laws on deadly force and self defense. It is an overview of what has occurred in the past. It is not a predictor of the future or of the results of any case you may be involved in. You are accepting substantial legal risks when you choose to use deadly force.

If you are ever involved in a shooting, and the evidence at the scene clearly shows a self-defense situation, you may find that you will not be charged with anything. This is sometimes referred to as a "no-bill," and you are free to get on with the rest of your life (though you still might be sued). It occurs with some frequency, and reflects the fact that legitimate self defense is not a violation of anything.

If on the other hand the evidence at the scene is not clear or raises questions, you may be charged with a felony. If a death resulted, the charge will be for a homicide, which includes manslaughter, negligent homicide, and murder.

The charges may be dropped if further investigation and forensic evidence shows that you acted in self defense, or if a clear case of criminal action cannot be made. If you are charged and the case goes to trial, then you must present all the evidence you have to convince the jury that your particular situation comes within the legal definition of self defense. No matter how justified you believed you were at the critical moment, your fate now rests with the legal system.

When you are charged with a crime such as murder or manslaughter, two sections of law are available for your defense.

Section 776.012 says you are justified in the use of deadly force only if you reasonably believe such force is necessary to prevent:

1–imminent death to yourself or another person,

2–great bodily harm to yourself or another person, or

3–the imminent commission of a forcible felony. Read the letter of this law in Appendix D.

Section 782.02 says you are justified in the use of deadly force:

1–if you are resisting someone's attempt to murder you,

2–to prevent the commission of any felony against you, or

3–to prevent the commission of any felony on or in a dwelling house if you are in it. Read the letter of this law in Appendix D.

The two sections seem to be clear in allowing the use of deadly force to protect yourself from being killed unlawfully.

There are some interesting differences in these two sections. For example, 776.012 mentions *forcible* felony, while 782.02 says *any* felony. Also, 776.012 allows you to defend someone else, while 782.02 does not. Section 782.02 mentions dwelling houses, while 776.012 does not.

In addition to these statutory differences, there are a number of requirements that the courts, through the use of common law or precedents, have decided are critical to the justifiable use of deadly force. The statute a person relies upon as a legal defense will depend on the circumstances of the event and decisions made by the attorneys.

Clearly, you cannot simply respond with deadly force for every felony. Excessive use of force, even if defending against a violent felony, can lead to charges against you. The law specifically provides for this in s. 782.11, which says that unnecessarily killing a person while resisting an attempted felony or any unlawful act, or after such an attempt has failed, is manslaughter, a second degree felony.

The statues say on one hand that you may use deadly force to protect yourself, and on the other hand that if you do it may be manslaughter.

A special justification for killing or wounding, when done by officials involved in stopping a riot or other serious breech of law and order, during a declared emergency, is provided in s. 870.05.

Every deadly force and self-defense situation is different. In this discussion we are presuming that a firearm is involved.

THE LANGUAGE OF THE LAW

The self-defense laws use phrases such as *deadly force, reasonably believe, imminent death, great bodily harm, forcible felony* and more. Each word in these statutes has specific meaning and is important to understand in the same sense that the authorities do.

Deadly Force

Deadly force is defined by statute, under s. 776.06, as any "force that is likely to cause death or great bodily harm".

The statute says that deadly force includes, but isn't limited to:

1–shooting in the direction of a person to be arrested, and

2–shooting at a vehicle that has a person to be arrested in it.

Any time you fire a gun in such a way that a person might be killed or wounded, this could be viewed as use of deadly force. Each situation is different, and the many people involved in bringing charges look at each specific case in order to decide on whether a given set of actions were legal or not.

The examples given in the statue refer to a person *to be arrested*. This may mean someone who has apparently committed a crime, or may be examples for law enforcement officers. Since justifiable use of force provisions for law enforcement officers are specifically set out in the next section, s. 776.07, the definition examples here appear to apply to civilians. Case law has not clarified the purpose or application of the phrase *to be arrested*. A person actually committing a sufficiently criminal act to justify your response with a gun would seem to fit well the definition of a person subject to arrest.

Deadly force doesn't always actually cause death or great bodily harm. It just must be something capable of causing it. A gunshot in the direction of a person represents that level of force, even if there is no intent to cause injury. Shooting such a "warning" is deadly force under s. 776.06 and this applies even if you shoot into the air (Miller v. State).

A *warning shot* is a Hollywood concept, and not generally recommended by experienced professionals. If there is no immediate need for deadly force, such a shot is unjustified and you should hold your fire. Such a shot may ricochet, and will eventually come down where you least expect it, perhaps a mile or more away; if it hits someone other than the suspect you were warning, the result may be a criminal charge related to improper use of deadly force.

There are other reasons not to fire a warning shot. If you fire a warning when you are truly in imminent danger you are wasting ammunition and time that would be better spent stopping the actual danger. A warning shot exposes you to liability for the death or injury of an innocent bystander because of your negligence or lack of justification for shooting. At the very least, shooting in public without justification is a first degree misdemeanor.

If you merely display a firearm without shooting it, this is not deadly force. The mere display of a gun isn't likely to cause death or great bodily harm, in and of itself. In once case, during an argument between two people in their cars in a parking lot, one waved an unloaded, holstered pistol in the air and drove off. The court held that merely displaying the gun without firing it was not deadly force (Stewart v. State, 1996; and Toledo v. State, 1984) .

In self defense you may only use an amount of force necessary to stop the imminent commission of death, great bodily harm, or a forcible felony. This doesn't always require deadly force. If you use excessive force and cause a death you may be found guilty of at least manslaughter, under s. 782.07. In two cases, where a person disarmed and then shot an attacker, the court found that this was excessive force and the shooter was guilty of manslaughter (Roberts v. State, 1983; Sanders v. State, 1978). If the attacker was still armed when the person shot, it might have been self defense instead, but you never know until well after the event occurs.

Reasonable Belief

There are two basic standards in American law for determining what amounts to a *reasonable belief*. One is based on what you believe at the moment you act, sometimes called the subjective standard. The other is what "a reasonably cautious and prudent person would do in the same situation," sometimes referred to as the objective standard.

In the first case, it is your thoughts, or more precisely, what you can convince someone else that your thoughts actually were at the time, that are the determining factor. In the other case, it is the opinion of someone else that determines the outcome, and what you may have thought is not an issue.

The Florida self-defense statute indicates that it is you who must reasonably believe your actions are necessary. However, court precedent here has established that justifiable use of deadly force is judged by the objective standard—literally, what the jury thinks would have been reasonable—and not by what you thought at the time.

The objective standard must be applied, however, to the facts and circumstances as they appeared at the time (Price v. Gray's Guard Service, 1974).

This objective standard makes it critical that you present evidence to the jury of what you experienced at the time, so they can find that a reasonable person in your situation would have used deadly force the same as you did, and therefore you were justified.

You must present evidence of your reasonable belief (Stewart v. State, 1996). The evidence can include many things, including, for example, that your attacker had a weapon, was bigger and stronger than you, had begun to actually attack, or had previously attacked or threatened you.

There must be evidence of an overt act that would cause a reasonable person to believe the attacker has an intention to immediately cause harm, and the victim will suffer death or serious injury if deadly force is not used in defense (State v. Coles, 1956). The actions of an aggressor may give you reasonable belief in one situation but not in another. The situation must be viewed in its entirety to determine if deadly force was justifiable. All the facts related to your decision to use deadly force are critical to a finding of not guilty by reason of justification.

A belief can be reasonable even if the danger isn't real as long as it appears to be real at the time (Harris v. State, 1958). For example, if someone put their hand on their hip during an argument, depending on what you know about the person, if they moved like they were going to draw a gun, if you could see something that looked like a gun, you might be justified in using deadly force.

However, if you knew the person didn't own a gun, the movement wasn't similar to a draw, or you didn't see anything to make you think there was a gun (or other lethal weapon), you might not be justified in using deadly force. You need to show that the conditions at the time would make a reasonable person believe it was necessary to use deadly force (Lightbourn v. State, 1937).

The danger can't be something you just imagine, there must be something you see, hear, or perceive that makes you think you are in immediate danger (Raneri v. State, 1971). For example, if an assailant has a toy gun that looks real in the situation you may be justified in using deadly force. But it should be obvious that the further you are from truly needing to defend yourself, the weaker your case will be.

If you make a mistake because you don't use good judgment, are frightened, negligent, or unduly excited, and primarily because of this you decide to use deadly force, you cannot rely on self defense as justification (Crockett v. State, 1939).

The reputation of the attacker may be important. If the attacker has attacked you in the past this can add to your reasonable belief that you are in imminent danger if the person attacks or threatens you again (Deeb v. State, 1938). If you know that the attacker has a reputation for violence against you or others this may give evidence to show why you formed a reasonable belief that you needed to use deadly force (Garner v. State, 1991).

Threats alone usually aren't enough. Mere words do not justify your use of deadly force, no matter how insulting or abusive (Harris v. State, 1958). Even if a person threatens to kill you, but doesn't do anything else, this doesn't give you justification to use deadly force. There must also be some overt act that shows that the person making the threats plans to immediately carry them out (State v. Coles, 1956).

Disparity of force can make a difference in determining what is reasonable. Disparity of force is something that gives one person an advantage over another and makes a fight uneven. The person with a disadvantage in strength, size, or numbers can use this when making the decision to use deadly force. In one case, a karate expert kept advancing toward and making threatening gestures to a partially disabled man who was cornered and saying he didn't want to fight. When the cornered man used a knife and killed the unarmed attacker the court held it was self defense (Bacom v. State, 1975).

It is the combination of these many factors and more that a jury must take into account when deciding if your use of force seems reasonable to them, regardless of if it seemed reasonable to you. While all this decision making takes place, your family perhaps reads about you in the paper, wondering how it will all turn out.

Imminent Danger

Deadly force may only be used in self defense to prevent an *imminent danger* of death or great bodily harm. One Florida case showed that making an attempt to draw a gun is imminent danger (Howell v. State, 1913). Imminent means that an attack is immediately about to happen or is actually occurring right now, right here, and that you will suffer harm if the attack continues.

If the danger is past, it is not imminent and the right to use deadly force evaporates immediately. You cannot shoot at someone driving away and claim justification (Pressley v. State, 1981). You can't shoot someone who is walking away even if they had just pulled a gun and threatened to shoot you (McKinney v. State, 1972). You generally can't use deadly force against someone you have disarmed (Huntley v. State, 1953).

Using deadly force while chasing someone, even on the heels of a crime that was just committed or attempted, is generally illegal—pursuit is not defense. Once the threat is over, the justification to use deadly force ends. Let it end and give thanks that you're safe and it's over. In a somewhat bizarre turn of logic, a criminal who is escaping may be able to defend against you if you give chase, since you have now become the aggressive party. A criminal's retreat, even immediately after committing a crime, is not an attack.

The requirement that danger be imminent means that you can't lay a trap or wait for someone to attack and then claim self defense. You may not set a spring gun and claim that it was self defense. A spring gun, not defined by law, is generally a gun set to go off from a trip wire or similar device. There is no statute regarding this but it is covered in case law.

Even if your home or business was previously broken into, the use of a trap or spring gun is unjustified. Spring guns are arbitrary, cannot make a decision, and shoot anyone who trips the firing mechanism. The use of a spring gun that caused a death has been found to be manslaughter (Falco v. State, 1981). Likewise, you can't lie in wait and ambush someone even if they have threatened your life (Barnhill v. State, 1908).

You also have a legal and moral duty to prevent a danger from becoming imminent if you can. If you see or anticipate a bad situation you must avoid it if possible. If a danger suddenly or gradually appears, you generally must try to get away before you stand your ground and defend yourself.

Great Bodily Harm

An injury which creates a substantial risk of death, causes permanent loss of a limb or organ, which causes disfigurement, or from which the victim may never fully recover, is generally considered great bodily harm. An injury which is likely to heal completely in a reasonable amount of time is probably not great bodily harm.

Duty to Retreat

You may have a *duty to retreat* from danger before resorting to deadly force. While the statutes here don't require that you retreat from danger before using force or deadly force, as some states do, the courts have sometimes decided that you should have done so. You can at least expect prosecutors to question your decision to shoot if you could have just as easily gotten away. From a tactical standpoint, escaping an attack may be a better choice than entering mortal combat.

If you don't take any measures to avoid an attack but could have, and instead use deadly force when it might have been avoided, you may be guilty of manslaughter (Gainer v. State, 1976). At least one case determined that you must do whatever you reasonably can to avoid using deadly force (Scholl v. State, 1927). This may mean avoiding a danger or retreating as long as you safely can. In a case where a person was in a car with the engine running and was not blocked from driving out of the parking space, the court found he could have retreated and was liable for using deadly force. He should have retreated because the option was available to him (Reimel v. State, 1988).

There is *no duty to retreat* if it increases the danger to you (Prudential v. Marullo). If you will be put in greater danger by retreating (for example, you must turn your back to the attacker, or you are backed up against a steep drop you may stand your ground.

The law views your home as a special case, and you don't have to retreat if you are attacked in your own home (Pell v. State, 1929). This is the so-called *castle doctrine*, which says your home is your castle, and you are allowed to stand your ground to defend yourself in it. This is seen in statute in s. 782.02. However, if you are attacked by someone who shares your home with you and who has an equal right to be there, then once again you must try to avoid the danger or retreat, unless it will increase the danger to you or someone else (Rippie v. State, 1981).

The castle doctrine may also apply at work. You typically don't have to retreat if attacked at your place of business (State v. Smith, 1979). This applies if you own the business or if you are just an employee. Employees however may have legal exposure or face firing for being armed if the boss has prohibited this.

Forcible Felonies

The use of deadly force is permissible by statute to prevent a *forcible felony*. These felonies are listed in the statute, under s. 776.08, and include:

- treason
- murder
- manslaughter
- sexual battery
- carjacking
- home-invasion
- robbery
- burglary

- arson
- kidnapping
- aggravated assault
- aggravated battery
- aggravated stalking
- aircraft piracy
- unlawful throwing, placing, or discharging of a destructive device or bomb
- any other felony which involves the use or threat of physical force or violence against any individual

Although a deadly-force response may be allowed by statute, this doesn't mean you may automatically use deadly force. Common sense and good judgment are required and should be used. A person setting off a small explosive in a deserted place may be violating the law, but responding with gunfire may well be seen as excessive force when it reaches a jury. The same might apply for a lethal response to any person who is threatening violence, depending on the circumstances. You should always avoid shooting if safely possible, if for no other reason than the legal risk it represents to you.

Protecting Property

The use of deadly force to protect property is generally restricted to property crimes that also include an element of potential harm to a person. Property crimes such as theft are not included for this reason. The list of forcible felonies includes some crimes against property, such as carjacking, home-invasion, burglary, and arson. Each of these property crimes however also includes an element of potential harm to any person who is at the scene.

Section 776.031 says you may use force (but not deadly force) to protect real and personal property that is lawfully in your possession, or in the possession of your immediate family or members of your household, or if you have a legal duty to protect the property. You are only justified in using deadly force if you reasonably believe it is necessary to prevent the imminent commission of a forcible felony.

Impairment

Section 790.151, making it a second degree misdemeanor to use a firearm while impaired by alcohol or drugs, makes an exception for anyone who legally uses a firearm for personal protection or protection of their property.

Limits on the Claim of Self Defense

Generally, you must be free from fault and cannot be the aggressor to be successful in a claim of self defense (Gaff v. State, 1931). This basically means you are minding your own business and doing nothing illegal at the moment when an illegal attack occurs.

If you initially provoke a fight you may not use the confrontation to justify your use of deadly force in self defense, under s. 776.041. A person, whose unprovoked aggressive acts set into motion a chain of events that lead to the death of another person, was found to be guilty of manslaughter (Perkins v. State, 1991).

There are two possible exceptions to this however. If you had a role in creating the confrontation, you still may be able to justify the use of deadly force if:

1–the person you are fighting uses such force that you are in imminent danger of death or serious bodily injury and you cannot escape, or

2–if you withdraw from the fight and clearly indicate that you are stopping, but the other person keeps fighting.

See s. 776.041 for the letter of the law. A precedent on this principle was also set in the case of Padgett v. State, 1898.

Self Defense As an Exception to Other Offenses

The possession or use of a firearm may be a criminal offense in certain situations, but if self defense is the reason for having the firearm, then there is no offense.

1–It is a first degree misdemeanor to have or carry a firearm in the presence of others and exhibit it in a rude, careless, angry, or threatening manner, unless it is done in self defense (s. 790.10).

2–It is a first degree misdemeanor to shoot in a public place, on or over a right-of-way or any paved public road, or over an occupied premises unless done in lawful defense of life or property (s. 790.15).

3–It is a second degree misdemeanor to use a firearm while impaired by alcohol or drugs unless in lawful self defense or defense of your property (s. 790.151).

4–It is a second degree felony to discharge a firearm on school property, a school bus, or at a school bus stop unless it is in lawful defense of yourself or another person, or for other lawful purpose (s. 790.115).

5–It is a third degree felony to improperly display a firearm on school property, a school bus, at a school bus stop, or within 1,000 feet of school property (with an exception for private property within the 1,000 feet), during school hours or events, except in self defense (s. 790.115).

6–Section 780.07 makes it manslaughter to kill a human being by the act, procurement, or culpable negligence of another person, without lawful justification under the provisions of Chapter 776. This means that if you kill someone when you *are* legally justified in using deadly force the charge of manslaughter cannot be made.

CIVIL LIABILITY FOR SELF DEFENSE

Florida protects you from a civil lawsuit brought by someone you shoot in self defense. See s. 776.085 for the letter of the law. If you are sued by a person (or the estate of a person) you shot in self defense, showing that the person was committing or attempting a forcible felony at the time invalidates their case.

If there was no conviction you may prove the criminal activity by a "preponderance of evidence." This civil degree of proof is easier to show than the "beyond a reasonable doubt" evidence to get a criminal conviction. If you can show either of these the court will dismiss the action against you.

In one case a man who was alone at home heard a noise and suspected burglars. Three men had pried off the lock to the security bars on his sliding glass door with crowbars. When the man approached the door he saw the three men and what he believed was a weapon. He shot and killed one of them. The dead burglar's estate sued him for damages, and he got a summary judgment to stop the suit. They appealed. The court of appeal said:

"The record supports the trial court's findings that Perez (the criminal) was attempting to commit a forcible felony at the time Valdes (the homeowner) discharged the weapon; the burglars had not repudiated the crime prior to the shooting."

The court held that it was proper to enter a summary judgment, that is, to dismiss the case, in favor of the homeowner (Gonzales v. Liberty Mutual, 1994). The comment that the burglars "had not repudiated the crime" points out that if the burglars had given up or fled, there would have been no justification to shoot.

Bystanders

Your liability for killing or injuring an innocent bystander may depend on the circumstances or on the court. Some early cases held that if you intended to use deadly force in legitimate self defense, and your shot missed your attacker and killed an innocent bystander, that this comes within justifiable use of deadly force and you won't be liable (McCray v. State, 1925; Brown v. State, 1922; Pinder v. State, 1891). A more recent case held that if you shoot, even though you have no intention of hitting or killing someone, if you kill a bystander, you may be guilty of second degree murder (Pressley v. State, 1981).

RELATED LAWS

Use of firearms can lead to charges being brought against you if your actions are not justified by law. Here are the basic charges a person with a gun may face, if the possession or use is found by the authorities to be unlawful. Remember that self defense is only determined after an incident of gun use occurs. Creative prosecutors may come up with additional charges.

- *Open Carry (790.053)* Despite apparent constitutional guarantees, the mere possession of a firearm, if carried improperly (in this case, openly in public, with some exceptions) is a second degree misdemeanor.

- *Concealed Carry (s. 790.01)* Despite apparent constitutional guarantees, the mere possession of a firearm, if carried improperly (in this case, concealed without a government license or other valid exception) is a third degree felony.

- *Impairment (s. 790.151)* Shooting or holding a loaded gun is a second degree misdemeanor if you're under the influence of alcohol or illegal drugs (with an exception for self defense).

- *Reckless Display (s. 790.10)* It's a first degree misdemeanor to display a gun in a rude, careless, angry or threatening manner, except in self defense.

- *Threatening (s. 790.10)* It's a first degree misdemeanor to threaten a person with a gun except in self defense.

- *Warning Shots (S. 776.06)* There is no statute that allows for warning shots, and under this statute may be considered the use of deadly force. Any such shot in public could be a first degree misdemeanor under s. 790.15, and other charges could be brought. Because warning shots are dangerous to bystanders (even a mile away when the round comes down) they are ill advised, and causing an injury could be a felony.

The justification to shoot in self defense or in resisting certain crimes does not in any way allow using a firearm as an audible warning device, and it can attract more police attention to you (since the bad guys will have long since split) than you ever wanted.   The firearm used may be subject to confiscation, and you really don't want to have to explain your innocence to uniformed officers at your door.

If the situation isn't immediately life or death, don't fire.   If you really are locked in mortal combat, don't waste a potentially life-saving shot, and time, making scary noises. Firing a warning may serve as evidence that you didn't believe the situation presented an immediately deadly threat, and that you really did fire without justification. Warning shots are an instrument of Hollywood, that have little place in the real world.

- *Paramilitary Organizations and Marches (s. 870.06)* It's a second degree misdemeanor for a group of people to get together to drill or parade in public with firearms, or to form such a group.

- *Unlawful Assembly (s. 790.29)*   A fine line is drawn between conducting legitimate firearms training with other people, which is guaranteed by law, groups of two or more people getting together with firearms for unlawful training, and three or more people causing a public disturbance involving acts of violence. A violation is a third degree felony.

- *Aggravated Assault (s. 784.021)*   Unlawfully threatening a person with a gun, in a way that causes a well-founded fear of violence, without intent to kill, or with intent to commit a felony, is a third degree felony.   Using a gun to "leverage" an argument, even without pulling it, can lead to this very serious charge.

- *Threats and Extortion (s. 836.05)* Maliciously threatening anyone, verbally or in writing, with injury, or to compel them to act against their will, is a second degree felony.

- *Resisting an Officer (s. 843.01)* Knowingly and willfully resisting anyone performing a legal duty, by doing violence to them, is a third degree felony.

- *Arresting Escaped Convicts (s. 843.04)* You must help authorities search for and arrest escapees if you are called upon to do so, or face a first degree misdemeanor charge.

- *Aiding Peace Officers (s. 843.06 and 901.18)* If asked, you must help any peace officer in preserving the peace, assisting in a criminal case, or in capturing or arresting a person. Failure to do so is a second degree misdemeanor. When commanded by a peace officer, you have the same authority to make an arrest as the officer does, and you are shielded against civil liability for reasonable conduct.

- *Stop and Frisk Law (s. 901.151)* A peace officer can temporarily detain you, and seize any dangerous weapon you may have, if the officer reasonably believes a crime may have been committed or is imminent.

Certain other state laws have a bearing on your personal ownership, possession and use of firearms.

- *Using Force to Deter Trespass (s. 810.08)* It is legal for a property owner or other person authorized by the owner to use reasonable force to detain or take a person into custody, if you reasonably believe the person is committing armed trespass. You must contact the authorities as soon as practical in such an event.

- *Body Armor (s. 775.0846)* It is legal to own or wear bullet resistant garments, but committing a serious crime while wearing one is a third degree felony.

- *Reporting Gunshot Wounds (s. 790.24)* Medical personnel must report gunshot wounds to the local sheriff, if violence is indicated, or face a first degree misdemeanor charge.

- *Assisting Self Murder (s. 782.08)* It is second degree felony manslaughter to help a person commit suicide.

- *Minors and Incompetents (s. 790.17)* It is a third degree felony to illegally transfer a firearm to a minor. It is a first degree misdemeanor to transfer a weapon to a minor or person of unsound mind.

- *Keeping Control of Your Firearms* There is an increasing risk of civil action (a lawsuit) against a person whose firearm is taken, lawfully or otherwise, and used illegally by another person. Such suits seek to transfer the responsibility for illegal actions from the person committing the crime to a person who otherwise lawfully owns a piece of property, in this case, a firearm.

IF YOU SHOOT A CROOK OUTSIDE YOUR HOUSE DO YOU HAVE TO DRAG HIM INSIDE?

IF YOU SHOOT A CROOK OUTSIDE YOUR HOUSE
DO YOU HAVE TO DRAG HIM INSIDE?

IF YOU SHOOT A CROOK OUTSIDE YOUR HOUSE DO YOU HAVE TO DRAG HIM INSIDE?

No! Acting on this wide-spread myth is a completely terrible idea. You're talking about tampering with evidence and obstructing justice. If you're involved in a shooting, leave everything at the scene just as it is and call for the police, an ambulance and your attorney.

Don't think for a minute that modern forensics won't detect an altered scene of a crime. At any shooting a crime has been committed. Either the shooting is justified, which means you were in your rights and the victim was acting illegally, or you exceeded your rights in the shooting, regardless of the victim's circumstance. The situation will be investigated to determine the facts, and believe it, the facts will come out. Police tell time-worn jokes about finding "black heel marks on the linoleum." Once you're caught in a lie, your credibility is shot.

If you tamper with the evidence, you have to lie to all the authorities to back it up. Then you have to commit perjury to follow through. One illegal act leads to another and you may end up in far greater trouble than if you just tell the truth, after you calm down a little, with your attorney present.

If the guy with the mask was shot from the front, armed as he is, the homeowner has a good case for self defense. If the thief was leaving, hands full of loot, there may not have been justification to shoot at all, and this homeowner is in trouble. Either way, he's better off leaving the body where it falls.

Suppose you shoot an armed intruder coming through your window, and the body falls outside the house. You'll have a better time convincing a jury that you were scared to death, than trying to explain how the dead crook in your living room got blood stains on your lawn.

The reason this fable gets so much play is because there is a big difference between a homeowner shooting a crook in the kitchen, and one person shooting another outdoors. Shooting at a stranger outside your house can be murder.

CAN YOU POINT A GUN AT SOMEONE?

CAN YOU POINT A GUN AT SOMEONE?

CAN YOU POINT A GUN AT SOMEONE?

No matter how many aces a person is holding, you can't settle the matter with a gun. This also shows how the law can be interpreted in more than one way.

Unless you have solid legal grounds for doing so (and the character here does not), using a gun to threaten another person is *aggravated assault,* a third degree felony. Merely showing a gun so a person can see you do it is enough to bring on this very serious charge. This could even occur by accidentally pointing a gun at someone through careless handling.

If the guy with the gun is angry enough to take back his money, it could become *robbery with a firearm,* a first degree felony, punishable by up to 30 years imprisonment.

A common charge for pulling a firearm in a rude, careless, angry or threatening manner, when it's not necessary for self defense, is *improper exhibition*, a first degree misdemeanor.

By drawing your gun, the other guy may be able to shoot you dead and legally claim self defense. You may never pull a gun to leverage an argument.

If someone pointed a gun at you, would you get angry and want to see them arrested? Consider how someone would feel if roles were reversed and it was you who pulled the gun out of some passion other than the will to survive, when it wasn't absolutely necessary to prevent a life-threatening situation.

Despite all this, the law recognizes your right to defend yourself, your loved ones, and other people. These cases, when you *can* point a gun at another person, are described in this chapter.

HUNTING REGULATIONS 6

The Florida Constitution, in Article IV Section 9, creates the five member Game and Fresh Water Fish Commission. This body is delegated the authority to regulate hunting and fresh water fishing in Florida. The legislature enacts laws to assist the Commission with its decisions.

Rules for hunting in Florida are found primarily in Florida Statutes, Chapter 372 Wildlife, and in Title 39 of the Florida Administrative Code (the regulations enacted by the Commission). Appendix D of *The Florida Gun Owner's Guide* contains the hunting statutes dealing with firearms. Hunters need to know much more than just the firearms details provided here. For detailed hunting regulations contact the Game and Fresh Water Fish Commission at one of the phone numbers listed in Appendix C.

You should also refer to the Hunting Handbook Regulations Summary published by the Commission each year. This is free of charge and you can find a copy wherever hunting licenses are sold. Be aware that the handbook is a *summary* and does not contain all the regulations and laws you need to know. You can contact the Commission for exact legal questions you may have, and of course, exercise reasonable caution with any information you get verbally. Get a new handbook every year because bag limits and dates of seasons may change.

Hunting Licenses

Hunting licenses are sold across the state. You can get one at the county tax collector's office or a subagent of the tax collector. Subagents are often gun stores, sporting-goods retailers, and hunting and fishing stores. You can get a federal waterfowl stamp at the U.S. Post Office.

A hunting license is required for anyone who is going to hunt, except:

1–a child under 16 years old (who must be accompanied);

2–anyone who is hunting in their county of residence on their homestead or the homestead of their spouse or minor child;

3–a minor child hunting on their parent's homestead;

4–a resident who is a member of the US armed forces, who is not stationed in Florida, but who has orders and is home on leave for 30 days or less;

5–a resident who is 65 years or older who has a free senior citizen's hunting license or who has proof of age and residency;

6–certain Native American tribe members.

In addition, no license is needed by a landowner to take mammals (except deer or bear) that are damaging personal property, in the immediate vicinity where the damage is occurring. However, the use of a gun and a light at night are not allowed.

Hunting licenses may be obtained by residents and non-residents. Non-resident licenses have substantially higher fees. To qualify for a resident hunting license you must have lived in Florida for the six months before applying for the license and intend to continue to live in Florida as your permanent residence. Many people who live in the northern states and Canada live in Florida during the winter to avoid the cold and snow. The definition of *resident* prevents these "snowbirds" from obtaining resident hunting licenses. Members of the U.S. armed forces stationed in Florida are residents for the purpose of obtaining hunting licenses.

Hunter Education Course

Everyone born on or after June 1, 1975 must take a hunter safety course and have their hunter safety certification card in their possession to get a hunting license (though a child under 16 may hunt without taking the course, but must be accompanied). Florida allows the use of a hunter safety certification card issued by any state or Canadian province.

The Commission is required by statute to offer a free hunter education course. Fall classes are the most crowded, as many hunters wait until just before the season opens to get their certification. You can avoid the rush by attending a summer or spring session. The Florida course is between 12 and 16 hours long and covers:

- Firearms law;
- Firearms safety;
- Marksmanship;
- Blackpowder basics;
- Archery basics;
- Wildlife identification and management;
- Survival;
- First aid;
- Florida Wildlife Code;
- Outdoor ethics.

At the completion of the course, those who pass the written examination are issued a permanent hunter safety certification card. You need this card to obtain a hunting license in this or any other state. If you lose it you may contact the Commission for a replacement.

While hunting you must have proof of taking a hunter safety course with you (unless you are under 16 years old). This may be either the certification card or your valid hunting license. Anyone who was issued a lifetime license before hunter safety certification numbers were written on them, must also carry their hunter safety certification card along with their license. Anyone who does not need a license for hunting does not have to possess a hunter safety certification card.

Starting in 1997, the Commission is required to develop a special, free, hunter safety course for children between the ages of 5 and 16 years of age. This course must include safe handling of firearms, conservation, and hunter ethics, and it must be appropriate for the ages of the children. It is voluntary and in addition to the standard hunter education course in which a certification card is issued. This course is to provide this important training at a level more easily understood by these young children who sometimes have difficulty following the regular course.

Obtaining a License

In 1997 major changes in the hunting license application and form were introduced. Stamps were eliminated and replaced by permits. A single new form was introduced that includes all the hunting and fishing license options.

The form requires more information than before, including name, address and phone number; statistical data of race and sex; and identification information of hair and eye color, height, weight, and hunter safety certification number and state.

Included are questions for anyone who hunts migratory birds and the species hunted. Then you select which hunting licenses you want, and you may choose from among:

1–Freshwater Fishing/Hunting (complete permit);

2–Hunting (complete permit);

3–Trapping;

4–Management Area Permit;

5–Archery Permit;

6–Muzzleloading Permit;

7–Waterfowl Permit (complete permit);

8–Turkey Permit;

9–Migratory Bird Permit.

Upon payment of the fees you are issued one of the multiple pages as your license, which you may fold up to carry. You may buy all your permits at once, or complete a new application each time you want to add a new permit.

License subagents are liable under the new system for paying the Commission the total fees listed on the application if they lose an application. Some retailers, unhappy with the new system, are no longer selling hunting and fishing licenses. Call to see if your hunting retailer still sells licenses before you stop to get your license on the first morning of hunting season.

Wildlife Alert

The Commission has a Wildlife Alert Reward program. Anyone may confidentially report a wildlife violation by calling a toll-free phone number 24 hours a day. Since this program started in 1979 more than 700 arrests a year have been made because of reports by conscientious individuals. The phone numbers for each of the five hunting regions is listed in Appendix C.

SOME KEY STATE HUNTING REGULATIONS

Below you'll find the main general rules about the use of firearms while hunting. Remember, hunting regulations are not limited to guns and include archery, falconry, trapping and more. Be sure to check with the Florida Game and Fresh Water Fish Commission before undertaking any hunting activity.

It is generally illegal to:

• Shoot while hunting if it is prior to one-half hour before sunrise or more than one-half hour after sunset; special rules apply for spring turkey, migratory game birds, ducks, coots and others;

• Hunt with a centerfire semi-automatic rifle that has a magazine capacity of more than 5 rounds;

• Hunt deer, or accompany someone hunting deer, on public lands unless each person is wearing at least 500 square inches of daylight fluorescent orange above the waistline;

• Hunt deer with a muzzleloader less than .40 caliber or less than 20-gauge;

- Hunt deer with non-expanding, full metal jacket ammunition; expanding solid copper alloy bullets are allowed;
- Hunt deer with any rimfire ammunition;
- Display or use a light when in possession of a firearm customarily used for taking deer;
- Take fish with a firearm in fresh or salt water;
- Hunt migratory game birds with a shotgun that is not plugged to a three-shell capacity; the plug must not be removable without disassembly of the gun;
- Hunt migratory game birds with a shotgun larger than 10-gauge;
- Use rifles or pistols for hunting migratory game birds;
- Hunt with a machine gun;
- Hunt with a firearm that has a silencer;
- Use set guns (a firearm not held by a person, which is fired by the use of a string or other remote means);
- Shoot from any vehicle, power boat, or sailboat which is moving under power;
- Shoot turkeys while they are on the roost;
- Use any firearm other than a legal muzzleloading gun during muzzleloading season;
- Shoot (or in any way injure) any alligator or crocodile;
- Wantonly or willfully waste any wildlife. Edible portions that cannot be consumed may be donated to charitable causes.

Denial of the Right to Bear Arms

Some hunting regulations may attempt to prohibit possession of firearms, or certain types of firearms, based upon hunting season, location, the type of game, or other considerations. The authority for such prohibitions may not be clear, but you are advised that violations may have serious repercussions. Questions related to concealed weapons licensees vs. hunting requirements may not have clear answers, and since a firearm violation can cause you to lose or become ineligible for a concealed weapons license, extra caution is advisable.

Examples of firearm prohibitions under the general banner of hunting rules include:

• Possession of a gun while hunting fox (fox may be chased by dogs, but not taken);

• Use or possession of firearms not authorized for particular hunting seasons;

• Possession of loaded firearms in vehicles while engaged in hunting activities;

• Possession of firearms in specially designated hunting areas during closed season;

• Being within reach or in possession of firearms while catching, cutting off, or waiting for dogs while on a right-of-way of a federal, state or county road. (Hunters who must catch dogs on a right-of-way are advised to leave firearms with a companion, or unloaded and out of reach);

• Possession of guns while training deer dogs.

Firearms used in violation of hunting laws may be subject to seizure. If the firearm is owned by someone other than the person committing the violation, it may be returned to its lawful owner on proof of ownership. On conviction of a violation, the firearm may be forfeited to the state.

Civil Liability

Hunters may be liable in a civil suit brought by someone who was injured by an act of the hunter. This is in addition to any criminal charges that may apply. Civil cases generally arise from the negligence of a hunter. If you sue or get sued for a hunting incident in Florida, the suit is handled under Florida law, regardless of the residence of the persons involved.

If you injure someone while hunting, you can be both charged with a crime and sued by the injured person. If you are guilty in a criminal case you may lose your hunting license, have to pay a fine, forfeit your property, or go to jail. If you lose in a civil case you won't go to jail, but you may have to pay large amounts of money to the person you injured.

Basically, negligence involves three elements:

1–There must be a *duty of care* to others;

2–There must be a breach of that duty of care;

3–An injury must result from that breach.

As a hunter you owe a duty of care not to injure other people with firearms (or in any other way related to the hunting activity). That duty of care is to follow the ordinary care customary with hunting practices. A good guideline is to follow all the firearms and hunting safety practices taught in the Florida Game and Fresh Water Fish Commission hunter safety course.

Generally, you may be liable if someone is injured or killed:

1–If your firearm accidentally discharges;

2–If you mistake a person for game and shoot;

3–If you don't hit your target and the stray shot hits someone.

A HUNTER'S PLEDGE

Responsible hunting provides unique challenges and rewards. However, the future of the sport depends on each hunter's behavior and ethics. Therefore, as a hunter, I pledge to:

- Respect the environment and wildlife;
- Respect property and landowners;
- Show consideration for non hunters;
- Hunt safely;
- Know and obey the law;
- Support wildlife and habitat conservation;
- Pass on an ethical hunting tradition;
  Strive to improve my outdoor skills and understanding of wildlife;
- Hunt only with ethical hunters.

By following these principles of conduct each time I go afield, I will give my best to the sport, the public, the environment and myself. The responsibility to hunt ethically is mine; the future of hunting depends on me.

The Hunter's Pledge was created cooperatively by:

International Association of Fish and Wildlife Agencies
Izaak Walton League of America
National Rifle Association
Rocky Mountain Elk Foundation
Tread Lightly! Inc.
Sport Fishing Institute
Times Mirror Magazines Conservation Council
U.S. Dept. of Agriculture Extension Service
Wildlife Management Institute

NOTES ON FEDERAL LAW 7

Although federal laws regulate firearms to a great degree, the same laws prohibit the federal and local governments from encroaching on the right to bear arms. This is seen in the 2nd, 4th 9th and 14th Amendments to the Constitution, and in federal statutory laws, which number about 230.

Dealers of firearms must be licensed by the Bureau of Alcohol, Tobacco and Firearms (ATF). Federal law requires licensed dealers to keep records of each sale, but prohibits using this information in any sort of national registration plan. The information is permanently saved by the dealer and is not centrally recorded by the federal authorities. If a dealer goes out of business the records are sent to a central federal depository for storage (or a state site if approved by the Treasury Dept.). Although federal law prohibits using these records to establish a national firearms registration system, several federal attempts to do so have apparently been made. In addition, fingerprints submitted for background checks to the FBI are stored by that agency until the individual reaches 99 years of age.

Paperwork required by the Brady Law must be destroyed shortly after it is used to conduct background checks, and by law, no records of the checks may be kept. Local authorities are required to certify their compliance with record destruction to the U.S. Attorney General every six months. (The Justice Dept. reports that compliance with this requirement has been quite low.)

In theory, this means there's no central place for anyone to go and see if a given person owns a firearm (except perhaps in the case of those people who have registered for a concealed weapons license, if you assume they all own guns). Firearm ownership in America is traditionally a private matter. For someone to find out if you have a gun they would have to check all the records of all the dealers in the country, a daunting task. As a practical matter, though, it is increasingly easy for the authorities to tell who is armed and who isn't.

Only ATF is authorized to check the records of manufacture, importation and sale of firearms nationally. Local authorities occasionally ask to see a dealer's records, and dealers may feel it's in their best interests to cooperate, even if it isn't required by law.

The dealer's records allow guns to be *traced,* a very different and important matter. When a gun is involved in a crime, ATF can find out, from the manufacturer's serial number, which licensed dealer originally received the gun. The dealer can then look through the records and see who purchased the weapon. It's a one-way street—a gun can be linked to a purchaser but owners can't be traced to their guns. One study of successful traces showed that four out of five were of some value to law enforcement authorities.

When President Reagan was shot by John Hinckley Jr., the weapon was traced and in fourteen minutes time, a retail sale to Hinckley was confirmed.

Buying, selling, having, making, transferring and transporting guns is in many cases regulated by federal laws. These regulations are covered in *The Florida Gun Owner's Guide,* but for the most part, only state penalties are noted. There may be federal penalties as well.

Under the Assimilative Crimes Act, state law controls if there is no federal law covering a situation. It is important to recognize that there can be a question of jurisdiction in some cases. Additional federal requirements may be found in the Code of Federal Regulations and the United States Code.

A long history of federal regulation exists with regard to firearms and other weapons. The main laws include:

- 2nd, 4th and 9th Amendments to the Constitution (1791)
- Fourteenth Amendment to the Constitution (1868)
- National Firearms Act (1934)
- Federal Firearms Act (1938)
- Omnibus Crime Control and Safe Streets Act (1968)
- Gun Control Act (1968)
- Organized Crime Control Act (1970)
- Omnibus Crime Control Act (1986)
- Firearms Owners' Protection Act (1986)
- Brady Handgun Violence Prevention Act (1993)
- Public Safety and Recreational Firearms Use Protection Act (The Crime Bill) (1994)
- Promotion of Rifle Practice and Firearms Safety Act (1996)
- Antiterrorism and Effective Death Penalty Act (1996)
- Omnibus Consolidated Appropriation Act for FY 1997 (Domestic Violence Gun Ban, Gun Free School Zones)

Additional federal requirements may be found in the Code of Federal Regulations (CFR) and the United States Code (USC).

FEDERAL FIREARMS TRANSPORTATION GUARANTEE

Passed on July 8, 1986 as part of the Firearms Owners' Protection Act, federal law guarantees that a person may legally transport a firearm from one place where its possession is legal to another place where possession is legal, provided it is unloaded and the firearm and ammunition are not readily accessible from the passenger compartment of the vehicle. The law doesn't say it in so many words, but the only non-accessible spot in the average passenger car is the trunk. If a vehicle has no separate compartment for storage, the firearm and ammunition may be in a locked container other than the glove compartment or console.

There have been cases, especially in Eastern states, where local authorities have not complied with this law, creating a degree of risk for people otherwise legally transporting firearms. To avoid any confusion, the text of the federal guarantee is printed here word for word:

Federal Law Number 18 USC § 926A
Interstate transportation of firearms

Notwithstanding any other provision of any law or any rule or regulation of a State or any political subdivision thereof, any person who is not otherwise prohibited by this chapter from transporting, shipping, or receiving a firearm shall be entitled to transport a firearm for any lawful purpose from any place where he may lawfully possess and carry such firearm to any other place where he may lawfully possess and carry such firearm if, during such transportation the firearm is unloaded, and neither the firearm nor any ammunition being transported is readily accessible or is directly accessible from the passenger compartment of such transporting vehicle: Provided, That in the case of a vehicle without a compartment separate from the driver's compartment the firearm or ammunition shall be contained in a locked container other than the glove compartment or console.

Anyone interested in a complete copy of the federal gun laws, with plain English summaries of every law, can get a copy of *Gun Laws of America*, published by Bloomfield Press. See the back section of this book for details.

The Brady Law

The Brady Handgun Violence Prevention Act was signed into law on Nov. 30, 1993. Its provisions for common carriers, reporting multiple handgun sales and license fee increases are among the rules affecting private individuals that took effect immediately. The waiting-period provisions took effect on Feb. 28, 1994, and were set to expire on Nov. 30, 1998. Because Florida had its own 3-day waiting period and instant criminal history check system in place, the waiting and background provisions of the Brady law do not apply in Florida.

Under the "temporary" Brady provisions, waiting periods may be required, only handguns are involved, and background checks are conducted by local authorities. When the permanent requirements come on line (scheduled for 1998), all gun sales from dealers will be subject to national criminal background checks, which will be conducted by the FBI from a single location in Clarksburg, West Virginia. They plan to charge a fee for this service.

In addition to the regulation of private individuals described below, the Brady Law: places special requirements on dealers, sets timetables and budgets for the U.S. Attorney General to implement the law, provides funding, sets basic computer system requirements, mandates criminal-history record sharing among authorities, enhances penalties for gun thieves and more. Your federal legislators can send you the full 12-page Brady Law.

The Brady Law refers to a "chief law enforcement officer," defined as the chief of police, the sheriff, an equivalent officer or their designee. The description below refers to such persons as "the authorities." Where the law refers to an individual who is unlicensed under §923 of USC Title 18, this description says "private individual" or "you." Federally licensed dealers, manufacturers and importers are referred to as "dealers." The act of selling, delivering or transferring is called "transferring." The law defines *handgun* as, "a firearm which has a short stock and is designed to be held and fired by the use of a single hand." A combination of parts which can be assembled into a handgun counts as a handgun.

Most states, the same as Florida, are basically exempt from the Brady law. News reports are generally inaccurate in describing the bureaucratic procedures of this statute, often referring to a mandatory five-day waiting period when in fact no such thing is required (in Florida, same-day purchases are allowed for law-abiding residents). To legally obtain a handgun from a dealer under the Brady law, you must provide:

- A valid picture ID for the dealer to examine;
- A written statement with only the date the statement was made, notice of your intent to obtain a handgun from the dealer, your name, address, date of birth, the type of ID you used and a statement that you are not: 1–under indictment and haven't been convicted of a crime which carries a prison term of more than one year, 2–a fugitive from justice, 3–an unlawful user of or addicted to any controlled substance, 4–an adjudicated mental defective, 5–a person who has been committed to a mental institution, 6–an illegal alien (but legal alien is OK), 7–dishonorably discharged from the armed forces, 8–a person who has renounced U.S. citizenship.

Then, before transferring the handgun to you, the dealer must:

- Within one day, provide notice of the content and send a copy of the statement to the authorities where you live;
- Keep a copy of your statement and evidence that it was sent to the authorities;
- Wait up to five days during which state offices are open, from the day the dealer gave the authorities notice, and during that time,
- Receive no information from the authorities that your possession of the handgun would violate federal, state or local laws.

The waiting period ends early if the authorities notify the dealer early that you're eligible. The federal mandate that local authorities "shall make a reasonable effort" to check your background in local, state and federal records, was overturned by the Supreme Court in 1997, on 10th amendment grounds. Long guns are unaffected by the Brady Law until the National Instant Check described below comes on line.

You are excluded from the Brady waiting-period process:

1–If you have a written statement from the authorities, valid for 10 days, that you need a handgun because of a threat to your life or a member of your household's life (Florida law has a similar provision, see Chapter 1); or

2–With a handgun permit, in the state which issued it, if the permit is less than five years old and required a background check (the Florida concealed weapons license qualifies);

3–In states which have their own handgun background check (Florida has an instant check, making all Florida residents exempt from the Brady delay and paperwork); or

4–If the transfer is already regulated by the National Firearms Act of 1934, as with Class III weapons; or

5–If the dealer has been certified as being in an extremely remote location of a sparsely populated state and there are no telecommunications near the dealer's business premises (written for Alaska, but other localities may qualify).

If a dealer is notified after a transfer that your possession of the handgun is illegal, the dealer must, within one business day, provide any information they have about you to the authorities at the dealer's place of business and at your residence. The information a dealer receives may only be communicated to you, the authorities, or by court order. If you are denied a handgun, you may ask the authorities why, and they are required to provide the reason in writing within 20 business days of your request.

Unless the authorities determine that the handgun transfer to you would be illegal, they must, within 20 days of the date of your statement, destroy all records of the process. The authorities are expressly forbidden to convey or use the information in your statement for anything other than what's needed to carry out the Brady process.

The authorities may not be held liable for damages for either allowing an illegal handgun transfer or preventing a legal one. If you are denied a firearm unjustly, you may sue the political entity responsible and get the information corrected or have the transfer approved, and you may collect reasonable attorney's fees.

National Instant Check: Under Part 2 of the Brady law the U.S. Attorney General (AG) must establish a National Instant Criminal Background Check System (NICS) before Nov. 30, 1998. Once this is in effect (30 days after the U.S. Attorney General tells FFLs that the system is operational), the previous waiting process is eliminated. In order to transfer *any firearm, not just handguns,* when the NICS system is in place, a dealer must:

- verify your identity from a valid photo-ID card, contact the system, identify you and receive a unique transfer number, or
- wait up to three days during which state offices are open and the system provides no notice that the transfer would violate relevant laws.

The NICS system is required to issue the transfer number if the transfer would violate no relevant laws, and it is supposed to destroy all records of approved inquiries except for the identifying number and the date it was issued. If the transfer is legal, the dealer includes the transfer number in the record of the transaction. The NICS system is bypassed under conditions similar to 2, 4 and 5 listed above as exceptions to the waiting period (with number 2 broadened to include "firearms" permit).

Whoever violates these requirements is subject to a fine of up to $1,000 and a jail term of up to 1 year.

If you are denied a firearm under NICS, you may request the reason and the system must present you with a written answer within five business days. You may also request the reason from the AG, who must respond immediately. You may provide information to fix any errors in the system, and the AG must immediately consider the information, investigate further, correct any erroneous federal records and notify any federal or state agency that was the source of the errors.

Multiple sales of handguns (two or more from the same dealer in a five day period) have long been reported to the Bureau of Alcohol, Tobacco and Firearms, and must now be reported to local authorities as well. Local authorities may not disclose the information, must destroy the records within 20 days from receipt if the transfer is not illegal and must certify every six months to the AG that they are complying with these provisions.

Common or contract carriers (airlines, buses, trains, etc.) are prohibited under Brady from labeling your luggage or packages to indicate that they contain firearms. The long-time labeling practice had been responsible for the frequent theft of luggage containing firearms. Federal law requires you to notify the carrier in writing if you are transporting firearms or ammunition, but in actual practice verbal notification is frequently accepted. Carriers are also required to give you a written receipt when you reclaim such luggage, but this provision of the Brady law is largely ignored.

Licensing fees for obtaining a new federal firearms license are increased to $200 for three years. The fee for renewing a currently valid license is $90 for three years.

Brady Law Note

While the Brady Law is new it would be prudent to anticipate a degree of confusion, inconsistent policies and enforcement, conflicting regulations and jurisdictions, regulations which do not match the letter of the law, denials of responsibility, and court cases to clarify the intent, practicalities and legality of the law. With the law being challenged in federal courts, changes to it, repeal or partial repeal are possible.

As we go to press, many unanswered questions remain with regard to the national instant check system, which is not yet operational. Bloomfield Press will have details on this and more, available on our website and by mail on request. The addresses are on page two.

Public Safety and Recreational Firearms Use Protection Act

This law, popularized as the 1994 Crime Bill and sometimes referred to as the assault-weapons ban, affected three areas of existing firearms law: 1–Possession and use of firearms by juveniles; 2–Possession of firearms by people under domestic violence restraining orders; and 3–It created a new class of regulated firearms and accessories. The information on juveniles is found in Chapter 1 since it relates to who can bear arms. The new class of prohibited purchasers (for domestic violence cases) is also in Chapter 1, as part of the list for federal form 4473—the form dealers use with all sales.

The portion of the law that creates the legal *assault-weapons* category, has been poorly reported and many people have an inaccurate notion of what this law accomplished. Nothing is actually banned—Americans may still buy, own, sell, trade, have and use any of the millions of affected firearms and accessories.

What the law actually did was to prohibit *manufacturers and importers* from selling newly made goods of that type to the public (and it's a crime for the public to get them). Maybe that is a ban, but not in the sense that's been popularized. Contrary to news reports, the law did nothing about the very real problem of getting armed criminals off the street. The list of affected weapons is in Chapter 3.

The net effect of the law was to motivate manufacturers to create stockpiles before the law took affect, then to introduce new products that are not affected and to step up marketing efforts overseas for affected products. In addition, demand and prices skyrocketed for the now fixed supply of goods domestically, and then adjusted downward when it became obvious that supplies were still available. None of this applies after the law expires in 2004. If this is all news to you, it's time to question your source of news.

Rifle Practice and Firearms Safety Act (1996)

The Civilian Marksmanship Program, run by the U.S. Army, has served as the federal government's official firearms training, supply and competitions program for U.S. citizens, since 1956. Its history traces back to the late 1800s, when programs were first established to help ensure that the populace could shoot straight, in the event an army had to be raised to defend the country. The program is privatized by this act.

The federal government transfers the responsibility and facilities for training civilians in the use of small arms to a 501(c)(3) non-profit corporation created for this purpose. All law-abiding people are eligible to participate, and priority is given to reaching and training youth in the safe, lawful and accurate use of firearms.

Functions formerly performed for this program by the Army are now the responsibility of this new corporation. The Army is required to provide direct support and to take whatever action is necessary to make the program work in its privatized form. The stated program goals are:

1–Teaching marksmanship to U.S. citizens;

2–Promoting practice and safety in the use of firearms;

3–Conducting matches and competitions;

4–Awarding trophies and prizes;

5–Procuring supplies and services needed for the program;

6–Securing and accounting for all firearms, ammunition and supplies used in the program;

7–Giving, lending or selling firearms, ammunition and supplies under the program. Priority must be given to training youths, and reaching as many youths as possible.

Any person who is not a felon, hasn't violated the main federal gun laws, and does not belong to a group that advocates violent overthrow of the U.S. government, may participate in the Civilian Marksmanship Program.

What do you think would happen if Americans everywhere knew of this fine new law, and enrolled their children in programs that teach responsible use of firearms and gun safety? It would build understanding and self-esteem, replacing the gun ignorance fostered by wildly violent senseless TV shows, with knowledge and respect for the power and proper use of firearms. The Civilian Marksmanship Program in listed in Appendix C.

Antiterrorism Act of 1996

A wide variety of gun-law changes were introduced in this 48,728-word act. Eight sections introduce new law, and other sections make 17 amendments to existing federal law. Much of it deals with intentional criminal acts, and so falls outside the scope of *The Florida Gun Owner's Guide*. Other sections could give rise to unexpected results and are included.

Section 702. Using a firearm in an assault on any person in the U.S. is a federal crime if: 1–the assault involves "conduct transcending national boundaries" (described below) and 2–if any of the following also exist: A–any perpetrator uses the mail or interstate or foreign commerce in committing the crime; B–the offense in any way affects interstate or foreign commerce; C–the victim is anyone in the federal government or the military; D–any structure or property damaged is owned in any part by the federal government, or E–the offense occurs in special U.S. territorial jurisdictions. The maximum penalty in a non-lethal assault with a firearm is 30 years.

Causing a serious risk of injury to anyone, by damaging any structure or property in the U.S., is a federal crime if the conditions described in 1 and 2 above exist. The maximum penalty is 25 years.

Threatening, attempting or conspiring to commit the above acts is a crime, and various penalties are defined.

The phrase "conduct transcending national boundaries" means "conduct occurring outside of the United States in addition to the conduct occurring in the United States." It is not clear what this might include.

The Attorney General is in charge of investigating "federal crimes of terrorism." Such crimes occur when any of a long list of felonies is committed to influence the government by intimidation or coercion, or to retaliate against government actions. An assault involving conduct transcending national boundaries, described in the first part of this law, is one of the felonies.

Section 727. Using or attempting to use deadly force against anyone in the federal government or the military, if the attack is because of the person's government role, is a federal crime (in addition to existing assault and homicide laws). All former personnel are included. Federal penalties for an attack on anyone in this protected class are defined. In the case of such an assault, a gun is considered a gun, even if it jams due to a defective part.

Omnibus Consolidated Appropriation Act for Fiscal Year 1997

Section 657, Gun-Free School Zone. Congress was stopped in its attempt to exercise police powers at the state level by the U.S. Supreme Court, when the court declared the 1991 Gun-Free School Zone law unconstitutional, in 1995 (U.S. v. Lopez). That law was reenacted, to the surprise of many observers, as an unnoticed add-on to a 2,000-page federal spending bill in 1996, in a form essentially identical to the one the Supreme Court overturned.

The law makes it a federal crime to knowingly have a firearm within 1,000 feet of any school. An exemption is granted to anyone willing to register with the government for a specified license to carry the firearm, and the prohibition does not apply to: 1–Firearms while on private property that is not part of the school grounds; 2–Any firearm that is unloaded and in a locked container; 3–Any firearm unloaded and locked in a firearms rack on a motor vehicle; 4–Possession of a firearm for use in an approved school program; 5–Possession under a contract with the school; 6–Possession by law enforcement officers in an official capacity; and 7–An unloaded firearm, while crossing school premises to public or private land open to hunting, if crossing the grounds is authorized by the school.

It is also illegal to fire a gun (or attempt to fire a gun), knowingly or with reckless disregard for safety, in a place you know is a school zone, with the following exceptions: 1–On private property that is not part of the school grounds; 2–As part of a program approved by the school; 3–Under contract with the school; 4–By law enforcement acting in an official capacity.

An exemption for self defense is conspicuously absent, creating a shocking suggestion that self defense or defense of a third person within 1,000 feet of a school could be a federal crime (two actually, for possession and for discharge). An offense is designated as a misdemeanor, but carries a five year federal prison term. States are not prohibited from passing their own laws.

America had 121,855 public and private schools as of 1994. In effect, this law criminalizes the actions of nearly anyone who travels in a populated area with a legally possessed firearm, creating millions of federal offenses every day. As with its overturned predecessor, its affect on the very real problem of youth violence is unclear, and of course, any firearm used illegally in America, whether it is near a school or not, is already a serious crime with penalties.

Section 658. Misdemeanor Gun Ban for Domestic Violence Offense. Anyone convicted of a state or federal misdemeanor involving the use or attempted use of physical force, or the threatened use of a deadly weapon, among family members (spouse, parent, guardian, cohabiter or similar) is prohibited from possessing a firearm under federal law. This marks the first time that a misdemeanor offense serves as grounds for denial of the constitutional right to keep and bear arms. The number of people affected is unknown, and no provision is made for the firearms such men and women might already possess. Firearms possession by a prohibited possessor is a five-year federal felony.

A number of narrow conditions may exempt a person from this law, including whether they were represented by an attorney, the type of trial and plea, an expungement or set aside, or a pardon or other restoration of civil rights. Because such offenses are often handled in courts-not-of-record, such a determination may not be possible.

The current congressional practice of placing unrelated laws in larger acts, in order to get them passed without debate (or even unnoticed), has raised concerns among many observers. This law, sometimes referred to as the Lautenberg amendment, is an extreme example of such a practice, and caught both firearms-rights advocates and adversaries by surprise.

The law is drafted broadly, affecting sworn police officers nationwide, the armed forces, and agencies such as the FBI, CIA, Secret Service, Forest Service and others, most of whom are accustomed to being exempted from such laws. Many of these groups are currently battling to get themselves exempted from the law. They don't believe they should be prevented from defending themselves or others because of prior minor infractions. Some police departments have begun laying off members who are in violation.

So many problems exist with respect to this legislation that is has raised concerns unlike any recent act of Congress. Indeed, some members reportedly were told before voting that this language had been deleted from the final version, and the vote was held before copies of the 2,000-page act were available for review. Experts close to the issues cite numerous constitutional conflicts, including:

1–It is *ex post facto*—a law passed after the fact to affect your former actions (prohibited by Art. 1, Sec. 9);

2–It impacts the right to keep and bear arms (2nd Amendment);

3–Legally owned property becomes subject to automatic seizure (prohibited by the 4th Amendment);

4–It holds people accountable to a felony without a Grand Jury indictment, represents a second punishment for a single offense creating a double jeopardy, and it requires dispossession of personal property without compensation or due process (all prohibited by the 5th Amendment);

5–It denies your right to be informed of an accusation, and to counsel and a public jury trial because an existing state misdemeanor automatically becomes a federal felony (prohibited by the 6th Amendment);

6–Using a misdemeanor (a minor infraction) instead of a felony (a serious crime) to deny civil rights may be cruel and unusual punishment (8th Amendment);

7–Federal authorities enter an arena (family conflicts) historically governed exclusively by the states (controlled by the 10th Amendment); and

8–It denies due process, abridges the rights of U.S. citizens by state law, and denies equal protection under the law (violates 14th Amendment guarantees).

Domestic violence does not have a single definition at the state level. Some states' laws require the arrest of at least one party if the police respond to an apparent domestic-violence report. This raises all the issues of judicial process and plea-bargaining after an arrest. A parent who pays a small fine rather than endure a long expensive trial can now be charged with a federal felony; domestic violence pleas have been a standard ploy in divorce proceedings for decades; these charges now deny your right to keep and bear arms, to vote, to hold office and more.

An analogy to cars crystallizes this law's affects. It is as if a former speeding ticket were now grounds for felony arrest if you own a car or gasoline. When a law is scrutinized for constitutionality it is typically held up to a single constitutional provision. The eight constitutional issues in this short piece of legislation may set a record.

The Changing Federal Landscape

Court challenges are actively underway with regard to the Brady law and other federal firearms issues. Despite pronouncements about a moratorium on new gun laws, federal gun law grew by more than 13% in 1996. That's more new federal law in one year than we've seen in almost any *decade*.

Failure to comply with new laws and regulations can have serious consequences to you personally, even if you believe your Constitutional rights have been compromised. In fact, many experts have noted that increasing latitudes are being taken by some governmental authorities with respect to Constitutional guarantees. Legislative and regulatory changes present serious risks to currently law-abiding people, since what is legal today may not be tomorrow. The entire body of U.S. law is growing at a significant rate and it represents some potential for threats to freedoms Americans have always enjoyed. It is prudent to take whatever steps you feel are reasonable to minimize any risks.

New laws may be passed at any time, and it is your responsibility to be fully up-to-date when handling firearms under all circumstances. The information contained in this book is guaranteed to age.

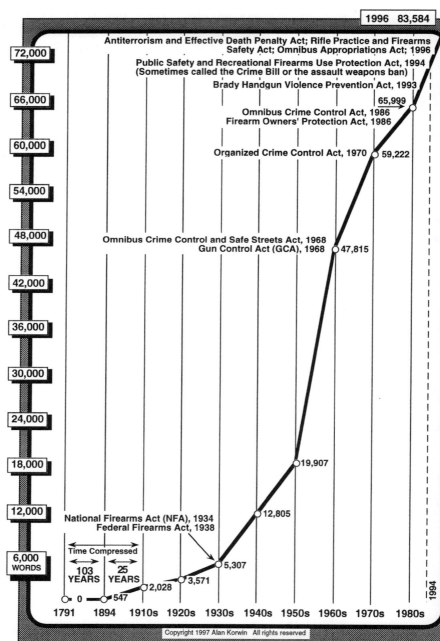

1996 83,584

Antiterrorism and Effective Death Penalty Act; Rifle Practice and Firearms Safety Act; Omnibus Appropriations Act; 1996

Public Safety and Recreational Firearms Use Protection Act, 1994 (Sometimes called the Crime Bill or the assault weapons ban)

Brady Handgun Violence Prevention Act, 1993

Omnibus Crime Control Act, 1986
Firearm Owners' Protection Act, 1986   65,999

Organized Crime Control Act, 1970   59,222

Omnibus Crime Control and Safe Streets Act, 1968
Gun Control Act (GCA), 1968   47,815

National Firearms Act (NFA), 1934
Federal Firearms Act, 1938

Time Compressed

103 YEARS   25 YEARS

0   547   2,028   3,571   5,307   12,805   19,907

1791 1894 1910s 1920s 1930s 1940s 1950s 1960s 1970s 1980s

1994

Growth in Federal Gun Laws

72,000
66,000
60,000
54,000
48,000
42,000
36,000
30,000
24,000
18,000
12,000
6,000 WORDS

GUN SAFETY and Self-Defense Training 8

Many fine books and classes exist which teach the current wisdom on gun safety and use. In Florida, some of the best public classes are given by the Game and Fresh Water Fish Commission and the National Rifle Association, both listed in Appendix C. Basic and advanced firearms classes are available from private instructors and schools.

When studying firearm safety (and every gun owner should), you will likely come across the Ten Commandments of Gun Safety. These well-intentioned lists have serious drawbacks—no two lists are ever the same and there are many more than ten rules to follow for safe gun use. In addition, hunters must learn many rules which don't apply to other shooters. For instance, a hunter should never openly carry game—it makes you an unwitting target of other hunters.

The Commandments of Safety are actually a way of saying, "Here's how people have accidents with guns." Each rule implies a kind of mishap. It's good exercise to look at each rule and read between the lines to find its counterpart—the potential disaster the rule will help you avoid. For example, Rule 1 translates into, "People have accidents with guns which they think are empty." Always keep in mind the prime directive: Take time to be safe instead of forever being sorry.

THE GUN OWNER'S COMMANDMENTS OF SAFETY

1–Treat every gun as if it is loaded until you have personally proven otherwise.

2–Always keep a gun pointed in a safe direction.

3–Don't touch the trigger until you're ready to fire.

4–Be certain of your target and what is beyond it before pulling the trigger.

5–Keep a gun you carry discretely holstered or otherwise concealed unless you're ready to use it.

6–Use but never rely on the safety.

7–Never load a gun until ready to use. Unload a gun immediately after use.

8–Only use ammunition which exactly matches the markings on your gun.

9–Always read and follow manufacturers' instructions carefully.

10–At a shooting range, always keep a gun pointed downrange.

11–Always obey a range officer's commands immediately.

12–Always wear adequate eye and ear protection when shooting.

13–If a gun fails to fire: a) keep it pointed in a safe direction; b) wait thirty seconds in case of a delayed firing; c) unload the gun carefully, avoiding exposure to the breech.

14–Don't climb fences or trees, or jump logs or ditches with a chambered round.

15–Be able to control the direction of the muzzle even if you stumble.

16–Keep the barrel and action clear of obstructions.

17–Avoid carrying ammunition which doesn't match the gun you are carrying.

18–Be aware that customized guns may require ammunition which doesn't match the gun's original markings.

19–Store guns with the action open.

20–Store ammunition and guns separately, and out of reach of children and careless adults.

21–Never pull a gun toward you by the muzzle.

22–Never horseplay with a firearm.

23–Never shoot at a hard flat surface, or at water, to prevent ricochets.

24–Be sure you have an adequate backstop for target shooting.

25–On open terrain with other people present, keep guns pointed upwards, or downwards and away from the people.

26–Never handle a gun you are not familiar with.

27–Learn to operate a gun empty before attempting to load and shoot it.

28–Be cautious transporting a loaded firearm in a vehicle.

29–Never lean a firearm where it may slip and fall.

30–Do not use alcohol or mood-altering drugs when you are handling firearms.

31–When loading or unloading a firearm, always keep the muzzle pointed in a safe direction.

32–Never use a rifle scope instead of a pair of binoculars.

33–Always remember that removing the magazine (sometimes called the clip) from semi-automatic and automatic weapons may still leave a live round, ready to fire, in the chamber.

34–Never rely on one empty cylinder next to the barrel of a revolver as a guarantee of safety, since different revolvers rotate in opposite directions.

35–Never step into a boat holding a loaded firearm.

36–It's difficult to use a gun safely until you become a marksman.

37–It's difficult to handle a gun safely if you need corrective lenses and are not wearing them.

38–Know the effective range and the maximum range of a firearm and the ammunition you are using.

39–Be sure that anyone with access to a firearm kept in a home understands its safe use.

40–Don't fire a large caliber weapon if you cannot control the recoil.

41–Never put your finger in the trigger guard when drawing a gun from a holster.

42–Never put your hand in front of the cylinder of a revolver when firing.

43–Never put your hand in back of the slide of a semi-automatic pistol when firing.

44–Always leave the hammer of a revolver resting over an empty chamber.

45–Never leave ammunition around when cleaning a gun.

46–Clean firearms after they have been used. A dirty gun is not as safe as a clean one.

47–Never fire a blank round directly at a person. Blanks can blind, maim, and at close range, they can kill.

48–Only use firearms in good working condition, and ammunition which is fresh.

49–Accidents don't happen, they are caused, and it's up to you and you alone to prevent them in all cases. Every "accident" which ever happened could have been avoided. Where there are firearms there is a need for caution.

50–Always think first and shoot second.

It is the responsibility of every American to prevent firearms from being instruments of tragedy.

TEACH YOUR CHILDREN WELL

Keeping Children Safe

Choosing to own a firearm—or choosing not to—has serious implications for the safety of your children and family. Your ability to respond in an emergency or not, and a child's dangerous access to a loaded firearm without your approval, should motivate you to take serious precautions for safety where firearms are concerned.

Firearms are dangerous; they're supposed to be dangerous; they wouldn't be very valuable if they weren't dangerous. The same as with power tools, automobiles, medicines, kitchen knives, balconies, swimming pools, electricity and everything else, it is up to responsible adults and their actions to help ensure the safety of those they love and the rest of the community.

In Florida these are not just good ideas, it's the law. A firearm owner has a legal responsibility to control a child's access to a loaded firearm, under s. 790.174. If you know that a child under 16 years of age is likely to find your gun (whether your own child or a visitor) you must keep it in a securely locked box or container, in a secure location, or locked with a trigger lock. There is an exception for when you are carrying it on your person or when you have it so nearby you can retrieve it as easily as if it were on you personally . Failing to secure it is a second degree misdemeanor, if a child gets it and has it, without proper supervision, in a public place, or displays it in a rude, careless, angry or threatening way except for use in self defense.

These requirements do not apply if the gun was obtained by an unlawful entry to your home.

Firearms dealers must display warning signs, under s. 790.175, about the safe-storage law and must give a written notice about safe-storage requirements to everyone who buys a gun.

Although it is not specifically required by the statute you should also keep your firearms away from careless and untrained adults. Another safety rule can be added to the list—always control access to your firearms.

A delicate balance exists between keeping a gun immediately ready for response in an emergency, and protecting it from careless adults and children. This is the paradox of home-defense firearms. The more out-of-reach a gun is for safety's sake, the less accessible it is for self defense (also for safety's sake).

Secured Storage

Leaving a loaded gun out *in the open* where careless adults or children could get at it is not being responsible and may subject you to criminal charges if an accident occurs.

Putting a loaded gun in *a hard-to-find spot* may fool some kids (and it's better than doing nothing), but remember how easily you found your folks' stuff when you were a kid.

Putting a gun in *a hard-to-get-to spot* (like the top of a closet) has advantages over hard-to-find spots when small children (like toddlers) are involved. Remember that kids reach an age where they like to climb. And you really have no idea what goes on when the baby-sitter is around.

Hinged *false picture frames,* when done well, provide a readily available firearm that most people will simply never notice. The frame must be in a spot that can't be bumped, and if ever the frame is detected its value is completely and immediately compromised.

Trigger guards warn that a gun is loaded, but they provide a low level of child-proofing since they are typically designed to be removed easily.

Gun locks can be effective in preventing accidents but are completely compromised if a child can get at the key. The location of the key then becomes the paradox factor in keeping the gun at-the-ready yet safe. The closer together you keep the gun and its key the less safety the lock provides.

Combination gun locks eliminate the key problem, but

mustn't be forgotten. If written down somewhere handy they too may be discovered. Many are difficult or impossible to operate in the dark. A number of push-button lock designs have been introduced which are made to fit directly into a handgun's mechanism.

Gun safes used properly can prevent accidents and provide reasonable access to personal firearms, but it is an expensive option. Many people with gun collections keep their firearms in a floor-standing safe, for theft and fire protection, simultaneously providing a high degree of accident proofing. Single-gun handgun safes are made for floor or wall mounting and use finger touch buttons that can be operated quickly in the dark. This is an excellent option for keeping a gun available yet highly protected from unauthorized use. Be sure to never let the batteries run down in the electronic models.

A home that doesn't have many visitors and never has kids around has a different challenge than a home with four kids growing up, when it comes to staying safe. Be sure that your home is safe for your kids and kids who may visit you—safe from those who would do you harm, and safe from the potential for harm your own home holds.

Disabling

Disabling a gun provides a safety margin. The more disabled a gun is the greater the safety, but the more difficult it becomes to bring the gun to bear if it should be needed.

The least disabled condition, and hence the least safe (though better than nothing), is *a safety lever engaged* on a semi-automatic or an appropriate empty cylinder on a revolver.

An *unloaded* firearm is disabled in a sense, and incapable of firing, though that reverses completely upon the presence of ammunition. The margin of safety here, for both preventing accidents and providing defense, is as wide as the distance between the gun and its ammunition, very similar to the key and lock relationship.

Removing a bolt or firing pin or otherwise disassembling a firearm represents a high degree of disabling, essentially lowering chances of accidents to zero, and removing the possibility of putting the weapon to use in an emergency.

Keeping *no firearm at home* eliminates the ability to respond for safety if necessary, and still leaves a child at risk when visiting friends or when friends visit (especially if the child is not firearms aware).

The bottom line is that there are no perfect solutions, and that life has risks. You trade some for others, and make personal choices that affect everything you do. Be sure you make the hard choices necessary to keep your family safe in your own home.

One Man's Approach

Internationally recognized firearms instructor and author Massad Ayoob believes it's wiser to educate your children than attempting to childproof your gun. For a detailed discussion of this approach to guns and child safety, read his booklet, *Gun-Proof Your Children,* available from Bloomfield Press.

THE EDDIE EAGLE PROGRAM

If you look behind all the hot political rhetoric, you'll notice that the main provider of firearms safety training in America is the National Rifle Association. They are literally the Red Cross of gun safety, fulfilling a century-old historic tradition that is actually embodied in federal law (10 USC §4312 and 40 USC §314). Handgun Control, Inc., and the NRA agree that child accidents are tragic and that responsible citizens must take steps to protect youngsters.

In response to this well perceived need, the NRA developed its highly acclaimed and widely used Eddie Eagle Safety Program. If your local school system doesn't teach gun safety, perhaps it should. For teacher lesson plans, class materials, parent kits, video tapes, coloring books, posters and more, contact the NRA, listed in the Appendix.

THE EDDIE EAGLE SAFETY RULES FOR KIDS —

If you find a gun:

STOP!

Don't touch.

Leave the area.

Tell an adult.

HOW WELL DO YOU KNOW YOUR GUN?

Safe and effective use of firearms demands that you understand your weapon thoroughly. This knowledge is best gained through a combination of reading, classes and practice with a qualified instructor. The simple test below will help tell you if you are properly trained in the use of firearms. If you're not sure what all the terms mean, can you be absolutely sure that you're qualified to handle firearms safely?

- ☐ Action
- ☐ Ammunition
- ☐ Automatic
- ☐ Ballistics
- ☐ Barrel
- ☐ Black powder
- ☐ Bolt
- ☐ Bore
- ☐ Break action
- ☐ Breech
- ☐ Buckshot
- ☐ Bullet
- ☐ Butt
- ☐ Caliber
- ☐ Cartridge
- ☐ Case
- ☐ Casing
- ☐ Centerfire
- ☐ Chamber
- ☐ Checkering
- ☐ Choke
- ☐ Clip
- ☐ Cock
- ☐ Comb
- ☐ Cylinder
- ☐ Discharge
- ☐ Dominant eye
- ☐ Effective range
- ☐ Firearm
- ☐ Firing Pin
- ☐ Firing Line
- ☐ Forearm
- ☐ Fouling
- ☐ Frame
- ☐ Gauge
- ☐ Grip
- ☐ Grip panels
- ☐ Grooves
- ☐ Gunpowder
- ☐ Half cock
- ☐ Hammer
- ☐ Handgun
- ☐ Hangfire
- ☐ Hunter orange
- ☐ Ignition
- ☐ Kneeling
- ☐ Lands
- ☐ Lever action
- ☐ Magazine
- ☐ Mainspring
- ☐ Maximum range
- ☐ Misfire
- ☐ Muzzle
- ☐ Muzzleloader
- ☐ Pattern
- ☐ Pistol
- ☐ Powder
- ☐ Primer
- ☐ Projectile
- ☐ Prone
- ☐ Pump action
- ☐ Receiver
- ☐ Repeater
- ☐ Revolver
- ☐ Rifle
- ☐ Rifling
- ☐ Rimfire
- ☐ Safety
- ☐ Sear
- ☐ Semi-automatic
- ☐ Shell
- ☐ Shooting positions
- ☐ Shot
- ☐ Shotgun
- ☐ Sights
- ☐ Sighting-in
- ☐ Sitting
- ☐ Smokeless powder
- ☐ Smoothbore
- ☐ Standing
- ☐ Stock
- ☐ Trigger
- ☐ Trigger guard
- ☐ Unplugged shotgun

CONCEALED WEAPON TRAINING

Florida law requires you to receive training if you want to obtain a license to carry a concealed weapon. You can meet this requirement, under s. 790.06, in any one of seven ways:

1–Complete any hunter education or hunter safety course offered in Florida or another state;

2–Complete any National Rifle Association firearms safety or training course;

3–Complete any firearms safety or training course open to the public offered by a law enforcement, junior college, college, or private or public organization that uses instructors certified by the National Rifle Association, Criminal Justice Standards and Training Commission, or the Dept. of State;

4–Complete any law enforcement firearms safety or training course offered for security guards, investigators, special deputies, or any division or subdivision of law enforcement or security enforcement;

5–Present evidence of equivalent experience with a firearm through participation in organized shooting competition or military service. You can use a letter from the president of the group offering the competitions or your military discharge papers;

6–Show that you have had a Florida concealed weapons license or a county license under the previous law, unless your license was revoked;

7–Take any firearm training or safety course conducted by a state-certified or National Rifle Association certified firearms instructor. There is no requirement to take an NRA course, only that the instructor has at least one NRA instructor certification.

You may use a photocopy of a certificate of any course, or an affidavit from the instructor, school, club, organization, or group that conducted the course, or a letter from a gun club president.

The procedure for obtaining a license is described in Chapter

2, and the degree of training is left in large measure up to you. Be smart and take a large measure of training.

Even though you can legally make do with less, it makes sense for you personally to get a high degree of training. Some states expect two full days of training or more to obtain a carry license. Many experts consider this a bare minimum if you're serious about bearing arms.

On the other hand, it can be argued that requiring training in order to exercise your constitutional rights is difficult to justify. No training is required, for example, to speak your mind or circulate your written words, and everyone knows words can cause harm or topple governments as readily as force of arms.

Some people buy a handgun, a box of ammo, load it up and put it in the night stand, and give it no further thought. Some will go so far as to run a few rounds through the gun to make sure it works, and then put it in the night stand. This does not constitute a commitment to firearms proficiency. Commitment is as essential to responsible firearms ownership as a command of the language is to the exercise of free speech.

Take the time to get good training. The NRA offers firearms programs for all levels of experience. Contact them and attend a few of their excellent courses. The Florida Game and Fresh Water Fish Commission hunter safety course is another good place to start for basic firearms safety. The hunter safety course is accepted as training for a concealed weapons license, but keep in mind that it doesn't cover many basic concealed weapons practices and laws you should want to know.

Private trainers are spread all across the state. Check on the qualifications of those offering courses—some people have only basic qualifications and offer simple programs, while others have impressive credentials and will really bring you up to speed. Take a class that teaches you the gun laws as well as firearms safety and how to shoot. Whatever training you receive, consider it as a beginning. Try a variety of trainers—you will learn something new from each. Seek out a particular trainer whose reputation crosses your path. Then practice frequently throughout your life to keep the needed skills. If this seems like too much bother, maybe you should reconsider your readiness to use deadly force in an emergency.

A thorough course would include (at least) training in firearms laws and the laws on deadly force, ammunition and how it works, firearms parts and workings, shooting with right, left and both hands, mental control including dealing with stress and decision making, how to conceal a gun on your body, types of equipment available for concealed carry, how to make a home and personal safety plan, crime avoidance techniques, non-violent dispute resolution, judgmental shooting and more.

Mistakes made with firearms can be tragic. The effect on your life and your loved ones can be devastating. And every mistake made is fuel for those who seek to deny your right to firearms. As a gun owner you must rise to a higher level of responsibility.

When you sign the concealed-weapons application form and have it notarized you are making a sworn statement that you have received a copy of Chapter 790 (the weapons and firearms laws, supplied with your application) and know what it says. This means that you know the primary gun laws of the state. But as you saw in Chapter 1, there are scores of other laws involved too, and federal laws. Here's a little self test to check your knowledge of Florida's gun laws.

1–What is the waiting period to buy a firearm in Florida? What are the exceptions? See Chapter 1

2–Is a starter gun a firearm? See Chapter 1

3–If you have a concealed weapons license may you carry more than one gun? Are there weapons you may not carry?
See Chapter 2

4–If you own a farm or a large piece of property may you openly wear a handgun while on your land? How about a concealed firearm without a license while on your property?
See Chapter 2

5–What are the four things you must show to obtain a concealed weapons license? Who is prohibited from getting one? See Chapter 2

6–Do you have to be a resident of Florida to get a concealed weapons license? See Chapter 2

7–Name seven places where you cannot legally carry a firearm, even with a concealed weapons license. See Chapter 2

8–If you don't have a concealed weapons license, may you carry a handgun in your car? Can it be loaded? What if you do have a license? See Chapter 2

9–Can you legally carry a firearm and drink alcohol? See Chapters 1 & 2

10–When is it legal to use deadly force? See Chapter 5

11–When and where can you legally shoot a machine gun? See Chapter 4

12–Is it legal to own a sawed-off shotgun and a silencer? See Chapter 3

13–Do you need a hunting license to hunt on your own property? See Chapter 6

14–May you pick up your child at elementary school if you have a loaded handgun in the glove compartment of your car? See Chapters 2 & 7

15–Does the Anti-Terrorism Act affect you as a private gun owner? See chapter 7

16–Is there any guarantee that you may transport a firearm nationally without being arrested? See Chapter 7

Make the smart choice and exceed the minimum training by reading extensively, practicing regularly, keeping up on the important issues, and taking additional training programs.

JUDGMENTAL SHOOTING

All gun owners, and concealed weapons license holders in particular, should study issues related to judgmental shooting. Anyone considering armed response needs an understanding of the issues involved.

The decision to use deadly force is rarely a clear-cut choice. Regardless of your familiarity with the laws, your degree of training, the quality of your judgmental skills and your physical location and condition at the time of a deadly threat, the demands placed on you at the critical moment are as intense as anything you will normally experience in your life, and your actual performance is an unknown.

Every situation is different. The answers to many questions relating to deadly force are subject to debate. To be prepared for armed response you must recognize that such situations are not black or white, and that your actions, no matter how well intentioned, will be evaluated by others, probably long after you act.

The chances that you will come away from a lethal encounter without any scars—legal, physical or psychological—are small, and the legal risks are substantial. That's why it's usually best to practice prevention and avoidance rather than confrontation, whenever possible.

Most people can think about it this way: You've gotten along this far in life without ever having pulled a weapon on someone, much less having fired it. The odds of that changing once you have a concealed weapons license are about the same, practically zero.

A concealed handgun may make you feel more secure, but it doesn't change how safe your surroundings actually are, in the places you normally travel, one bit. And it certainly isn't safe to think of a firearm as a license (or a talisman) for walking through potentially dangerous areas you would otherwise avoid like the plague.

Remember that the person holding a gun after a shooting is

frequently thought of as the bad guy—the perpetrator—even if it's you and you acted in self defense. The person who is shot often gets a different, more sympathetic name—the victim— and gets the benefit of a prosecutor even if, perhaps, you learn later it's a hardened criminal with a long record.

Maybe your legal standing will improve if it is indeed a serious repeat offender, but you won't know that until after the fact, and don't count on it. If you ever have to raise a gun to a criminal, you'll find out quickly how good they can be at portraying you as the bad guy and themselves as the helpless innocents, at the mercy of a crazed wacko—you.

Situational Analysis
Think about the deadly-force encounters described below, and consider discussing them with your personal firearms-safety trainer:

1–If you are being seriously attacked by a man with a club, is it legal for you to aim for his leg so you can stop the attack without killing him?

2–If you enter your home and find a person looting your possessions are you justified in shooting?

3–If you enter your home and find a person looting your possessions, who runs out the back door as he hears you arrive, can you shoot him to stop him from escaping?

4–If you enter your home and find a person looting your possessions, who turns and whirls toward you when you enter, literally scaring you to death, may you shoot and expect to be justified?

5–If you enter your home and find a stranger in it who charges you with a knife, may you shoot?

6–A stranger in your home has just stabbed your spouse and is about to stab your spouse again. May you shoot the stranger from behind to stop the attack?

7–As you walk past a park at night, you notice a woman tied to a tree and a man tearing off her clothing. May you use deadly force to stop his actions?

8–A police officer is bleeding badly and chasing a man in prison coveralls who runs right past you. May you shoot the fleeing suspect while he is in close range to you?

9–You're in your home at night when a man with a ski mask on comes through an open window in the hallway. May you shoot?

10–You're in your home at night, sleeping, when a noise at the other end of the house awakens you. Taking your revolver you quietly walk over to investigate and notice a short person going through your silverware drawer, 45 feet from where you're standing. The person doesn't notice you. May you shoot?

11–As you approach your parked car in a dark and remote section of a parking lot, three youthful toughs approach you from three separate directions. You probably can't unlock your vehicle and get in before they reach you and you're carrying a gun. What should you do?

12–From outside a convenience store you observe what clearly appears to be an armed robbery—four people are being held at gun point while the store clerk is putting money into a paper bag. You're armed. What should you do?

13–You're waiting to cross the street in downtown and a beggar asks you for money. He's insistent and begins to insult you when you refuse to ante up. Finally, he gets loud and belligerent and says he'll kill you if you don't give him ten dollars. May you shoot him?

14–You get in your car, roll down the windows, and before you can drive off a man sticks a knife in the window and orders you to get out. Can you shoot him?

15-You get in your car and before you start it a man points a gun at you and tells you to get out. You have a gun in the pocket on the door, another under the seat, and a gun in a holster in your pants. What should you do?

16–Before you get in your car, a man with a gun comes up from behind, demands your car keys, takes them, and while holding you at gun point, starts your car and drives away. Can you shoot at him while he's escaping?

17–You're walking to your car in the mall parking lot after a movie when two armed hoods jump out of a shadow and demand your money. You've got a gun in your back pocket. What should you do?

18–A masked person with a gun stops you on the street, demands and takes your valuables, then flees down the street on foot. You're carrying a concealed handgun. What should you do?

19–A youngster runs right by you down the street and an old lady shouts, "Stop him, he killed my husband!" May you shoot to stop his getaway?

20–You're at work when two ornery-looking dudes amble in. You can smell trouble, so you walk to a good vantage point behind a showcase. Sure enough, they pull guns and announce a stick-up. You and your four employees are armed and there are several customers in the store. What's your move?

21–Your friend and you have been drinking, and now you're arguing over a football bet. You say the spread was six points, he says four. There's $500 hanging in the balance of a five-point game, and it represents your mortgage payment. He pulls a knife and says, "Pay me or I'll slice you up." You've got a gun in your pocket. What should you do?

22–At a gas station, the lines are long, it's hot, and the guy next in line starts getting surly. You're not done pumping and he hits you in the face and tells you to finish up. He shuts off your pump and says he'll kick your butt if you don't move on. Should you pull your gun to put him in his place?

Observations about the situations presented:

1–The Hollywood-promoted idea of *shoot to wound* is incredibly poor in the real world for a host of reasons. If you wing an arm but hit an artery the person can die anyway—there is no such thing as "wounding-level force." Hitting the limb of a moving person is among the most difficult shots known, especially in the stressful emotional state where such a shot would be justified. If you miss you are jeopardizing your life which is severely threatened in the first place or you would have no justification to shoot at all. It wastes valuable ammunition and time that may be critical to stopping the lethal attack you face. It's an unlikely case where the justification to use deadly force would be justification to intentionally wound a person. Firing and missing is a different story, but a prosecutor can argue that if the threat wasn't truly sufficient to apply deadly force then there was no justification to shoot at all.

2–Not enough information is provided to make an informed choice.

3–No. The penalty for burglary is jail, not death, and you almost never have the right to kill to prevent a criminal from escaping. Once the danger to you is over—and it generally is once the criminal is fleeing—your right to use deadly force ends.

4–You need more information to make a responsible choice. Do you always enter your home prepared for mortal combat? Does your story have other holes a prosecutor will notice?

5–It's hard to imagine not being justified in this situation, but stranger things have happened.

6–It's hard to imagine not being justified in this situation, but stranger things have happened. Will the bullet exit the attacker and wound your spouse? In one bizarre case (Arizona 1996), the attacker was actually the husband, wearing a ski mask, and the shooter was the wife's father-in-law—the husband's dad. They didn't even suspect what really happened until they were at the hospital, where the wife learned she was a widow and the shooter realized he had killed his own son.

7–Probably not, since you don't know if the people are consenting adults who like this sort of thing. Even if a crime is being committed, shooting might be viewed as excessive force. A seasoned police officer might cautiously approach the couple, weapon drawn, and with words instead of force determine what's happening, and then make further choices depending on the outcome.

8–Not enough information is provided to make an informed choice. Keep in mind that you do not have the obligation to apprehend criminals that police have.

9–Probably, though a well-trained expert might instead confront the intruder from a secure position and succeed in holding the person for arrest, which is no easy task. The longer you must hold the suspect the greater the risk to you. Armed and from good cover, you might just convince the intruder to leave the way he came.

10–Probably not. The distance and lack of immediate threat will make for a difficult explanation when the police arrive, and if the perpetrator has an accomplice that you didn't notice, the danger to you is severe. If it turns out that the intruder is 11 years old your court defense will be extremely difficult. Remember, you're obligated to not shoot if you don't absolutely have to. A shot would be in conflict with a prime safety rule—clearly identify your target before firing. Has your training prepared you for this?

11–That's a good question, and you should never have parked there in the first place.

12–Call for assistance, go to a defensible position, continue to observe, and recognize that charging into such a volatile situation is incredibly risky for all parties.

13–You are never justified in using deadly force in response to verbal provocation alone, no matter how severe.

14–The prosecutor will make it clear that if you could have stepped on the gas and escaped, the threat to you would have ended, and the need to shoot did not exist. If you were boxed into a parking space, the need to defend yourself would be hard for a prosecutor to refute. These things often come down to the exact circumstances and the quality of the attorneys.

15–Get out quietly and don't provoke someone who has the drop on you. All your guns are no match for a drawn weapon. This is where a real understanding of tactics comes into play.

16–No. Once the threat to you is over, the justification for using lethal force ends.

17–Not enough information is provided to make an informed choice.

18–Anyone crazy enough to rob you at gun point must be considered capable of doing anything, and the smart move is to avoid further confrontation and stay alive. Chasing after him is extremely unwise and risky to you.

19–You don't have enough information. When in doubt, don't shoot.

20–This is where strategy and tactics are critical. If you allow your employees to carry and are prepared for armed defense of your premises you better get plenty of advanced training in gun fighting and self defense. You'll need it to survive, and you'll need it to meet the legal challenges later. If a customer gets shot by one of your own, even if you get the villains, you're in for big time trouble and grief. If no one gets hurt but the criminals, you'll be a hero, though the media might paint you as a wild-eyed vigilante. Either outcome remains burned in memory. Tough choice.

21–Too many killings occur between people who know each other. Your chance of a successful legal defense in a case like this are remote, and if you're drunk or in a bar you've already broken the law. Would he really have killed you? Probably not. Did you have any other options besides killing him? Probably so. Have you fought like this before? Maybe. What would the witnesses say? Nothing you could count on, and probably all the wrong things. The fact that you have a firearm and can use it doesn't mean you should, the likelihood of absolutely having to use it is small, and using it to settle a bet with a half-soused friend over a point spread may not be the worst thing you can do, but it's close.

22–Cap your tank and move on, you don't need the grief. When you are armed you must be even more reluctant to enter into a conflict than you otherwise might be. Your pride is not worth the price and lifelong repercussions of an armed conflict.

RECOMMENDED READING

Knowledge is power, and the more you have the better off you are likely to be. Everyone concerned with personal safety, and gun owners in particular, should read books on crime avoidance, self defense and the use of deadly force. **If you have a firearm for self defense, decide to read about this critical subject.** A selection of some of the most highly regarded books on these topics appears at the back of *The Florida Gun Owner's Guide* and are easily available directly from the publisher. If your instructor doesn't include these in your course, get them yourself. The single best book on the subject is probably *In The Gravest Extreme*, by Massad Ayoob.

You may also choose to look up and read the Florida Statutes, since the laws reproduced in *The Florida Gun Owner's Guide* are a selected excerpt of gun laws only. Remember that no published edition of the law is complete without the legislation passed during the most recent session of the state congress, and that new federal laws may be passed at any time. An annotated edition of the law, available in major libraries, provides critical information in the form of court case summaries that clarify and expand on the meaning of the actual statutes.

THE NOBLE USES OF FIREARMS

THE NOBLE USES OF FIREARMS

In the great din of the national firearms debate it's easy to lose sight of the noble and respectable place firearms hold and have always held in American life. While some gun use in America is criminal and despicable, other applications appeal to the highest ideals our society cherishes, and are enshrined in and ensured by the statutes on the books:

- Protecting your family in emergencies
- Personal self defense
- Preventing and deterring crimes
- Detaining criminals for arrest
- Guarding our national borders
- Preserving our interests abroad
- Helping defend our allies
- Overcoming tyranny
- Emergency preparedness
- Obtaining food by hunting
- Historical preservation and study
- Olympic competition
- Sporting pursuits
- Target practice
- Recreational shooting
- Firearms collecting

News reports, by focusing almost exclusively on criminal misuse of firearms, create the false impression that firearms and crime are causally linked, when in fact almost all guns never have any link to crime whatsoever. The media judiciously ignore stories concerning legitimate self defense, which occur almost daily according to the FBI. There is silence on the effect the industry has on jobs in the manufacturing sector, contributions to the tax base, capital and investments, scientific advances, national trade and balance of payments, ballistics, chemistry, metallurgy, and, of course, the enjoyment of millions of decent people who use firearms righteously. <u>Some people associate guns with crime, fear and danger, and want them to go away. Those who associate guns with liberty, freedom, honor, strength and safety understand the irreplaceable role firearms play in our lives.</u>

APPENDIX A
GLOSSARY OF TERMS

Words, when used in the law, often have special meanings you wouldn't expect from simply knowing the English language. For the complete legal description of these and other important terms, see each chapter of the Florida Statutes and other legal texts dealing with language. The following plain-English descriptions are provided for your convenience only.

AMMUNITION = Cartridge, pellet, ball, missile or projectile adapted for use in a firearm.

ANTIQUE FIREARM = means any firearm manufactured in or before 1918, including any matchlock, flintlock, percussion cap, or similar early type of ignition system, or a replica of one of these firearms, whether it was actually manufactured before or after the year 1918. Also any firearm using fixed ammunition that was manufactured in or before 1918, that you can't buy a firearm or ammunition except from a collector.

ARMOR-PIERCING AMMUNITION = Handgun ammunition designed primarily for penetrating metal or body armor. Referred to as *restricted* ammunition in statute.

ASSAULT FIREARM = Any semi-automatic center-fire rifle or pistol equipped with a magazine which will hold more than twenty rounds of ammunition or accept a silencer or has a folding stock.

BALLISTIC KNIFE = any knife with a detachable blade that is propelled by a spring-operated mechanism.

BILLIE = a small bludgeon that can be carried in a pocket.

CHEMICAL WEAPON OR DEVICE = all such weapons except a compact self-defense chemical spray with up to two ounces of chemical, carried solely for lawful self defense.

CIVIL DISORDER = any public disturbance within the United States or any territorial possessions thereof involving acts of violence by assemblages of three or more persons, which causes an immediate danger of or results in damage or injury to the property or person of any other individual.

CONCEALED FIREARM = means any firearm which is carried on or about a person in such a manner as to conceal the firearm from the ordinary sight of another person.

CONCEALED WEAPON = means any dirk, metallic knuckles, slungshot, billie, tear gas gun, chemical weapon or device, or other deadly weapon carried on or about a person in such a manner as to conceal the weapon from the ordinary sight or another person.

CONVICTED = Found guilty of an offense by a court, even if the sentence is probation, the offender is discharged from community supervision, or the offender is pardoned, unless the pardon is granted for proof of innocence.

CONSERVATOR OF THE PEACE = Anyone duly appointed with legal authority to make arrests. Includes all law enforcement officers, judges, clerks of court, and persons in charge of maintaining order in public areas such as private security guards, ship's captains, game wardens, prison guards, train conductors, airline pilots and bus drivers.

CRIME OF VIOLENCE = Committing or attempting to commit any of the following: murder, manslaughter, kidnapping, rape, mayhem, assault.

CRIMINAL INSTRUMENT = Anything which is normally legal but which is put to illegal use.

CULPABLE MENTAL STATE = An accountable state of mind. Specifically and in decreasing order of seriousness: intentionally, knowingly, recklessly or with criminal negligence, in the sense described by law.

CURTILAGE = The land and buildings immediately surrounding a house or dwelling.

DEALER = Anyone licensed as a firearms dealer by the federal government. The federal description of a dealer appears in Chapter 1.

DEADLY FORCE = means force which is likely to cause death or great bodily harm and includes, but is not limited to: (1) The firing of a firearm in the direction of the person to be arrested, even though no intent exists to kill or inflict great bodily harm; and (2) The firing of a firearm at a vehicle in which the person to be arrested is riding.

DEADLY WEAPON = Anything made or adapted for lethal use or for inflicting serious bodily injury, including a firearm.

DIRK = a double edged knife.

ELECTRIC WEAPON OR DEVICE = any device which, through the application or use of electrical current, is designed, redesigned, used, or intended to be used for offensive or defensive purposes, the destruction of life, or the infliction of injury.

EXPLOSIVE DEVICE = Dynamite and all other forms of high explosive. Any incendiary, fire bomb or similar device including "Molotov cocktails."

FIREARM any weapon (including a starter gun) which will, is designed to, or may readily be converted to expel a projectile by the action of an explosive; the frame or receiver of any such weapon; any firearm muffler or firearm silencer; any destructive device; or any machine gun. The term "firearm" does not include an antique firearm unless the antique firearm is used in the commission of a crime.

FIREARM SHOW = Any gathering, open to the public, not on the premises of a firearm dealer, for the purpose of trading or selling firearms.

FIREARM SILENCER = Any device that can muffle the sound of a firearm.

FELONY = A serious crime, with jail time served in the state penitentiary, for a period of more than one year.

FORCIBLE FELONY = treason; murder; manslaughter; sexual battery; carjacking; home-invasion; robbery; burglary; arson; kidnapping; aggravated assault; aggravated battery; aggravated stalking; aircraft piracy; unlawful throwing, placing, or discharging of a destructive device or bomb; and any other felony which involves the use or threat of physical force or violence against any individual.

GOVERNMENT = The recognized political structure within the state.

HANDGUN = any pistol or revolver or other firearm originally designed, made and intended to fire a projectile by means of an explosion from one or more barrels when held in one hand.

HARM = Loss, disadvantage or injury to a person or someone for whom that person is responsible.

ILLEGAL ALIEN = a non-US citizen who is in the United States without a valid visa or status issued by the Immigration and Naturalization Service.

INDIVIDUAL = A living human being.

INTOXICATED = Having an alcohol concentration of 0.08 or more, or having had enough alcoholic beverages to observably affect manner, disposition, speech, muscular movement, general appearance or behavior.

KNIFE = Any bladed hand instrument that can inflict serious bodily injury or death by cutting or stabbing.

LAW = Formal rules by which society attempts to control itself. In Florida, the law means the Florida state statutes, the state Constitution, the U.S. Constitution and federal statutes, city ordinances, county commissioners court orders, county ordinances, published court precedents and more. "The law" is a thing too large for any one individual to know, but everyone is deemed to know the law so ignorance of the law is not a defense to a crime.

MACHINE GUN = any firearm which shoots, or is designed to shoot, automatically more than one shot, without manually reloading, by a single function of the trigger.

METALLIC KNUCKLES = A device made of hard material, designed to be worn on a hand to increase the effect of a blow, sometimes called brass knuckles.

MISDEMEANOR = A crime less serious than a felony. An offense against the law that carries a sentence of imprisonment of up to one year. Misdemeanor fines can run up to $2,500. Misdemeanors are classified as class 1 (most serious) to class 4 (least serious).

MUTATIS MUTANDIS = "When what must be changed has been changed." A legal term used to apply the provisions of one statute to a second statute, once the specifics such as section number have been changed.

PLACE OF NUISANCE = generally includes a house of prostitution and a place where illegal gambling occurs.

PRIMA FACIE = A legal presumption meaning "on the face of it" or "at first sight." Prima facie evidence is presumed to be accurate unless convincing contradicting evidence is presented.

REASONABLE = The admittedly interpretable notion of what is "fair, proper, just, moderate, suitable to the end in view... being synonymous with rational, honest, equitable, fair, suitable, moderate, tolerable." (Black's Law Dictionary)

READILY ACCESSIBLE FOR IMMEDIATE USE = that a firearm or other weapon is carried on the person or within such close proximity and in such a manner that it can be retrieved and used as easily and quickly as if carried on the person.

REMOTE STUN GUN = A nonlethal device with a 16-foot tethered range, that disperses a tracer that can be traced to the purchaser through records the manufacturer keeps and makes available to law enforcement.

RESTRICTED AMMUNITION = See armor-piercing ammunition.

SAWED-OFF RIFLE = A rifle with a barrel length less than 16 inches or an overall length of less than 26 inches.

SAWED-OFF SHOTGUN = A smooth bore shotgun with a barrel length less than 18 inches. A rifled barrel shotgun with a length of less than 16 inches and a caliber greater than .225 (federal rules make no distinction as to caliber).

SECURELY ENCASED = in a glove compartment, whether or not locked; snapped in a holster; in a gun case, whether or not locked; in a zippered gun case; or in a closed box or container which requires a lid or cover to be opened for access.

SERIOUS BODILY INJURY = Injury that causes permanent damage to or loss of a limb or organ, or creates a reasonable risk of death or death itself. Also, injury that causes serious and permanent disfigurement or impairment.

SHORT-BARRELED RIFLE = a rifle having one or more barrels less than 16 inches in length and any weapon made from a rifle (whether by alteration, modification, or otherwise) if such weapon as modified has an overall length of less than 26 inches.

SHORT-BARRELED SHOTGUN = a shotgun having one or more barrels less than 18 inches in length and any weapon made from a shotgun (whether by alteration, modification, or otherwise) if such weapon as modified has an overall length of less than 26 inches.

SLUNGSHOT = a small mass of metal, stone, sand, or similar material fixed on a flexible handle, strap, or the like, used as a weapon.

SPRING GUN = Any firearm or deadly weapon set to activate or discharge by means of a trip wire or any other remote device.

STERILE AREA = the area of an airport to which access is controlled by the inspection of persons and property in accordance with federally approved airport security programs.

STUN WEAPON = Any mechanism that is designed to emit an electronic, magnetic, or other type of charge used for the purpose of temporarily incapacitating a person.

SWITCHBLADE KNIFE = A knife with a blade that comes out of its handle automatically by centrifugal force, by gravity, or by pressing a button or other device on the handle.

TEAR GAS GUN = See *Chemical Weapon or Device*

UNLAWFUL = Anything that's criminal or a tort.

UNSOUND MIND = The mental condition of someone who has been judged mentally incompetent or mentally ill, who has been found not guilty of a crime by reason of insanity, or who has been diagnosed by a licensed physician as being unable to manage themselves or their personal affairs.

WEAPON = any dirk, metallic knuckles, slungshot, billie, tear gas gun, chemical weapon or device, or other deadly weapon except a firearm or a common pocketknife, as defined by statute.

APPENDIX B
Crime and Punishment Chart

Type of Crime: Illegal activities are divided into categories to match the punishment to the crime. Chapter 775 of *Florida Statutes* describes the elements of offenses and the punishments. Courts may vary sentences depending on how a crime is committed and the history of the offender. A court may also decree forfeiture of property, suspension or cancellation of a license, removal from office, or other civil penalties. Anyone who commits more than one offense during a criminal episode may be sentenced separately for each conviction.

Jail Term: These are the general ranges for a first offense involving a gun; many crimes have special sentences. A capital felony, in addition to life imprisonment, carries a possible death penalty for first degree murder, which is administered by electrocution.

Fines: These are maximums, which may be lowered at court discretion. Fines may be payable immediately or a court may grant permission to pay by a certain date or in installments.

Statute of Limitations: A complex set of rules describes the length of time within which a person may be charged for a crime. The most serious crimes have no time limit for bringing a prosecution.

Offenses: The chart provides a partial list of offenses in each category, and exceptions often apply.

Crime and Punishment
FELONIES
Imprisonment in State Penitentiary

TYPE OF CRIME	MAXIMUM SENTENCE FOR A FIRST OFFENSE	MAXIMUM FINE
Capital Felony Premeditated murder.	**Death**	
Life Felony	**Life Imprisonment**	**$15,000**
1st Degree Felony Shoot a machine gun in public with intent to do harm; Treason.	**30 Years**	**$10,000**
2nd Degree Felony Shoot into a building, sell a firearm to a minor by a dealer, illegal possession of short barreled rifle or shotgun, illegal possession of machine gun, discharge firearm on school grounds	**15 Years**	**$10,000**
3rd Degree Felony Commit certain crimes while carrying concealed weapon, carry concealed firearm with no license, provide firearm to minor, possession of prohibited ammo, buy firearm for prohibited possessor, exhibit weapon in threatening way or on school grounds, sell firearm to prohibited possessor by dealer, concealed firearm in pharmacy, remove the serial number from firearm, provide false ID to dealer to obtain firearm, dealer requests criminal history under false pretense.	**5 Years**	**$5,000**

Crime and Punishment
MISDEMEANORS
Imprisonment in County Jail

TYPE OF CRIME	JAIL SENTENCE FOR A FIRST OFFENSE	MAXIMUM FINE
1st Degree Misdemeanor	**Up to 1 Year**	**$1,000**

Illegal discharge of firearm in public place, medical personnel fails to report gunshot wound, provide weapon to minor, sell or possess firearm with serial number removed, carry concealed weapon or electric device, threatening with firearm or weapon

2nd Degree Misdemeanor	**Up to 60 Days**	**$500**

Use firearm under influence of alcohol, provide BB gun to minor under 16, carry firearm in National Forest, carry firearm or electric weapon openly, make or sell slungshot or metal knuckles, business fails to post sign regarding children

Noncriminal Violation	**None**	**$500**

Failure of a concealed weapons license holder to notify the Dept., of State of a lost or destroyed license, or change of address, within 30 days; failure of a concealed weapons license holder to possess license and other ID while armed.

THE PROPER AUTHORITIES C

Regulations on guns and their use come from a lot of places. Listed with each authority are the addresses and phones of the nearest offices. Several useful resource numbers are included. All cities are in Florida unless indicated.

American Self Defense Institute 800-700-8525

Bureau of Alcohol, Tobacco and Firearms 202-927-8410
    650 Massachusetts Ave. NW, Washington, DC 20226
      Florida Main Office 305-597-4800
        5225 NW 87th Ave., Miami 33178
      State Capitol Office 850-942-9660
        2671 Executive Center Cir. W., #201
        Tallahassee 32301

Bureau of Indian Affairs 202-208-7163
    1849 C St. NW, Washington, DC 20240

Bureau of Land Management 202-452-5120
    18th & C St. NW, Washington D.C. 20240

Director of Civilian Marksmanship 703-924-0502
    6551 Loisdale Ct. #714, Springfield, VA 22150

Florida Attorney General 904-487-1963
    The Capitol-PL 01, Tallahassee 32399

Florida Dept. of Law Enforcement, PO Box 1489, Tallahassee 32302 904-488-7880
    Firearm Purchase Program 904-488-7651
    General Counsel 904-488-8323
    Public Information Office 904-488-8771
    Regional Operations/Field Offices
      Ft. Myers 941-768-4880
      Jacksonville 904-359-6480
      Miami 305-470-5500
      Orlando 407-245-0801

Pensacola   904-470-2000
Tallahassee   904-488-1040
Tampa Bay   813-878-7300

Florida Dept. of State, Concealed Weapon Service Representative, Div. of Licensing,
  PO Box 6687, Tallahassee 32314   904-488-5381
  Florida Dept. of State, Regional Offices
    Fort Walton, 184 Elgin Pkwy #2, 32548   904-833-9146
    Jacksonville, 1965 Beachway Rd., 32207   904-348-2660
    Miami, 401 NW 2nd Ave. #720N, 33128   305-377-5950
    Orlando, 400 W. Robinson St. #110, 32801   407-245-0883
    Tallahassee, Box 6687, 32314   904-488-6474
    Tampa, 1313 Tampa St. #712, 33602   813-272-2552
    West Palm Beach, 1675 Palm Beach Lakes Blvd. #A-100, 33401   407-640-6144

Florida Game and Fresh Water Fish Commission, Licenses
  1-800-FISHFLORIDA (1-800-347-4356)   Credit card sales for hunt/fish licenses

Florida Game and Fresh Water Fish Commission, Offices
  Headquarters (Region #6)   904-488-4676
    Farris Bryant Bldg., 620 S. Meridian St., Tallahassee 32399
    Everglades Region (#4)   800-432-2046
      551 N Military Tr., W. Palm Beach 33415   561-640-6100
    Central Region (#5)   800-342-9620
      1239 SW 10th St., Ocala 34474   352-732-1225
    NE Region (#2)   800-342-8105
      RFD 7 Box 440, Lake City 32055   904-758-0525
    NW Region (#3)   800-342-1676
      3911 Hwy 2321, Panama City   904-265-3676
    So. Region (#1)   800-282-8002
      3900 Drain Field Rd., Lakeland 33811   941-648-3203

Florida Game and Fresh Water Fish Commission, Ranges
  Columbia County, Osceola Shooting Range   904-758-0525
  Palm Beach County   407-624-6928
  Marion County, Ocala Shooting Range   352-732-1225 or 352-625-2520

Florida Shooting Sports Association   850-894-6224, www.flfsa.org

National Rifle Association   800-336-7402
  11250 Waples Mill Rd., Fairfax 22030
  Locally, see Florida Shooting Sports Association

So. Florida Firearms Owners, Box 4607, Boynton Beach 33424   561-735-4102

Unified Sportsmen of Florida, 904-222-9518
  110-A S. Monroe St., Box 6565, Tallahassee 32314

U.S. Forest Service, U.S. Dept. of. Agriculture   202-205-8333
  PO Box 96090, Washington, D.C. 20090

APPENDIX D
THE FLORIDA GUN LAWS

On the following pages are excerpts from official Florida state law.

Florida law covers a broad spectrum of subjects but **only gun laws for private individuals are included in this appendix**. A complete copy of the state law is available in major libraries, but keep in mind that those copies are incomplete (and in many instances inaccurate) without the new material from the last legislative session (which this book includes for 1998).

The laws reproduced here are *excerpts*. Only material related to keeping and bearing arms has been included. In some cases this means substantial portions of laws may have been edited. **For official legal proceedings do not rely on these excerpts**—obtain unedited texts and competent professional assistance. Florida's statutes are available from the state's legislative web site. Any errors occurring there may appear here as well.

The Florida "gun laws," as represented by the following statutes, contain 47,116 words of law. In addition, gun owners are regulated by the 83,584 words of federal gun law.

How State Law Is Arranged

Each numbered part of Florida Statutes is called a "section," and is abbreviated "s.". This makes it easy to refer to any particular statute—just call it by its title and section numbers. For instance, Florida Statutes s. 790.06 is the part about concealed weapons. You say it like this, "Florida Statutes, section seven ninety point oh six."

Excerpt from the Constitution of the State of Florida

ARTICLE I

SECTION 8. Right to bear arms

(a) The right of the people to keep and bear arms in defense of themselves and of the lawful authority of the state shall not be infringed, except that the manner of bearing arms may be regulated by law.

(b) There shall be a mandatory period of three days, excluding weekends and legal holidays, between the purchase and delivery at retail of any handgun. For the purposes of this section, "purchase" means the transfer of money or other valuable consideration to the retailer, and "handgun" means a firearm capable of being carried and used by one hand, such as a pistol or revolver. Holders of a concealed weapon permit as prescribed in Florida law shall not be subject to the provisions of this paragraph.

(c) The legislature shall enact legislation implementing subsection (b) of this section, effective no later than December 31, 1991, which shall provide that anyone violating the provisions of subsection (b) shall be guilty of a felony.

(d) This restriction shall not apply to a trade in of another handgun.

ARTICLE X

SECTION 2. Militia

(a) The militia shall be composed of all able bodied inhabitants of the state who are or have declared their intention to become citizens of the United States; and no person because of religious creed or opinion shall be exempted from military duty except upon conditions provided by law.

(b) The organizing, equipping, housing, maintaining, and disciplining of the militia, and the safekeeping of public arms may be provided by law.

(c) The governor shall appoint all commissioned officers of the militia, including an adjutant general who shall be chief of staff. The appointment of all general officers shall be subject to confirmation by the senate.

(d) The qualifications of personnel and officers of the federally recognized national guard, including the adjutant general, and the grounds and proceedings for their discipline and removal shall conform to the appropriate United States army or air force regulations and usages.

FLORIDA GUN LAWS

EXCERPTS FROM FLORIDA STATUTES

<Cross-references and explanatory remarks appear in pointed brackets
and are not part of the statutes.>

CHAPTER 27
STATE ATTORNEYS; PUBLIC DEFENDERS; RELATED OFFICES

27.53 Appointment of assistants and other staff; method of payment

(1) The public defender of each judicial circuit is authorized to employ and establish, in such numbers as he or she shall determine, assistant public defenders, investigators, and other personnel who shall be paid from funds appropriated for that purpose. Notwithstanding the provisions of s. 790.01, s. 790.02, or s. 790.25(2)(a), an investigator employed by a public defender, while actually carrying out official duties, is authorized to carry concealed weapons if the investigator complies with s. 790.25(3)(o). However, such investigators are not eligible for membership in the Special Risk Class of the Florida Retirement System. The public defenders of all judicial circuits shall jointly develop a coordinated classification and pay plan which shall be submitted on or before January 1 of each year to the Justice Administrative Commission, the office of the President of the Senate, and the office of the Speaker of the House of Representatives. Such plan shall be developed in accordance with policies and procedures of the Executive Office of the Governor established in s. 216.181. Each assistant public defender appointed by a public defender under this section shall serve at the pleasure of the public defender. Each investigator employed by a public defender shall have full authority to serve any witness subpoena or court order issued, by any court or judge, within the judicial circuit served by such public defender, in a criminal case in which such public defender has been appointed to represent the accused.

CHAPTER 112
PUBLIC OFFICERS AND EMPLOYEES; GENERAL PROVISIONS

112.193 Law enforcement, correctional, and correctional probation officers' commemorative service awards

(1) For the purposes of this section, the term:
(a) "Employer" means a state board, commission, department, division, bureau, or agency or a county or municipality.
(b) "Law enforcement, correctional, or correctional probation officer" means any full-time, part-time, or auxiliary officer as defined in s. 943.10(14).
(2) Each employer that employs or appoints law enforcement, correctional, or correctional probation officers may present to each such employee who retires under any provision of a state or municipal retirement system, including medical disability retirement, or who is eligible to retire under any such provision but, instead, resigns from one employer to accept an elected public office, one complete uniform including the badge worn by that officer, the officer's service handgun, if one was issued as part of the officer's equipment, and an identification card clearly marked "RETIRED."
(3) Upon the death of a law enforcement, correctional, or correctional probation officer, the employer may present to the spouse or other beneficiary of the officer, upon request, one complete uniform, including the badge worn by the officer. However, if a law enforcement, correctional, or correctional

probation officer is killed in the line of duty, the employer may present, upon request, to the spouse or other beneficiary of the officer the officer's service-issued handgun, if one was issued as part of the officer's equipment. If the employer is not in possession of the service-issued handgun, the employer may, within its discretion, and upon written request of the spouse or other beneficiary, present a similar handgun. The provisions of this section shall also apply in that instance to a law enforcement or correctional officer who died before May 1, 1993. In addition, the officer's service handgun may be presented by the employer for any such officer who was killed in the line of duty prior to this act becoming a law.

(4) Each uniform, badge, service handgun, and identification card presented under this section is to commemorate prior service and must be used only in such manner as the employer prescribes by rule. The provisions of this section shall also apply in that instance to a law enforcement officer who died before May 1, 1993.

CHAPTER 125
COUNTY GOVERNMENT

125.0107 Ordinances relating to possession or sale of ammunition

No county may adopt any ordinance relating to the possession or sale of ammunition. Any such ordinance in effect on June 24, 1983, is void.

CHAPTER 166
MUNICIPALITIES

166.044 Ordinances relating to possession or sale of ammunition

No municipality may adopt any ordinance relating to the possession or sale of ammunition. Any such ordinance in effect on June 24, 1983, is void

CHAPTER 230
DISTRICT SCHOOL SYSTEM

230.23 Powers and duties of school board

The school board, acting as a board, shall exercise all powers and perform all duties listed below:
(6) CHILD WELFARE
(d) *Code of student conduct.* Adopt a code of student conduct for elementary schools and a code of student conduct for secondary schools and distribute the appropriate code to all teachers, school personnel, students, and parents or guardians, at the beginning of every school year. A district may compile the code of student conduct for elementary schools and the code of student conduct for secondary schools in one publication and distribute the combined codes to all teachers, school personnel, students, and parents or guardians at the beginning of every school year. Each code of student conduct shall be developed by the school boards; elementary or secondary school teachers and other school personnel, including school administrators; students; and parents or guardians. The code of student conduct for elementary schools shall parallel the code for secondary schools. Each code shall be organized and written in language which is understandable to students and parents and shall be discussed at the beginning of every school year in student classes, school advisory councils, and parent and teacher associations. Each code shall be based on the rules governing student conduct and discipline adopted by the school board and be made available in the student handbook or similar publication. Each code shall include, but not be limited to:
5. Notice that the possession of a firearm, a knife, a weapon, or an item which can be used as a weapon by any student while the student is on school property or in attendance at a school function is grounds for disciplinary action and may also result in criminal prosecution.

230.2316 Dropout prevention

(4) STUDENT ELIGIBILITY AND PROGRAM CRITERIA
(e) *Second chance schools*
3. A student shall be assigned to a second chance school if the school district in which the student resides has a second chance school and if the student meets one of the following criteria:
c. The student has committed a serious offense which warrants suspension or expulsion from school according to the district code of student conduct. For the purposes of this program, "serious offense" is behavior which:
(III) Includes possession of weapons or drugs; or

CHAPTER 240
POSTSECONDARY EDUCATION

240.268 University police officers

(1) Each university is empowered and directed to provide for police officers for the university, and such police officers shall hereafter be known and designated as the "university police."
(2) The university police are hereby declared to be law enforcement officers of the state and conservators of the peace with the right to arrest, in accordance with the laws of this state, any person for violation of state law or applicable county or city ordinances when such violations occur on any property or facilities which are under the guidance, supervision, regulation, or control of the State University System, except that arrests may be made off campus when hot pursuit originates on campus. Such officers shall have full authority to bear arms in the performance of their duties and to execute search warrants within their territorial jurisdiction. University police, when requested by the sheriff or local police authority, may serve subpoenas or other legal process and may make arrest of any person against whom a warrant has been issued or any charge has been made of violation of federal or state laws or county or city ordinances.

240.38 Community college police

(1) Each community college is permitted and empowered to employ police officers for the college, who must be designated community college police.
(2) Each community college police officer is a law enforcement officer of the state and a conservator of the peace who has the authority to arrest, in accordance with the laws of this state, any person for a violation of state law or applicable county or municipal ordinance if that violation occurs on or in any property or facilities of the community college by which he or she is employed. A community college police officer may also arrest a person off campus for a violation committed on campus after a hot pursuit of that person which began on campus. A community college police officer may bear arms in the performance of his or her duties and carry out a search pursuant to a search warrant on the campus where he or she is employed. Community college police, upon request of the sheriff or local police authority, may serve subpoenas or other legal process and may make arrests of persons against whom arrest warrants have been issued or against whom charges have been made for violations of federal or state laws or county or city ordinances.

CHAPTER 242
SPECIALIZED STATE EDUCATIONAL INSTITUTIONS

242.343 Florida School for the Deaf and the Blind campus police

(1) The Board of Trustees for the Florida School for the Deaf and the Blind is permitted and empowered to employ police officers for the school, who must be designated Florida School for the Deaf and the Blind campus police.
(2) Each Florida School for the Deaf and the Blind campus police officer is a law enforcement officer of the state and a conservator of the peace, who has the authority to arrest, in accordance with the laws of this state, any person for a violation of state law or applicable county or municipal ordinance if that violation occurs on or in any property or facilities of the school A campus police officer may also arrest a person off campus after a hot pursuit of that person which began on campus. A campus police officer shall have full authority to bear arms in the performance of the officer's duties and carry out a

search pursuant to a search warrant on the campus. Florida School for the Deaf and the Blind campus police, upon request of the sheriff or local police authority, may serve subpoenas or other legal process and may make arrests of persons against whom arrest warrants have been issued or against whom charges have been made for violations of federal or state laws or county or municipal ordinances.

CHAPTER 252
EMERGENCY MANAGEMENT

252.36 Emergency management powers of the Governor

(5) In addition to any other powers conferred upon the Governor by law, she or he may:
(h) Suspend or limit the sale, dispensing, or transportation of alcoholic beverages, firearms, explosives, and combustibles.

CHAPTER 258
STATE PARKS AND PRESERVES

258.157 Prohibited acts in Savannas State Reserve

(2) It is unlawful for any person, except a law enforcement or conservation officer, to have in his or her possession any firearm while within the Savannas except when in compliance with regulations established by the Florida Game and Fresh Water Fish Commission applying to lands within the described boundaries.
(3) Any person who violates this section commits a misdemeanor of the second degree, punishable as provided in s. 775.082 or s. 775.083.

CHAPTER 281
SAFETY AND SECURITY SERVICES

281.02 Powers and duties of the Division of Capitol Police

(4) To employ:
(a) Agents who hold certification as police officers in accordance with the minimum standards and qualifications as set forth in s. 943.13 and the provisions of chapter 110, who shall have the authority to bear arms, make arrests, and apply for arrest warrants; and

281.20 Transportation and protective services

(1) The Department of Law Enforcement shall provide and maintain the security of the Governor, the Governor's immediate family, and the Governor's office and mansion and the grounds thereof.
(2) The department shall employ such personnel as may be necessary to carry out this responsibility, including uniformed and nonuniformed agents who shall have authority to bear arms and make arrests, with or without warrant, for violations of any of the criminal laws of the state, under the same terms and conditions as investigative personnel of the department, and who shall be considered peace officers for all purposes, including but not limited to, the privileges, protections, and benefits of ss. 112.19, 121.051, 122.34, and 870.05.

CHAPTER 285
INDIAN RESERVATIONS AND AFFAIRS

285.18 Tribal council as governing body; powers and duties

(2) The governing bodies of the special improvement districts shall have the duty and power:

(c) To employ personnel to exercise law enforcement powers, including the investigation of violations of any of the criminal laws of the state occurring on reservations over which the state has assumed jurisdiction pursuant to s. 285.16.

1. All law enforcement personnel employed shall be considered peace officers for all purposes and shall have the authority to bear arms, make arrests, and apply for, serve, and execute search warrants, arrest warrants, capias, and other process of the court, and to enforce criminal and noncriminal traffic offenses, within their respective special improvement districts.

CHAPTER 316
MOTOR VEHICLES

316.640 Enforcement

(1) STATE

(b)2.a. The Department of Transportation shall develop training and qualifications standards for toll enforcement officers whose sole authority is to enforce the payment of tolls pursuant to s. 316.1001. Nothing in this subparagraph shall be construed to permit the carrying of firearms or other weapons, nor shall a toll enforcement officer have arrest authority.

(2) COUNTIES

(b) The sheriff's office of each county may employ as a traffic accident officer . . . This paragraph does not permit the carrying of firearms or other weapons, nor do such officers have arrest authority other than for the issuance of a traffic citation as authorized in this paragraph.

(c) The sheriff's office of each of the several counties of this state may employ as a parking enforcement specialist . . .

2. A parking enforcement specialist employed pursuant to this subsection shall not carry firearms or other weapons or have arrest authority.

(3) MUNICIPALITIES

(b) The police department of a chartered municipality may employ as a traffic accident investigation officer . . . Nothing in this paragraph shall be construed to permit the carrying of firearms or other weapons, nor shall such officers have arrest authority other than for the issuance of a traffic citation as authorized above.

(c)2. A parking enforcement specialist employed by a chartered municipality or its authorized agency or instrumentality is authorized to enforce all state, county, and municipal laws and ordinances governing parking within the boundaries of the municipality employing the specialist, by appropriate state, county, or municipal traffic citation. Nothing in this paragraph shall be construed to permit the carrying of firearms or other weapons, nor shall such a parking enforcement specialist have arrest authority.

(4)(c) This subsection does not permit the carrying of firearms or other weapons, nor do traffic control officers have arrest authority.

(5)(a) Any sheriff's department or police department of a municipality may employ, as a traffic infraction enforcement officer...

(c) This subsection does not permit the carrying of firearms or other weapons, nor do traffic infraction enforcement officers have arrest authority other than the authority to issue a traffic citation as provided in this subsection.

CHAPTER 321
HIGHWAY PATROL

321.05 Duties, functions, and powers of patrol officers

The members of the Florida Highway Patrol are hereby declared to be conservators of the peace and law enforcement officers of the state, with the common-law right to arrest a person who, in the presence of the arresting officer, commits a felony or commits an affray or breach of the peace constituting a misdemeanor, with full power to bear arms; and they shall apprehend, without warrant, any person in the unlawful commission of any of the acts over which the members of the Florida Highway Patrol are given jurisdiction as hereinafter set out and deliver him or her to the sheriff of the country that further proceedings may be had against him or her according to law. In the performance of any of the powers, duties, and functions authorized by law, members of the Florida Highway Patrol shall have the same protections and immunities afforded other peace officers, which shall be recognized by all courts having jurisdiction over offenses against the laws of this state, and shall have authority to apply for, serve, and execute search warrants, arrest warrants, capias, and other process of the court in those matters in which patrol officers have primary responsibility as set forth in subsection (1)...

321.24 Members of an auxiliary to Florida Highway Patrol

(2) Members of an auxiliary serving with the Florida Highway Patrol shall at all times serve under the direction and supervision of the director and members of the Florida Highway Patrol. After approval by the director on an individual basis and after completion of a firearms course approved by the director, members of an auxiliary, while serving under the supervision and direction of the director, or a member of the Florida Highway Patrol, shall have the power to bear arms. Members of an auxiliary shall have the same protection and immunities afforded regularly employed highway patrol officers, which shall be recognized by all courts having jurisdiction over offenses against the laws of this state.

CHAPTER 354
SPECIAL OFFICERS FOR CARRIERS

354.02 Powers

Each special officer shall have and exercise throughout every county in which the common carrier for which he or she was appointed, shall do business, operate, or own property, the power to make arrests for violation of law on the property of such common carrier, and to arrest persons, whether on or off such carrier's property, violating any law on such carrier's property, under the same conditions under which deputy sheriffs may by law make arrests, and shall have authority to carry weapons for the reasonable purpose of their offices.

CHAPTER 370
SALTWATER FISHERIES

370.08 Fishers and equipment; regulations

(5) THROWING EXPLOSIVES OR USE OF FIREARMS IN WATER FOR PURPOSE OF KILLING FOOD FISH PROHIBITED. No person may throw or cause to be thrown, into any of the waters of this state, any dynamite, lime, other explosive or discharge any firearms whatsoever for the purpose of killing food fish therein. The landing ashore or possession on the water by any person of any food fish that has been damaged by explosives or the landing of headless jewfish or grouper, if the grouper is taken for commercial use, is prima facie evidence of violation of this section.

CHAPTER 372
WILDLIFE

372.025 Everglades recreational sites; definitions

(1) PURPOSE. It is the intent of the Legislature to provide for the development and management of recreational sites in the water conservation areas of the Florida Everglades when such development:
(d) Offers recreational potential for nature trails, bird study, picnic areas, boating, fishing, hunting, and target shooting.

372.07 Police powers of commission and its agents

(1) The Game and Fresh Water Fish Commission, the director and the director's assistants designated by her or him, and each wildlife officer are constituted peace officers with the power to make arrests for violations of the laws of this state when committed in the presence of the officer or when committed on lands under the supervision and management of the commission...
(2) Said officers shall have power and authority to enforce throughout the state all laws relating to game, nongame birds, freshwater fish, and fur-bearing animals and all rules and regulations of the Game and Fresh Water Fish Commission relating to wild animal life and freshwater aquatic life, and in connection with said laws, rules, and regulations, in the enforcement thereof and in the performance of their duties thereunder, to:
(d) Carry firearms or other weapons, concealed or otherwise, in the performance of their duties;

372.57 Licenses and stamps; exemptions; fees

(3) A resident or nonresident taking fur-bearing animals by the use of guns or dogs only and not by the use of traps or other devices, and not for commercial purposes, who has purchased the license provided for hunting in this section, received a no-cost license, or is exempt from the license requirements of this chapter is not required to purchase the license provided in paragraph (2)(h). A resident who is age 65 or older is not required to purchase the license provided in paragraph (2)(h).
(4) In addition to any license required by this chapter, the following permits and fees for certain hunting, fishing, and recreational uses, and the activities authorized thereby are:
(c) A muzzle-loading gun permit to hunt within this state with a muzzle-loading gun during those game seasons in which hunting with a modern firearm is not allowed is $5.
(d) An archery permit to hunt within this state with a bow and arrow during those game seasons in which hunting with a firearm is not allowed is $5.

372.5717 Hunter safety course; requirements; penalty

(1) This section may be cited as the Senator Joe Carlucci Hunter Safety Act.
(2) A person born on or after June 1, 1975, may not be issued a license to take wild animal life with the use of a firearm, gun, bow, or crossbow in this state without having first successfully completed a hunter safety course as provided in this section, and without having in his or her possession a hunter safety certification card, as provided in this section.
(3) The Game and Fresh Water Fish Commission shall institute and coordinate a statewide hunter safety course which must be offered in every county and consist of not less than 12 hours nor more than 16 hours of instruction which including, but not limited to, instruction in the competent and safe handling of firearms, conservation, and hunting ethics.
(4) The commission shall issue a permanent hunter safety certification card to each person who successfully completes the hunter safety course. The commission shall maintain permanent records of hunter safety certification cards issued and shall establish procedures for replacing lost or destroyed cards.
(5) A hunter safety certification card issued by a wildlife agency of another state, or any Canadian province, which shows that the holder of the card has successfully completed a hunter safety course approved by the commission is an acceptable substitute for the hunter safety certification card issued by the commission.
(6) All persons subject to the requirements of subsection (2) must have in their personal possession, proof of compliance with this section, while taking or attempting to take wildlife with the use of a firearm, gun, bow, or crossbow and must display a valid hunter safety certification card to county tax

collectors or their subagents in order to purchase a Florida hunting license. After the issuance of a license, the license itself shall serve as proof of compliance with this section. A holder of a lifetime license whose license does not indicate on the face of the license that a hunter safety course has been completed must have in his or her personal possession a hunter safety certification card, as provided by this section, while attempting to take wild animal life with the use of a firearm, gun, bow, or crossbow.

(7) The hunter safety requirements of this section do not apply to persons for whom licenses are not required under s. 372.57(1).

(8) A person who violates this section shall be cited for a noncriminal infraction, punishable as provided in s. 372.711.

372.5718 Hunter safety course for juveniles

The Game and Fresh Water Fish Commission shall develop a hunter safety course for juveniles who are at least 5 years of age but less than 16 years of age. The course must include, but is not limited to, instruction in the competent and safe handling of firearms, conservation, and hunting ethics. The course must be appropriate for the ages of the students. The course is voluntary and must be offered in each county in the state at least annually. The course is in addition to, and not in lieu of, the hunter safety course prescribed in s. 372.5717.

372.663 Illegal killing, possessing, or capturing of alligators or other crocodilia or eggs; confiscation of equipment.

(1) It is unlawful to intentionally kill, injure, possess, or capture, or attempt to kill, injure, possess, or capture, an alligator or other crocodilian, or the eggs of an alligator or other crocodilian, unless authorized by the rules of the Game and Fresh Water Fish Commission. Any person who violates this section is guilty of a felony of the third degree, punishable as provided in s. 775.082, s. 775.083, or s. 775.084, in addition to such other punishment as may be provided by law. Any equipment, including but not limited to weapons, vehicles, boats, and lines, used by a person in the commission of a violation of any law, rule, regulation, or order relating to alligators or other crocodilia or the eggs of alligators or other crocodilia shall, upon conviction of such person, be confiscated by the Game and Fresh Water Fish Commission and disposed of according to rules and regulations of the commission. The arresting officer shall promptly make a return of the seizure, describing in detail the property seized and the facts and circumstances under which it was seized, including the names of all persons known to the officer who have an interest in the property.

(2) The commission shall promptly fix the value of the property and make return to the clerk of the circuit court of the county wherein same was seized. Upon proper showing that any such property is owned by, or titled in the name of, any innocent party, such property shall be promptly returned to such owner.

(3) The provisions of this section shall not vitiate any valid lien, retain tile contract, or chattel mortgage on such property in effect as of the time of such seizure.

372.664 Prima facie evidence of intent to violate laws protecting alligators

Except as otherwise provided by rule of the Game and Fresh Water Fish Commission for the purpose of the limited collection of alligators in designated areas, the display or use of a light in a place where alligators might be known to inhabit in a manner capable of disclosing the presence of alligators, together with the possession of firearms, spear guns, gigs, and harpoons customarily used for the taking of alligators, during the period between 1 hour after sunset and 1 hour before sunrise shall be prima facie evidence of an intent to violate the provisions of law regarding the protection of alligators.

372.99 Illegal taking and possession of deer and wild turkey; evidence; penalty

(1) Whoever takes or kills any deer or wild turkey, or possesses a freshly killed deer or wild turkey, during the closed season prescribed by law or by the rules and regulations of the Game and Fresh Water Fish Commission, or whoever takes or attempts to take any deer or wild turkey by the use of gun and light in or out of closed season, is guilty of a misdemeanor of the first degree, punishable as provided in s. 775.082 or s. 775.083, and shall forfeit any license or permit issued to her or him under the provisions of this chapter. No license shall be issued to such person for a period of 3 years following any such violation on the first offense. Any person guilty of a second or subsequent violation shall be permanently ineligible for issuance of a license or permit thereafter.

(2) The display or use of a light in a place where deer might be found and in a manner capable of disclosing the presence of deer, together with the possession of firearms or other weapons customarily used for the taking of deer, between 1 hour after sunset and 1 hour before sunrise, shall be prima facie evidence of an intent to violate the provisions of subsection (1). This subsection does not apply to an owner or her or his employee when patrolling or inspecting the land of the owner, provided the employee has satisfactory proof of employment on her or his person.

372.9901 Seizure of illegal devices; disposition; appraisal; forfeiture.

(1) Any vehicle, vessel, animal, gun, light, or other hunting device used in the commission of an offense prohibited by s. 372.99, shall be seized by the arresting officer, who shall promptly make return of the seizure and deliver the property to the Director of the Game and Fresh Water Fish Commission. The return shall describe the property seized and recite in detail the facts and circumstances under which it was seized, together with the reason that the property was subject to seizure. The return shall also contain the names of all persons known to the officer to be interested in the property.

(2) The director of the commission, upon receipt of the property, shall promptly fix its value and make return thereof to the clerk of the circuit court of the county wherein the article was seized; after which on proper showing of ownership of the property by someone other than the person arrested the property shall be returned to the said owner.

(3) Upon conviction of the violator, the property, if owned by the person convicted, shall be forfeited to the state under the procedure set forth in ss. 372.312 through 372.318, where not inconsistent with this section. All amounts received from the sale or other disposition of the property shall be paid into the State Game Trust Fund. If the property is not sold or converted, it shall be delivered to the director of the Game and Fresh Water Fish Commission.

CHAPTER 394
MENTAL HEALTH

394.458 Introduction or removal of certain articles unlawful; penalty.

(1)(a) Except as authorized by law or as specifically authorized by the person in charge of each hospital providing mental health services under this part, it is unlawful to introduce into or upon the grounds of such hospital, or to take or attempt to take or send therefrom, any of the following articles, which are hereby declared to be contraband for the purposes of this section:

1. Any intoxicating beverage or beverage which causes or may cause an intoxicating effect;
2. Any controlled substance as defined in chapter 893; or
3. Any firearms or deadly weapon.

(b) It is unlawful to transmit to, or attempt to transmit to, or cause or attempt to cause to be transmitted to, or received by, any patient of any hospital providing mental health services under this part any article or thing declared by this section to be contraband, at any place which is outside of the grounds of such hospital, except as authorized by law or as specifically authorized by the person in charge of such hospital.

(2) A person who violates any provision of this section commits a felony of the third degree, punishable as provided in s. 775.082, s. 775.083, or s. 775.084.

CHAPTER 493
PRIVATE INVESTIGATIVE, PRIVATE SECURITY, AND REPOSSESSION SERVICES

493.6101 Definitions.

(9) "Unarmed" means that no firearm shall be carried by the licensee while providing services regulated by this chapter.

(14) "Firearm instructor" means any Class "K" licensee who provides classroom or range instruction to applicants for a Class "G" license.

493.6102 Inapplicability of parts I through IV of this chapter

This chapter shall not apply to:

(3) Any individual solely, exclusively, and regularly employed as an unarmed investigator or recovery agent in connection with the business of her or his employer, when there exists an employer-employee relationship.

(4) Any unarmed nonuniformed individual engaged in security services who is employed exclusively to work on the premises of her or his employer, or in connection with the business of her or his employer, when there exists an employer-employee relationship.

493.6105 Initial application for license

(1) Each individual, partner, or principal officer in a corporation, shall file with the department a complete application accompanied by an application fee not to exceed $60, except that the applicant for a Class "D" or Class "G" license shall not be required to submit an application fee. The application fee shall not be refundable.

(4) In addition to the application requirements outlined in subsection (3), the applicant for a Class "C," Class "CC," Class "E," Class "EE," or Class "G" license shall submit two color photographs taken within the 6 months immediately preceding the submission of the application, which meet specifications prescribed by rule of the department. All other applicants shall submit one photograph taken within the 6 months immediately preceding the submission of the application.

(6) In addition to the requirements outlined in subsection (3), an applicant for a Class "G" license shall satisfy minimum training criteria for firearms established by rule of the department, which training criteria shall include, but is not limited to, 24 hours of range and classroom training taught and administered by a firearms instructor who has been licensed by the department; however, no more than 8 hours of such training shall consist of range training. The department shall, effective October 1, 1992, increase the minimum number of hours of firearms training required for Class "G" licensure by 4 hours, and shall subsequently increase the training requirement by 4 hours every 2 years, up to a maximum requirement of 48 hours. If the applicant can show proof that he or she is an active law enforcement officer currently certified under the Criminal Justice Standards and Training Commission, or if the applicant submits one of the certificates specified in paragraph (7)(a), the department may waive the firearms training requirement referenced above.

(7) In addition to the requirements under subsection (3), an applicant for a Class "K" license shall:

(a) Submit one of the following certificates:

1. The Florida Criminal Justice Standards and Training Commission Firearms Instructor's Certificate.

2. The National Rifle Association Police Firearms Instructor's Certificate.

3. The National Rifle Association Security Firearms Instructor's Certificate.

4. A Firearms Instructor's Certificate from a federal, state, county, or municipal police academy in this State recognized as such by the Criminal Justice Standards and Training Commission or by the Department of Education.

(b) Pay the fee for and pass an examination administered by the department which shall be based upon, but is not necessarily limited to, a firearms instruction manual provided by the department.

493.6106 License requirements; posting.

(3) Each Class "C," Class "CC," Class "D," Class "DI," Class "E," Class "EE," Class "G," Class "K," Class "M," Class "MA," Class "MB," Class "MR, or Class "RI" licensee shall notify the division in writing within then days of a change in her or his residence or mailing address.

493.6107 Fees.

(1) The department shall establish by rule examination and biennial license fees which shall not exceed the following:

(a) Class "M" license -- manager Class "AB" agency: $75.

(b) Class "G" license -- statewide firearm license: $150.

(c) Class "K" license -- firearms instructor: $100.

(d) Fee for the examination for firearms instructor: $75.

(2) The department may establish by rule a fee for the replacement or revision of a license which fee shall not exceed $30.

(3) The fees set forth in this section must be paid by certified check or money order or, at the discretion of the department, by agency check at the time the application is approved, except that the applicant for

a Class "G" or Class "M" license must pay the license fee at the time the application is made. If a license is revoked or denied or if the application is withdrawn, the license fee shall not be refunded.
(4) The department may prorate license fees.
(5) Payment of any license fee provided for under this chapter authorizes the licensee to practice his or her profession anywhere in this state without obtaining any additional license, permit, registration, or identification card, any municipal or county ordinance or resolution to the contrary notwithstanding. However, an agency may be required to obtain a city and county occupational license in each city and county where the agency maintains a physical office.

493.6108 Investigation of applicants by Department of State.

(2) In addition to subsection (1), the department shall make an investigation of the general physical fitness of the Class "G" applicant to bear a weapon or firearm. Determination of physical fitness shall be certified by a physician currently licensed pursuant to chapter 458, chapter 459 or any similar law of another state authorized to act as a licensed physician by a federal agency or department. Such certification shall be submitted on a form provided by the department.
(3) The department shall also investigate the mental history and current mental and emotional fitness of any Class "G" applicant, and shall deny a Class "G" license to anyone who has a history of mental illness or drug or alcohol abuse.

493.6109 Reciprocity.

(1) The department may adopt rules for:
(a) Entering into reciprocal agreements with other states or territories of the United States for the purpose of licensing persons to perform activities regulated under this chapter who are currently licensed to perform similar services in the other states or territories; or
(b) Allowing a person who is licensed in another state or territory to perform similar services in this state, on a temporary and limited basis, without the need for licensure in state.
(2) The rules authorized in subsection (1) may be promulgated only if:
(a) The other state or territory has requirements which are substantially similar to or greater than those established in this chapter.
(b) The applicant has engaged in licensed activities for at least 1 year in the other state or territory with no disciplinary action against him or her.
(c) The Secretary of State or other appropriate authority of the other state or territory agrees to accept service of process for those licensees who are operating in this state on a temporary basis.

493.6111 License; contents; identification card.

(1) All licenses issued pursuant to this chapter shall be on a form prescribed by the department and shall include the licensee's name, license number, expiration date of the license, and any other information the department deems necessary. Class "C," Class "CC," Class "D," Class "E," Class "EE," Class "M," Class "MA," Class "MB," Class "MR," and Class "G" licenses shall be in the possession of individual licenses while on duty.
(2) Licenses shall be valid for a period of 2 years.
(3) The department shall, upon complete application and payment of the appropriate fees, issue a separate license to each branch office for which application is make.
(4) Notwithstanding the existence of a valid Florida corporate registration, no agency licensee may conduct activities regulated under this chapter under any fictitious name without prior written authorization from the department to use that name in the conduct of activities regulated under this chapter. The department may not authorize the use of a name which is so similar to that of a public officer or agency, or of that used by another licensee, that the public may be confused or misled thereby. The authorization for the use of a fictitious name shall require, as a condition precedent to the use of such name, the filing of a certificate of engaging in business under a fictitious name under s. 865.09. No licensee shall be permitted to conduct business under more than one name except as separately licensed nor shall the license be valid to protect any licensee who is engaged in the business under any name other than that specified in the license. An agency desiring to change its licensed name shall notify the department and, except upon renewal, pay a fee not to exceed $30 for each license requiring revision including those of all licensed employees except Class "D" or Class "G" licensees. Upon the return of such licenses to the department, revised licenses shall be provided.
(5) It shall be the duty of every agency to furnish all of its partners, principal corporate officers, and all licensed employees an identification card. The card shall specify at least the name and license

number, if appropriate, of the holder of the card and the name and license number of the agency and shall be signed by a representative of the agency and by the holder of the card.
(a) Each individual to whom a license and identification card have been issued shall be responsible for the safekeeping thereof and shall not loan, or let or allow any other individual to use or display, the license or card.
(b) The identification card shall be in the possession of each partner, principal corporate officer, or licensed employee while on duty.
(c) Upon denial, suspension, or revocation of a license, or upon termination of a business association with the licensed agency, it shall be the duty of each partner, principal corporate officer, manager, or licensed employee to return the identification card to the issuing agency.
(6) A licensed agency must include its agency license number in any advertisement in any print medium or directory, and must include its agency license number in any written bid or offer to provide services.

493.6113 Renewal application for licensure.

(1) A license granted under the provision of this chapter shall be renewed biennially by the department.
(2) No less than 90 days prior to the expiration date of the license, the department shall mail a written notice to the last known residence address for individual licensees and to the last known agency address for agencies.
(3) Each licensee shall be responsible for renewing his or her license on or before its expiration by filing with the department an application for renewal accompanied by payment of the prescribed license fee.
(a) Each Class "A," Class "B," or Class "R" licensee shall additionally submit on a form prescribed by the department a certification of insurance which evidences that the licensee maintains coverage as required under s. 493.6110.
(b) Each Class "G" licensee shall additionally submit proof that he or she has received during each year of the license period a minimum of 4 hours of firearms recertification training taught by a Class "K" licensee and has complied with such other health and training requirements which the department may adopt by rule. If proof of a minimum of 4 hours of annual firearms recertification training cannot be provided, the renewal applicant shall complete the minimum number of hours of range and classroom training required at the time of initial licensure.
(c) Each Class "DS" or Class "RS" licensee shall additionally submit the current curriculum, examination, and list of instructors.
(4) A licensee who fails to file a renewal application on or before its expiration must renew his or her license by fulfilling the applicable requirements of subsection (3) and by paying a late fee equal to the amount of the license fee.
(5) No license shall be renewed 3 months or more after its expiration date. The applicant shall submit a new, complete application and the respective fees.
(6) A renewal applicant shall not perform any activity regulated by this chapter between the date of expiration and the date of renewal of his or her license.

493.6114 Cancellation or inactivation of license.

(1) In the event the licensee desires to cancel her or his license, she or he shall notify the department in writing and return the license to the department within 10 days of the date of cancellation.
(2) The department, at the written request of the licensee, may place her or his license in inactive status. A license may remain inactive for a period of 3 years, at the end of which time, if the license has not been renewed, it shall be automatically canceled. If the license expires during the inactive period, the licensee shall be required to pay license fees and, if applicable, show proof of insurance or proof of firearms training before the license can be made active. No late fees shall apply when a license is in inactive status.

493.6115 Weapons and firearms.

(1) The provision of this section shall apply to all licensees in addition to the other provisions of this chapter.
(2) Only Class "C," Class "CC," Class "D," Class "M," Class "MA," or Class "MB" licensees are permitted to bear a firearm and any such licensee who bears a firearm shall also have a Class "G" license.
(3) No employee shall carry or be furnished a weapon or firearm unless the carrying of a weapon or firearm is required by her or his duties, nor shall an employee carry a weapon or firearm except in connection with those duties. When carried pursuant to this subsection, the weapon or firearm shall be encased in view at all times except as provided in subsection (4).
(4) A Class "C" or Class "CC" licensee 21 years of age or older who has also been issued a Class "G" license may carry, in the performance of her or his duties, a concealed firearm. A Class "D" licensee

21 years of age or older who has also been issued a Class "G" license may carry a concealed firearm in the performance of her or his duties under the conditions specified in s. 493.6305(2). The Class "G" license shall clearly indicate such authority. The authority of any such licensee to carry a concealed firearm shall be valid throughout the state, in any location, while performing services within the scope of the license.

(5) The Class "G" license shall remain in effect only during the period the applicant is employed as a Class "C," Class "CC," Class "D," Class "MA," Class "MB," or Class "M" licensee.

(6) Unless otherwise approved by the department, the only firearm a Class "CC," Class "D," class "M," or Class "MB" licensee who has been issued a Class "G" license may carry is a .38 or .357 caliber revolver with factory .38 caliber ammunition only. In addition to any other firearm approved by the department, a Class "C" and Class "MA" licensee who has been issued a Class "G" license may carry a .38 caliber revolver; or a .380 caliber or 9 millimeter semiautomatic pistol; or a .357 caliber revolver with .38 caliber ammunition only. A Class "C" licensee who also holds a Class "D" license, and who has been issued a Class "G" license, may carry a 9 millimeter semiautomatic pistol while performing security-related services. No licensee may carry more than two firearms upon her or his person when performing her or his duties. A licensee may only carry a firearm of the specific type and caliber with which she or he is qualified pursuant to the firearms training referenced in subsection (8) or s. 493.6113(3)(b).

(7) Any person who provides classroom and range instruction to applicants for Class "G" licensure shall have a Class "K" license.

(8) A Class "G" applicant must satisfy the minimum training criteria as set forth in s. 493.6105(6) and as established by rule of the department.

(9) Whenever a Class "G" licensee discharges her or his firearm in the course of her or his duties, the class "G" licensee and the agency by which she or he is employed shall, within 5 working days, submit to the department an explanation describing the nature of the incident, the necessity for using the firearm, and a copy of any report prepared by a law enforcement agency. The department may revoke or suspend the Class "G" licensee's license and the licensed agency's agency license if this requirement is not met.

(10) The department may promulgate rules to establish minimum standards to issue licenses for weapons other than firearms.

(11) The department may establish rules to require periodic classroom training for firearms instructors to provide updated information relative to curriculum or other training requirements provided by statute or rule.

(12) The department may issue a temporary Class "G" license, on a case-by-case basis, if:

(a) The agency or employer has certified that the applicant has been determined to be mentally and emotionally stable by either:

1. A validated written psychological test taken within the previous 12-month period.

2. An evaluation by a psychiatrist or psychologist licensed in this state or by the Federal Government made within the previous 12-month period.

3. Presentation of a DD form 214, issued within the previous 12-month period, which establishes the absence of emotional or mental instability at the time of discharge from military service.

(b) The applicant has submitted a complete application for a Class "G" license, with a notation that she or he is seeking a temporary Class "G" license.

(c) The applicant has completed all Class "G" minimum training requirements as specified in this section.

(d) The applicant has received approval from the department subsequent to its conduct of a criminal history record check as authorized in s. 593.6121(6).

(13) In addition to other fees, the department may charge a fee, not to exceed $25, for processing a Class "G" license application as a temporary Class "G" license request.

(14) Upon issuance of the temporary Class "G" license, the licensee is subject to all of the requirements imposed upon Class "G" licensees.

(15) The temporary Class "G" license is valid units the class "G" license is issued or denied. If the department denies the Class "G" license, any temporary Class "G" license issued to that individual is void, and the individual shall be removed from armed duties immediately.

(16) If the criminal history record check program referenced in Subsection 493.6121(6) is inoperable, the department may issue a temporary "G" license on a case-by-case basis, provided that the applicant has met all statutory requirements for the issuance of a temporary "G" license as specified in subsection (12), excepting the criminal history record check stipulated there; provided, that the department requires that the licensed employer of the applicant conduct a criminal history record check of the applicant pursuant to standards set forth in rule by the department, and provide to the department an affidavit containing such information and statements as required by the department, including a statement that the criminal history record check did not indicate the existence of any criminal history that would prohibit licensure. Failure to properly conduct such a check, or knowingly providing incorrect or misleading information or statements in the affidavit shall constitute grounds for

disciplinary action against the licensed agency, including revocation of license.

(17) No person is exempt from the requirements of this section by virtue of holding a concealed weapon or concealed firearm license issued pursuant to s. 790.06.

493.6118 Grounds for disciplinary action.

(1)(u) In addition to the grounds for disciplinary action prescribed in paragraph (a) - (t), Class "R" recovery agencies, Class "E" recovery agents, and Class "EE" recovery agent interns are prohibited from committing the following acts:

9. Carrying any weapon or firearm when he or she is on private property and performing duties under his or her license whether or not he or she is licensed pursuant to s. 709.06.

(4) Notwithstanding the provisions of paragraph (1)(c) and subsection (2):

(a) If the applicant or licensee has been convicted of a felony, the department shall deny the application or revoke the license unless and until civil rights have been restored by the State of Florida or by a state acceptable to Florida and a period of 10 years has expired since final release from supervision.

(b) A Class "G" applicant who has been convicted of a felony shall also have had the specific right to possess, carry, or use a firearm restored by the State of Florida.

(c) If the applicant or licensee has been found guilty of, entered a plea of guilty to, or entered a plea of nolo contendere to a felony and adjudication of guilt is withheld, the department shall deny the application or revoke the license until a period of 3 years has expired since final release from supervision.

(d) A plea of nolo contendere shall create a rebuttable presumption of guilt to the underlying criminal charges, and the department shall allow the person being disciplined or denied an application for a license to present any mitigating circumstances surrounding, his or her plea.

(e) The grounds for discipline or denial cited in this subsection shall be applied to any disqualifying criminal history regardless of the date of commission of the underlying charge. Such provisions shall be applied retroactively and prospectively.

493.6121 Enforcement; investigation

(6) The department shall be provided access to the program that is operated by the Department of Law Enforcement, pursuant to s. 790.065, for providing criminal history record information to licensed gun dealers, manufacturers, and exporters. The department may make inquiries, and shall receive responses in the same fashion as provided under s. 790.065. The department shall be responsible for payment to the Department of Law Enforcement of the same fees as charged to others afforded access to the program.

PART II PRIVATE INVESTIGATIVE SERVICES

493.6201 Classes of licenses.

(7) Only Class "M," Class "MA," Class "C," or Class "CC" licensees are permitted to bear a firearm, and any such licensee who bears a firearm shall also have a Class "G" license.

493.6203 License requirements.

(6) In addition to any other requirement, an applicant for a Class "G" license shall satisfy the firearms training set forth in s. 493.6115.

PART III PRIVATE SECURITY SERVICES

493.6301 Classes of licenses

(6) Only Class "M," Class "MB," or Class "D" licensees are permitted to bear a firearm, and any such licensee who bears a firearm shall also have a Class "G" license.

493.6303 License requirements.

In addition to the license requirements set forth elsewhere in this chapter, each individual or agency shall comply with the following additional requirements:

(5) An applicant for a Class "G" license shall satisfy the firearms training outlined in s. 493.6115.

493.6305 Uniforms, required wear; exceptions.

(1) Class "D" licensees shall perform duties regulated under this chapter in a uniform which bears at least one patch or emblem visible at all times clearly identifying the employing agency. Upon resignation or termination of employment, a class "D" licensee shall immediately return to the employer any uniform and any other equipment issued to him by the employer.

(2) Class "D" licensees may perform duties regulated under this chapter in nonuniform status on a limited special assignment basis, and only when duty circumstances or special requirements of the client necessitate such dress.

(3) Class "D" licensees who are also Class "G" licensees and who are performing limited, special assignment duties may carry their authorized firearm concealed in the conduct of such duties.

CHAPTER 534
LIVESTOCK; MARKS AND BRANDS; STAMPING BEEF

534.081 Duties of law enforcement officers; appointment of special officers.

(3)(c) In the enforcement of the provisions of this chapter and other criminal laws relating to livestock, farm equipment, livery tack, farm or citrus products, trespass, wild animal life, freshwater aquatic life, littering, forests, forest fires, open burning, theft of forest products, damage to forest products, or other crimes committed incidental or related thereto or crimes committed on property owned, managed, or occupied by the department, such officers may go upon all premises, posted or otherwise, as necessary for the enforcement of such laws. The department may, at any time for cause, withdraw the appointments as special officers from such investigators of the department. All such special officers shall, upon certification under s. 943.1395(1), have the same right and authority to carry arms as do the sheriffs of this state. The compensation of such special officers shall be fixed and paid by the department.

CHAPTER 552
MANUFACTURE, DISTRIBUTION, AND USE OF EXPLOSIVES

552.081 Definitions.

(2) "Explosives" means any chemical compound, mixture, or device, the primary purpose of which is to function by explosion. The term "explosives" includes, but is not limited to, dynamite, nitroglycerin, trinitrotoluene, other high explosives, black powder, pellet powder, detonating cord, igniter cord, and igniters. "Explosives" does not include cartridges for firearms and does not include fireworks as defined in chapter 791.

552.091 License or permit required of manufacturer-distributor, dealer, user, or blaster of explosives.

(5)(b) However, no fee shall be required for a dealer license if the only explosive sold by the dealer is black powder for recreational use.

552.22 Penalties.

(1) Any person who manufactures, purchases, transports, keeps, stores, possesses, distributes, sells, or uses any explosive with the intent to harm life, limb, or property is guilty of a felony of the second degree, punishable as provided in s. 775.082, s. 775.083, or s. 775.084. Manufacturing, purchasing, possessing, distributing, or selling an explosive under circumstances contrary to the provisions of this chapter or such regulations as are adopted pursuant thereto shall be prima facie evidence of an intent to use the explosive for destruction of life, limb, or property.

552.241 Limited exemptions.

The licensing, permitting, and storage requirements of this chapter shall not apply to:

(1) Dealers who purchase, sell, possess, or transport:

(a) Smokeless propellant or commercially manufactured sporting grades of black powder in quantities not exceeding 150 pounds, provided such dealer holds a valid federal firearms dealer's license.

(b) Small arms ammunition primers, percussion caps, safety and pyrotechnic fuses, quills quick and slow matches and friction primers intended to be used solely for sporting, recreational, and cultural purposes, provided such dealer holds a valid federal firearms dealer's license.

(2) Users who are natural persons and who purchase, possess, or transport:

(a) Smokeless propellant powder in quantities not to exceed 150 pounds, or commercially manufactured sporting grades of black powder not to exceed 25 pounds, provided such powder is for the sole purpose of handloading cartridges for use in pistols or sporting rifles, or handloading shells for use in shotguns, or for a combination of these or other purposes strictly confined to handloading or muzzle-loading firearms for sporting, recreational, or cultural use.

(b) Small arms ammunition primers, percussion caps, safety and pyrotechnic fuses, quills, quick and slow matches and friction primers, provided such small arms ammunition primers are for the sole purpose of handloading cartridges for use in pistols or sporting rifles, or handloading shells for use in shotguns, or for a combination of these or other purposes strictly confined to handloading or muzzle-loading firearms for sporting, recreational, or cultural use.

CHAPTER 626
INSURANCE FIELD REPRESENTATIVES AND OPERATIONS

626.989 Division of Insurance Fraud; definition; investigative, subpoena powers; protection from civil liability; reports to division; division investigator's power to execute warrants and make arrests.

(7) Division investigators shall have the power to make arrests for criminal violations established as a result of investigations only. The general laws applicable to arrest by law enforcement officers of this state shall also be applicable to such investigators. Such investigators shall have the power to execute arrest warrants and search warrants for the same criminal violations; to serve subpoenas issued for the examination, investigation, and trial of all offenses determined by their investigations; and to arrest upon probable cause without warrant any person found in the act of violating any of the provisions of applicable laws. Investigators empowered to make arrests under this section shall be empowered to bear arms in the performance of their duties. In such a situation, the investigator must be certified in compliance with the provisions of s. 943.1395 or must meet the temporary employment or appointment exemption requirements of s. 943.131 until certified.

CHAPTER 705
LOST OR ABANDONED PROPERTY

705.105 Procedure regarding unclaimed evidence

(1) Title to unclaimed evidence or unclaimed tangible personal property lawfully seized pursuant to a lawful investigation in the custody of the court or clerk of the court from a criminal proceeding or seized as evidence by and in the custody of a law enforcement agency shall vest permanently in the law enforcement agency 60 days after the conclusion of the proceeding.

(a) If the property is of appreciable value, the agency may elect to:

1. Retain the property for the agency's own use;

2. Transfer the property to another unit of state or local government;

3. Donate the property to a charitable organization;

4. Sell the property at public sale, pursuant to the provisions of s. 705.103.

(b) If the property is not of appreciable value, the law enforcement agency may elect to destroy it.

(2) Nothing in this section shall be construed to repeal or supersede the provisions of s. 790.08 relating to the disposition of weapons and firearms.

CHAPTER 713
LIENS

713.68 Liens for hotels, apartment houses, roominghouses, boardinghouses, etc.

In favor of any person conducting or operating any hotel, apartment house, rooming house, boarding house or tenement house where rooms or apartments are let for hire or rental on a transient basis. Such lien shall exist on all the property including trunks, baggage, jewelry and wearing apparel, guns and sporting goods, furniture and furnishings and other personal property of any person which property is brought into or placed in any room or apartment of any hotel, apartment house, lodging house, rooming house, boardinghouse or tenement house when such person shall occupy, on a transient basis, such room or apartment as tenant, lessee, boarder, roomer or guest for the privilege of which occupancy money or anything of value is to be paid to the person conducting or operating such hotel, apartment house, rooming house, lodging house, boardinghouse or tenement house. Such lien shall continue and be in full force and effect for the amount payable for such occupancy until the same shall have been fully paid and discharged.

CHAPTER 741
HUSBAND AND WIFE

741.28 Domestic violence; definitions.--As used in ss. 741.28-741.31:

(1) "Domestic violence" means any assault, aggravated assault, battery, aggravated battery, sexual assault, sexual battery, stalking, aggravated stalking, kidnapping, false imprisonment, or any criminal offense resulting in physical injury or death of one family or household member by another who is or was residing in the same single dwelling unit.

(2) "Family or household member" means spouses, former spouses, persons related by blood or marriage, persons who are presently residing together as if a family or who have resided together in the past as if a family, and persons who have a child in common regardless of whether they have been married or have resided together at any time.

741.29 Domestic violence; investigation of incidents; notice to victims of legal rights and remedies; reporting.

(1) Any law enforcement officer who investigates an alleged incident of domestic violence shall assist the victim to obtain medical treatment if such is required as a result of the alleged incident to which the officer responds. Any law enforcement officer who investigates an alleged incident of domestic violence shall advise the victim of such violence that there is a domestic violence center from which the victim may receive services. The law enforcement officer shall give the victim immediate notice of the legal rights and remedies available on a standard form developed and distributed by the department. As necessary, the department shall revise the Legal Rights and Remedies Notice to Victims to include a general summary of s. 741.30 using simple English as well as Spanish, and shall distribute the notice as a model form to be used by all law enforcement agencies throughout the state. The notice shall include:

(4)(b) If a law enforcement officer has probable cause to believe that two or more persons have committed a misdemeanor or felony, or if two or more persons make complaints to the officer, the officer shall try to determine who was the primary aggressor. Arrest is the preferred response only with respect to the primary aggressor and not the preferred response with respect to a person who acts in a reasonable manner to protect or defend oneself or another family or household member from domestic violence.

741.30 Domestic violence; injunction; powers and duties of court and clerk; petition; notice and hearing; temporary injunction; issuance of injunction; statewide verification system; enforcement.

(1) There is created a cause of action for an injunction for protection against domestic violence.

(a) Any person described in paragraph (e), who is the victim of any act of domestic violence, or has reasonable cause to believe he or she is in imminent danger of becoming the victim of any act of domestic violence, has standing in the circuit court to file a sworn petition for an injunction for protection against domestic violence.

(d) A person's right to petition for an injunction shall not be affected by such person having left a residence or household to avoid domestic violence.

(e) This cause of action for an injunction may be sought by family or household members. No person shall be precluded from seeking injunctive relief pursuant to this chapter solely on the basis that such person is not a spouse.

(6)(f) A final judgment on injunction for protection against domestic violence entered pursuant to this section must, on its face, indicate that it is a violation of s. 790.233, and a first degree misdemeanor, for the respondent to have in his or her care, custody, possession, or control any firearm or ammunition.

741.31 Violation of an injunction for protection against domestic violence.

(4)(b)1. It is a violation of s. 790.233, and a misdemeanor of the first degree, punishable as provided in s. 775.082 or s. 775.083, for a person to violate a final injunction for protection against domestic violence by having in his or her care, custody, possession, or control any firearm or ammunition.

2. It is the intent of the Legislature that the disabilities regarding possession of firearms and ammunition are consistent with federal law. Accordingly, this paragraph shall not apply to a state or local officer as defined in s. 943.10(14), holding an active certification, who receives or possesses a firearm or ammunition for use in performing official duties on behalf of the officer's employing agency, unless otherwise prohibited by the employing agency.

CHAPTER 772
CIVIL REMEDIES FOR CRIMINAL PRACTICES

772.102 Definitions

As used in this chapter, the term:

(1) "Criminal activity" means to commit, to attempt to commit, to conspire to commit, or to solicit, coerce, or intimidate another person to commit:

(a) Any crime which is chargeable by indictment or information under the following provisions:

16. Chapter 790, relating to weapons and firearms.

CHAPTER 775
CRIMES
DEFINITIONS; GENERAL PENALTIES; REGISTRATION OF CRIMINALS

775.012 General purposes

The general purposes of the provisions of the code are:

(1) To proscribe conduct that improperly causes or threatens substantial harm to individual or public interest.

(2) To give fair warning to the people of the state in understandable language of the nature of the conduct proscribed and of the sentences authorized upon conviction.

(3) To define clearly the material elements constituting an offense and the accompanying state of mind or criminal intent required for that offense.

(4) To differentiate on reasonable grounds between serious and minor offenses and to establish appropriate disposition for each.

(5) To safeguard conduct that is without fault or legitimate state interest from being condemned as criminal.

(6) To ensure the public safety by deterring the commission of offenses and providing for the opportunity for rehabilitation of those convicted and for their confinement when required in the interests of public protection.

775.08 Classes and definitions of offenses.--When used in the laws of this state:

(1) The term "felony" shall mean any criminal offense that is punishable under the laws of this state, or that would be punishable if committed in this state, by death or imprisonment in a state penitentiary. "State penitentiary" shall include state correctional facilities. A person shall be imprisoned in the state penitentiary for each sentence which, except an extended term, exceeds 1 year.

(2) The term "misdemeanor" shall mean any criminal offense that is punishable under the laws of this state, or that would be punishable if committed in this state, by a term of imprisonment in a county correctional facility, except an extended term, not in excess of 1 year. The term "misdemeanor" shall not mean a conviction for any noncriminal traffic violation of any provision of chapter 316 or any municipal or county ordinance.

(3) The term "noncriminal violation" shall mean any offense that is punishable under the laws of this state, or that would be punishable if committed in this state, by no other penalty than a fine, forfeiture, or other civil penalty. A noncriminal violation does not constitute a crime, and conviction for a noncriminal violation shall not give rise to any legal disability based on a criminal offense. The term "noncriminal violation" shall not mean any conviction for any violation of any municipal or county ordinance. Nothing contained in this code shall repeal or change the penalty for a violation of any municipal or county ordinance.

(4) The term "crime" shall mean a felony or misdemeanor.

775.081 Classifications of felonies and misdemeanors.

(1) Felonies are classified, for the purpose of sentence and for any other purpose specifically provided by statute, into the following categories:

(a) Capital felony;
(b) Life felony;
(c) Felony of the first degree;
(d) Felony of the second degree; and
(e) Felony of the third degree.

A capital felony and a life felony must be so designated by statute. Other felonies are of the particular degree designated by statute. Any crime declared by statute to be a felony without specification of degree is of the third degree, except that this provision shall not affect felonies punishable by life imprisonment for the first offense.

(2) Misdemeanors are classified, for the purpose of sentence and for any other purpose specifically provided by statute, into the following categories:

(a) Misdemeanor of the first degree; and
(b) Misdemeanor of the second degree.
A misdemeanor is of the particular degree designated by statute. Any crime declared by statute to be a misdemeanor without specification of degree is of the second degree.
(3) This section is supplemental to, and is not to be construed to alter, the law of this state establishing and governing criminal offenses that are divided into degrees by virtue of distinctive elements comprising such offenses, regardless of whether such law is established by constitutional provision, statute, court rule, or court decision.

775.083 Fines.

(1) A person who has been convicted of an offense other than a capital felony may be sentenced to pay a fine in addition to any punishment described in s. 775.082; when specifically authorized by statute, he or she may be sentenced to pay a fine in lieu of any punishment described in s. 775.082. A person who has been convicted of a noncriminal violation may be sentenced to pay a fine. Fines for designated crimes and for noncriminal violations shall not exceed:
(a) $15,000, when the conviction is of a life felony.
(b) $10,000, when the conviction is of a felony of the first or second degree.
(c) $5,000, when the conviction is of a felony of the third degree.
(d) $1,000, when the conviction is of a misdemeanor of the first degree.
(e) $500, when the conviction is of a misdemeanor of the second degree or a noncriminal violation.
(f) Any higher amount equal to double the pecuniary gain derived from the offense by the offender or double the pecuniary loss suffered by the victim.
(g) Any higher amount specifically authorized by statute.
If a defendant is unable to pay a fine, the court may defer payment of the fine to a date certain.

775.084 Violent career criminals; habitual felony offenders and habitual violent felony offenders; definitions; procedure; enhanced penalties

(1) As used in this act:
(c) "Violent career criminal" means a defendant for whom the court must impose imprisonment pursuant to paragraph (4)(c), if it finds that:
g. a felony violation of chapter 790 involving the use or possession of a firearm.

775.0846 Wearing bulletproof vest while committing certain offenses

(1) For the purposes of this section, the term "bulletproof vest" means a bullet-resistant soft body armor providing, as a minimum standard, the level of protection known as "threat level I," which shall mean at least seven layers of bullet-resistant material providing protection from three shots of 158-grain lead ammunition fired from a .38 caliber handgun at a velocity of 850 feet per second.
(2) A person is guilty of the unlawful wearing of a bulletproof vest when, acting alone or with one or more other persons and while possessing a firearm, he or she commits or attempts to commit any murder, sexual battery, robbery, burglary, arson, aggravated assault, aggravated battery, kidnapping, escape, breaking and entering with intent to commit a felony, or aircraft piracy and, in the course of and in furtherance of any such crime, he or she wears a bulletproof vest.
(3) Any person who is convicted of a violation of this section is guilty of a felony of the third degree, punished as provided in s. 775.082, s. 775.083, or s. 775.084.

775.087 Possession or use of weapon; aggravated battery; felony reclassification; minimum sentence.

(1) Unless otherwise provided by law, whenever a person is charged with a felony, except a felony in which the use of a weapon or firearm is an essential element, and during the commission of such felony the defendant carries, displays, uses, threatens, or attempts to use any weapon or firearm, or during the commission of such felony the defendant commits an aggravated battery, the felony for which the person is charged shall be reclassified as follows:
(a) In the case of a felony of the first degree, to a life felony.
(b) In the case of a felony of the second degree, to a felony of the first degree.
(c) In the case of a felony of the third degree, to a felony of the second degree.
For purposes of sentencing under chapter 921 and determining incentive gain-time eligibility under chapter 944, a felony offense which is reclassified under this section is ranked one level above the

ranking under s. 921.0012 or s. 921.0013 of the felony offense committed.
(2) Any person who is convicted of a felony or an attempt to commit a felony and the conviction was for:
(a) Murder;
(b) Sexual battery;
(c) Robbery;
(d) Burglary;
(e) Arson;
(f) Aggravated assault;
(g) Aggravated battery;
(h) Kidnaping;
(i) Escape;
(j) Aircraft piracy;
(k) Aggravated child abuse;
(l) Unlawful throwing, placing, or discharging of a destructive device or bomb;
(m) Carjacking;
(n) Home-invasion robbery; or
(o) Aggravated stalking
and during the commission of the offense, such person possessed a "firearm," as defined in s.
791.001(6), or "destructive device," as defined in s. 790.001(4), shall be sentenced to a minimum term
of imprisonment of 3 years. Notwithstanding the provisions of s. 948.01, adjudication of guilt or
imposition of sentence shall not be suspended, deferred, or withheld. An offender sentenced under
this subsection is not eligible for control release under s. 947.146.
(3)(a) Any person who is convicted of a felony or an attempt to commit a felony and the conviction was
for:
1. Murder;
2. Sexual battery;
3. Robbery;
4. Burglary;
5. Arson;
6. Aggravated assault;
7. Aggravated battery;
8. Kidnaping;
9. Escape;
10. Sale, manufacture, delivery, or intent to sell, manufacture, or deliver any controlled substance;
11. aircraft piracy;
12. Aggravated child abuse;
13. Unlawful throwing, placing, or discharging of a destructive device or bomb;
14. Carjacking;
15. Home-invasion robbery; or
16. Aggravated stalking
and during the commission of the offense, such person possessed a semiautomatic firearm and its high-
capacity detachable box magazine or a machine gun as defined in s. 790.001(9), shall be sentenced
to a minimum term of imprisonment of 8 years. Notwithstanding the provisions of s. 984.01,
adjudication of guilt or imposition of sentence shall not be suspended, deferred, or withheld. An
offender sentenced under this subsection is not eligible for control release under s. 947.146.
(b) As used in this subsection, the term:
1. "High-capacity detachable box magazine" means any detachable box magazine, for use in a
semiautomatic firearm, which is capable of being loaded with more than 20 centerfire cartridges.
2. "Semiautomatic firearm" means a firearm which is capable of firing a series of rounds by separate
successive depressions of the trigger and which uses the energy of discharge to perform a portion of
the operating cycle.

775.0875 Unlawful taking, possession, or use of law enforcement officer's firearm; crime reclassification; penalties.

(1) A person who, without authorization, takes a firearm from a law enforcement officer lawfully engaged
in law enforcement duties commits a felony of the third degree, punishable as provided in s. 775.082,
s. 775.083, or s. 775.084.
(2) If a person violates subsection (1) and commits any other crime involving the firearm taken from the
law enforcement officer, such crime shall be reclassified as follows:
(a)1. In the case of a felony of the first degree, to a life felony.
2. In the case of a felony of the second degree, to a felony of the first degree.
3. In the case of a felony of the third degree, to a felony of the second degree.

For purposes of sentencing under chapter 921 and determining incentive gain-time eligibility under chapter 944, a felony offense which is reclassified under this paragraph is ranked one level above the ranking under s. 921.0022 or s. 921.0023 of the felony offense committed.

(b) In the case of a misdemeanor, to a felony of the third degree. For purposes of sentencing under chapter 921 and determining incentive gain-time eligibility under chapter 944, such offense is ranked in level 2 of the offense severity ranking chart.

(3) A person who possesses a firearm which he or she knows was unlawfully taken from a law enforcement officer commits a misdemeanor of the first degree, punishable as provided in s. 775.082 or s. 775.083.

CHAPTER 776
JUSTIFIABLE USE OF FORCE

776.012 Use of force in defense of person.

A person is justified in the use of force, except deadly force, against another when and to the extent that the person reasonably believes that such conduct is necessary to defend himself or herself or another against such other's imminent use of unlawful force. However, the person is justified in the use of deadly force only if he or she reasonably believes that such force is necessary to prevent imminent death or great bodily harm to himself or herself or another or to prevent the imminent commission of a forcible felony.

776.031 Use of force in defense of others.

A person is justified in the use of force, except deadly force, against another when and to the extent that the person reasonably believes that such conduct is necessary to prevent or terminate such other's trespass on, or other tortious or criminal interference with, either real property other than a dwelling or personal property, lawfully in his or her possession or in the possession of another who is a member of his or her immediate family or household or of a person whose property he or she has a legal duty to protect. However, the person is justified in the use of deadly force only if he or she reasonably believes that such force is necessary to prevent the imminent commission of a forcible felony.

776.041 Use of force by aggressor.

The justification described in the preceding sections of this chapter is not available to a person who:

(1) is attempting to commit, committing, or escaping after the commission of, a forcible felony; or

(2) Initially provokes the use of force against himself or herself, unless:

(a) Such force is so great that the person reasonably believes that he or she is in imminent danger of death or great bodily harm and that he or she has exhausted every reasonable means to escape such danger other than the use of force which is likely to cause death or great bodily harm to the assailant; or

(b) in good faith, the person withdraws from physical contact with the assailant and indicates clearly to the assailant that he or she desires to withdraw and terminate the use of force, but the assailant continues or resumes the use of force.

776.05 Law enforcement officers; use of force in making arrest.

A law enforcement officer, or any person whom the officer has summoned or directed to assist him or her, need not retreat or desist from efforts to make a lawful arrest because of resistance or threatened resistance to the arrest. The officer is justified in the use of any force:

(1) Which he or she reasonably believes to be necessary to defend himself or herself or another from bodily harm while making the arrest;

(2) When necessarily committed in retaking felons who have escaped; or

(3) When necessarily committed in arresting felons fleeing from justice. However, this subsection shall not constitute a defense in any civil action for damages brought for the wrongful use of deadly force unless the use of deadly force was necessary to prevent the arrest from being defeated by such flight and, when feasible, some warning had been given, and:

(a) The officer reasonably believes that the fleeing felon poses a threat of death or serious physical harm to the officer or others; or

(b) The officer reasonably believes that the fleeing felon has committed a crime involving the infliction or threatened infliction of serious physical harm to another person.

776.051 Use of force in resisting or making an arrest; prohibition.

(1) A person is not justified in the use of force to resist an arrest by a law enforcement officer who is known, or reasonably appears, to be a law enforcement officer.

(2) A law enforcement officer, or any person whom the officer has summoned or directed to assist him or her, is not justified in the use of force if the arrest is unlawful and known by him or her to be unlawful.

776.06 Deadly force.

"Deadly force" means force which is likely to cause death or great bodily harm and includes, but is not limited to:

(1) The firing of a firearm in the direction of the person to be arrested, even though no intent exists to kill or inflict great bodily harm; and

(2) The firing of a firearm at a vehicle in which the person to be arrested is riding.

776.07 Use of force to prevent escape.

(1) A law enforcement officer or other person who has an arrested person in his or her custody is justified in the use of any force which he or she reasonably believes to be necessary to prevent the escape of the arrested person from custody.

(2) A correctional officer or other law enforcement officer is justified in the use of force, including deadly force, which he or she reasonably believes to be necessary to prevent the escape from a penal institution of a person whom the officer reasonably believes to be lawfully detained in such institution under sentence for an offense or awaiting trial or commitment for an offense.

776.08 Forcible felony.

"Forcible felony" means treason; murder; manslaughter; sexual battery; carjacking; home-invasion; robbery; burglary; arson; kidnaping; aggravated assault; aggravated battery; aggravated stalking; aircraft piracy; unlawful throwing, placing, or discharging of a destructive device or bomb; and any other felony which involves the use or threat of physical force or violence against any individual.

776.085 Defense to civil action for damages; party convicted of forcible or attempted forcible felony.

(1) It shall be a defense to any action for damages for personal injury or wrongful death, or for injury to property, that such action arose from injury sustained by a participant during the commission or attempted commission of a forcible felony. The defense authorized by this section shall be established by evidence that the participant has been convicted of such forcible felony or attempted forcible felony, or by proof of the commission of such crime or attempted crime by a preponderance of the evidence.

(2) For the purposes of this section., the term 'forcible felony' shall have the same meaning as in s. 776.08.

(3) Any civil action in which the defense recognized by this section is raised shall be stayed by the court on the motion of the civil defendant during the tendency of any criminal action which forms the basis for the defense, unless the court finds that a conviction in the criminal action would not form a valid defense under this section.

(4) In any civil action where a party prevails based on the defense created by this section:

(a) The losing party, if convicted of and incarcerated for the crime or attempted crime, shall, as determined by the court, lose any privileges provided by the correctional facility, including, but not limited to:

1. Canteen purchases;

2. Telephone access;

3. Outdoor exercise;

4. Use of the library; and

5. Visitation.

(b) The court shall award a reasonable attorney's fee to be paid to the prevailing party in equal amounts by the losing party and the losing party's attorney; however, the losing party's attorney is not personally responsible it he or she has acted in good faith, based on the representations of his or her client. If the losing party is incarcerated for the crime or attempted crime and has insufficient assets to cover payment of the costs of the action and the award of fees pursuant to this paragraph, the party shall, as determined by the court, be required to pay by deduction from any payments the prisoner receives while incarcerated.

(c) If the losing party is incarcerated for the crime or attempted crime, the court shall issue a written order containing its findings and ruling pursuant to para graphs (a) and (b) and shall direct that a certified copy be forwarded to the appropriate correctional institution or facility.

CHAPTER 777
PRINCIPAL; ACCESSORY; ATTEMPT; SOLICITATION; CONSPIRACY

777.04 Attempts, solicitation, and conspiracy. <effective Oct. 1, 1998>

(1) A person who attempts to commit an offense prohibited by law and in such attempt does any act toward the commission of such offense, but fails in the perpetration or is intercepted or prevented in the execution thereof, commits the offense of criminal attempt, ranked for purposes of sentencing as provided in subsection (4). Criminal attempt includes the act of an adult who, with intent to commit an offense prohibited by law, allures, seduces, coaxes, or induces a child under the age of 12 to engage in an offense prohibited by law.

(2) A person who solicits another to commit an offense prohibited by law and in the course of such solicitation commands, encourages, hires, or requests another person to engage in specific conduct which would constitute such offense or an attempt to commit such offense commits the offense of criminal solicitation, ranked for purposes of sentencing as provided in subsection (4).

(3) A person who agrees, conspires, combines, or confederates with another person or persons to commit any offense commits the offense of criminal conspiracy, ranked for purposes of sentencing as provided in subsection (4).

(4)(a) Except as otherwise provided in ss. 828.125(2), 849.25(4), 893.135(5), and 921.0022, the offense of criminal attempt, criminal solicitation, or criminal conspiracy is ranked for purposes of sentencing under chapter 921 and determining incentive gain-time eligibility under chapter 944 one level below the ranking under s. 921.0022 or s. 921.0023 of the offense attempted, solicited, or conspired to. If the criminal attempt, criminal solicitation, or criminal conspiracy is of an offense ranked in level 1 or level 2 under s. 921.0022 or s. 921.0023, such offense is a misdemeanor of the first degree, punishable as provided in s. 775.082 or s. 775.083.

(b) If the offense attempted, solicited, or conspired to is a capital felony, the offense of criminal attempt, criminal solicitation, or criminal conspiracy is a felony of the first degree, punishable as provided in s. 775.082, s. 775.083, or s. 775.084.

(c) Except as otherwise provided in s. 893.135(5), if the offense attempted, solicited, or conspired to is a life felony or a felony of the first degree, the offense of criminal attempt, criminal solicitation, or criminal conspiracy is a felony of the second degree, punishable as provided in s. 775.082, s. 775.083, or s. 775.084.

(d) Except as otherwise provided in s. 828.125(2) or s. 849.25(4), if the offense attempted, solicited, or conspired to is a:
1. Felony of the second degree;
2. Burglary that is a felony of the third degree; or
3. Felony of the third degree ranked in level 3, 4, 5, 6, 7, 8, 9, or 10 under s. 921.0022 or s. 921.0023, the offense of criminal attempt, criminal solicitation, or criminal conspiracy is a felony of the third degree, punishable as provided in s. 775.082, s. 775.083, or s. 775.084.

(e) Except as otherwise provided in s. 849.25(4) or paragraph (d), if the offense attempted, solicited, or conspired to is a felony of the third degree, the offense of criminal attempt, criminal solicitation, or criminal conspiracy is a misdemeanor of the first degree, punishable as provided in s. 775.082 or s. 775.083.

(f) If the offense attempted, solicited, or conspired to is a misdemeanor of the first or second degree, the offense of criminal attempt, criminal solicitation, or criminal conspiracy is a misdemeanor of the second degree, punishable as provided in s. 775.082 or s. 775.083.

(5) It is a defense to a charge of criminal attempt, criminal solicitation, or criminal conspiracy that, under circumstances manifesting a complete and voluntary renunciation of his or her criminal purpose, the defendant:

(a) Abandoned his or her attempt to commit the offense or otherwise prevented its commission;
(b) After soliciting another person to commit an offense, persuaded such other person not to do so or otherwise prevented commission of the offense; or
(c) After conspiring with one or more persons to commit an offense, persuaded such persons not to do so or otherwise prevented commission of the offense.

CHAPTER 782
HOMICIDE

782.02 Justifiable use of deadly force.

The use of deadly force is justifiable when a person is resisting any attempt to murder such person or to commit any felony upon him or her or upon or in any dwelling house in which such person shall be.

782.03 Excusable homicide.

Homicide is excusable when committed by accident and misfortune in doing any lawful act by lawful means with usual ordinary caution, and without any unlawful intent, or by accident and misfortune in the heat of passion, upon any sudden and sufficient provocation, or upon a sudden combat, without any dangerous weapon being used and not done in a cruel or unusual manner.

782.04 Murder.

(1)(a) The unlawful killing of a human being:
1. When perpetuated from a premeditated design to effect the death of the person killed or any human being; or
2. When committed by a person engaged in the perpetration of, or in the attempt to perpetrate any:
a. Trafficking offense prohibited by s. 893.135(1),
b. Arson,
c. Sexual battery,
d. Robbery,
e. Burglary,
f. Kidnaping,
g. Escape,
h. Aggravated child abuse,
i. Aggravated abuse of an elderly person or disabled adult,
j. Aircraft piracy,
k. Unlawful throwing, placing, or discharging of a destructive device or bomb,
l. Carjacking,
m. Home-invasion robbery,
n. Aggravated stalking, or
is murder in the first degree and constitutes a capital felony, punishable as provided in s. 775.082.

782.07 Manslaughter.

(1) The killing of a human being by the act, procurement, or culpable negligence of another, without lawful justification according to the provisions of chapter 776 and in cases in which such killing shall not be excusable homicide or murder, according to the provisions of this chapter, is manslaughter and shall constitute a felony of the second degree, punishable as provided in s. 775.082, s. 775.083, or s. 775.084.

782.08 Assisting self-murder.

Every person deliberately assisting another in the commission of self-murder shall be guilty of manslaughter, a felony of the second degree, punishable as provided in s. 775.082, s. 775.083, or s. 775.084.

782.11 Unnecessary killing to prevent unlawful act

Whoever shall unnecessarily kill another, either while resisting an attempt by such other person to commit any felony, or to do any other unlawful act, or after such attempt shall have failed, shall be deemed guilty of manslaughter, a felony of the second degree, punishable as provided in s. 775.082, s. 775.083, or s. 775.084.

CHAPTER 784
ASSAULT; BATTERY; CULPABLE NEGLIGENCE

784.011 Assault

(1) An "assault" is an intentional, unlawful threat by word or act to do violence to the person of another, coupled with an apparent ability to do so, and doing some act which creates a well-founded fear in such other person that such violence is imminent.

(2) Whoever commits an assault shall be guilty of a misdemeanor of the second degree, punishable as provided in s. 775.082 or s. 775.083.

784.021 Aggravated assault.

(1) An "aggravated assault" is an assault:
(a) With a deadly weapon without intent to kill; or
(b) With an intent to commit a felony.
(2) Whoever commits an aggravated assault shall be guilty of a felony of the third degree, punishable as provided in s. 775.082, s. 775.083, or s. 775.084.

784.03 Battery.

(1)(a) The offense of battery occurs when a person:
1. Actually and intentionally touches or strikes another person against the will of the other; or
2. Intentionally causes bodily harm to another person.

784.045 Aggravated battery.

(1)(a) A person commits aggravated battery who, in committing battery:
1. Intentionally or knowingly causes great bodily harm, permanent disability, or permanent disfigurement; or
2. Uses a deadly weapon.
(b) a person commits aggravated battery if the person who was the victim of the battery was pregnant at the time of the offense and the offender knew or should have known that the victim was pregnant.
(2) Whoever commits aggravated battery shall be guilty of a felony of the second degree, punishable as provided in s. 775.082, s. 775.083, or s. 775.084.

784.047 Penalties for violating protective injunction against repeat violators.

A person who willfully violates an injunction for protection against repeat violence, issued pursuant to s. 784.046, or a foreign protection order accorded full faith and credit pursuant to s. 741.315 by:
1) Refusing to vacate the dwelling that the parties share;
2) Going to the petitioner's residence, school, place of employment, or a specified place frequented regularly by the petitioner and any named family or household member;
3) Committing an act of repeat violence against the petitioner;
4) Committing any other violation of the injunction through an intentional unlawful threat, word, or act to do violence to the petitioner; or
5) Telephoning, contacting, or otherwise communicating with the petitioner directly or indirectly, unless the injunction specifically allows indirect contact through a third party;
commits a misdemeanor of the first degree, punishable as provided in s. 775.082 or s. 775.083.

784.05 Culpable negligence.

(1) Whoever, through culpable negligence, exposes another person to personal injury commits a misdemeanor of the second degree, punishable as provided in s. 775.082 or s. 775.083.

(3) Whoever violates subsection (1) by storing or leaving a loaded firearm within the reach or easy access of a minor commits, if the minor obtains the firearm and uses it to inflict injury or death upon himself or herself or any other person, a felony of the third degree, punishable as provided in s. 775.082, s. 775.083, or s. 775.084. However, this subsection does not apply:

(a) If the firearm was stored or left in a securely locked box or container or in a location which a reasonable person would have believed to be secure, or was securely locked with a trigger lock;

(b) If the minor obtains the firearm as a result of an unlawful entry by any person;

(c) To injuries resulting from target or sport shooting accidents or hunting accidents; or

(d) To members of the Armed Forces, National Guard, or State Militia, or to police or other law enforcement officers, with respect to firearm possession by a minor which occurs during or incidental to the performance of their official duties.

When any minor child is accidentally shot by another family member, no arrest shall be made pursuant to this subsection prior to 7 days after the date of the shooting. With respect to any parent or guardian of any deceased minor, the investigating officers shall file all findings and evidence with the state attorney's office with respect to violations of this subsection. The state attorney shall evaluate such evidence and shall take such action as he or she deems appropriate under the circumstances and may file an information against the appropriate parties.

(4) As used in this act, the term "minor" means any person under the age of 16.

784.07 Assault or battery of law enforcement officers, firefighters, emergency medical care providers, public transit employees or agents, or other specified officers; reclassification of offenses; minimum sentences.

(1) As used in this section, the term:

(a) "Law enforcement officer" includes a law enforcement officer, a correctional officer, a correctional probation officer, a part-time law enforcement officer, a part-time correctional officer, an auxiliary law enforcement officer, and an auxiliary correctional officer, as those terms are respectively defined in s. 943.10, and any county probation officer; employee or agent of the Department of Corrections who supervises or provides services to inmates; officer of the Parole Commission; and law enforcement personnel of the Game and Fresh Water Fish Commission, the Department of Environmental Protection, or the Department of Law Enforcement.

(b) "Firefighter" means any person employed by any public employer of this state whose duty it is to extinguish fires; to protect life or property; or to enforce municipal, county, and state fire prevention codes, as well as any law pertaining to the prevention and control of fires.

(c) "Emergency medical care provider" means an ambulance driver, emergency medical technician, paramedic, registered nurse, physician as defined in s. 401.23, medical director as defined in s. 401.23, or any person authorized by an emergency medical service licensed under chapter 401.

(d) "Public transit employees or agents" means bus operators, train operators, revenue collectors, security personnel, equipment maintenance personnel, or field supervisors, who are employees or agents of a transit agency as described in s. 812.015(1)(l).

(2) Whenever any person is charged with knowingly committing an assault or battery upon a law enforcement officer, a fire fighter, an emergency medical care provider, a traffic accident investigation officer as described in s. 316.640, a traffic infraction enforcement officer as described in s. 318.141, or a parking enforcement specialist as defined in s. 316.640, or a security officer employed by the board of trustees of a community college, while the officer, firefighter, emergency medical care provider, intake officer, traffic accident investigation officer, traffic infraction enforcement officer, parking enforcement specialist, public transit employee or agent, or security officer is engaged in the lawful performance of his or her duties, the offense for which the person is charged shall be reclassified as follows:

(a) In the case of assault, from a misdemeanor of the second degree to a misdemeanor of the first degree.

(b) In the case of battery, from a misdemeanor of the first degree to a felony of the third degree.

(c) In the case of aggravated assault, from a felony of the third degree to a felony of the second degree.

(d) In the case of aggravated battery, from a felony of the second degree to a felony of the first degree.
(3) Any person who is convicted of a battery under paragraph (2)(b) and, during the commission of the offense, such person possessed:
(a) A "firearm" or "destructive device" as those terms are defined in s. 791.001, shall be sentenced to a minimum term of imprisonment of 3 years.
(b) A semi-automatic firearm and its high-capacity detachable box magazine, as defined in s. 755.087(3), or a machine gun as defined in s. 790.001, shall be sentenced to a minimum term of imprisonment of 8 years.

Notwithstanding the provisions of s. 948.01, adjudication of guilt or imposition of sentence shall not be suspended, deferred, or withheld and the defendant is not eligible for statutory gain-time under s. 944.275 or any form of discretionary early release, other than pardon or executive clemency, or conditional medical release under s. 947.149, prior to serving the minimum sentence.

CHAPTER 787
KIDNAPING; FALSE IMPRISONMENT; LURING OR ENTICING A CHILD; CUSTODY OFFENSES

787.01 Kidnapping; kidnapping of child under age 13, aggravating circumstances.

(1)(a) The term "kidnaping" means forcibly, secretly, or by threat confining, abducting, or imprisoning another person against her or his will and without lawful authority, with intent to:
1. Hold for ransom or reward or as a shield or hostage.
2. Commit or facilitate commission of any felony.
3. Inflict bodily harm upon or to terrorize the victim or another person.
4. Interfere with the performance of any governmental or political function.
(b) Confinement of a child under the age of 13 is against her or his will within the meaning of this subsection if such confinement is without the consent of her or his parent or legal guardian.
(2) A person who kidnaps a person is guilty of a felony of the first degree, punishable by imprisonment for a term of years not exceeding life or as provided in s. 775.082, or s. 775.083, or s. 775.084.

CHAPTER 790
WEAPONS AND FIREARMS

790.001 Definitions

As used in this chapter, except where the context otherwise requires:

(1) "Antique firearm" means any firearm manufactured in or before 1918 (including any matchlock, flintlock, percussion cap, or similar early type of ignition system) or replica thereof, whether actually manufactured before or after the year 1918, and also any firearm using fixed ammunition manufactured in or before 1918, for which ammunition is no longer manufactured in the United States and is not readily available in the ordinary channels of commercial trade.

(2) "Concealed firearm" means any firearm, as defined in subsection (6), which is carried on or about a person in such a manner as to conceal the firearm from the ordinary sight of another person.

(3)(a) "Concealed weapon" means any dirk, metallic knuckles, slungshot, billie, tear gas gun, chemical weapon or device, or other deadly weapon carried on or about a person in such a manner as to conceal the weapon from the ordinary sight of another person.

(b) "Tear gas gun" or "chemical weapon or device" means any weapon of such nature, except a device known as a "self-defense chemical spray." "Self-defense chemical spray" means a device carried solely for purposes of lawful self-defense that is compact in size, designed to be carried on or about the person, and contains not more than two ounces of chemical.

(4) "Destructive device" means any bomb, grenade, mine, rocket, missile, pipebomb, or similar device containing an explosive, incendiary, or poison gas and includes any frangible container filled with an explosive, incendiary, explosive gas, or expanding gas, which is designed or so constructed as to explode by such filler and is capable of causing bodily harm or property damage; any combination of parts either designed or intended for use in converting any device into a destructive device and from which a destructive device may be readily assembled; any device declared a destructive device by the Bureau of Alcohol, Tobacco, and Firearms; any type of weapon which will, is designed to, or may readily be converted to expel a projectile by the action of any explosive and which has a barrel with a bore of one-half inch or more in diameter; and ammunition for such destructive devices, but not including shotgun shells or any other ammunition designed for use in a firearm other than a destructible device. "Destructive device" does not include:

(a) A device which is not designed, redesigned, used, or intended for use as a weapon'

(b) Any device, although originally designed as a weapon, which is redesigned so that it may be used solely as a signaling, line-throwing, safety, or similar device;

(c) Any shotgun other than a short-barreled shotgun; or

(d) Any nonautomatic rifle (other than a short-barreled rifle) generally recognized or particularly suitable for use for the hunting of big game.

(5) "Explosive" means any chemical compound or mixture that has the property of yielding readily to combustion or oxidation upon application of heat, flame, or shock, including but not limited to dynamite, nitroglycerin, trinitrotoluene, or ammonium nitrate when combined with other ingredients to form an explosive mixture, blasting caps, and detonators; but not including:

(a) Shotgun shells, cartridges, or ammunition for firearms;

(b) Fireworks as defined in s. 791.01;

(c) Smokeless propellant powder or small arms ammunition primers, if possessed, purchased, sold, transported, or used in compliance with s. 552.241;

(d) Black powder in quantities not to exceed that authorized by chapter 552, or by any rules or regulations promulgated thereunder by the Department of Insurance, when used for, or intended to be used for, the manufacture of target and sporting ammunition or for use in muzzle-loading flint or percussion weapons.

The exclusions contained in paragraphs (a)-(d) do not apply to the term "explosive" as used in the definition of "firearm" in subsection (6).

(6) "Firearm" means any weapon (including a starter gun) which will, is designed to, or may readily be converted to expel a projectile by the action of an explosive; the frame or receiver of any such weapon; any firearm muffler or firearm silencer; any destructive device; or any machine gun. The term "firearm" does not include an antique firearm unless the antique firearm is used in the commission of a crime.

(7) "Indictment" means an indictment or an information in any court under which a crime punishable by imprisonment for a term exceeding 1 year may be prosecuted.

(8) "Law enforcement officer" means:
(a) All officers or employees of the United States or the State of Florida or any agency, commission, department, board, division, municipality, or subdivision thereof, who have authority to make arrests;
(b) Officers or employees of the United States or the State of Florida, or any agency, commission, department, board, division, municipality, or subdivision thereof, duly authorized to carry a concealed weapon;
(c) Members of the Armed Forces of the United States, the organized reserves, state militia, or Florida National Guard, when on duty, when preparing themselves for, or going to or from, military duty, or under orders;
(d) An employee of the state prisons or correctional systems who has been so designated by the Department of Corrections or by a superintendent of an institution;
(e) All peace officers;
(f) All state attorneys and United States attorneys and their respective assistants and investigators.
(9) "Machine gun" means any firearm, as defined herein, which shoots, or is designed to shoot, automatically more than one shot, without manually reloading, by a single function of the trigger.
(10) "Short-barreled shotgun" means a shotgun having one or more barrels less than 18 inches in length and any weapon made from a shotgun (whether by alteration, modification, or otherwise) if such weapon as modified has an overall length of less than 26 inches.
(11) "Short-barreled rifle" means a rifle having one or more barrels less than 16 inches in length and any weapon made from a rifle (whether by alteration, modification, or otherwise) if such weapon as modified has an overall length of less than 26 inches.
(12) "Slungshot" means a small mass of metal, stone, sand, or similar material fixed on a flexible handle, strap, or the like, used as a weapon.
(13) "Weapon" means any dirk, metallic knuckles, slungshot, billie, tear gas gun, chemical weapon or device, or other deadly weapon except a firearm or a common pocketknife.
(14) "Electric weapon or device" means any device which, through the application or use of electrical current, is designed, redesigned, used, or intended to be used for offensive or defensive purposes, the destruction of life, or the infliction of injury.
(15) "Remote stun gun" means any nonlethal device with a tethered range not to exceed 16 feet and which shall utilize an identification and tracking system which, upon use, disperses coded material traceable to the purchaser through records kept by the manufacturer on all remote stun guns and all individual cartridges sold which information shall be made available to any law enforcement agency upon request.
(16) "Readily accessible for immediate use" means that a firearm or other weapon is carried on the person or within such close proximity and in such a manner that it can be retrieved and used as easily and quickly as if carried on the person.
(17) "Securely encased" means in a glove compartment, whether or not locked; snapped in a holster; in a gun case, whether or not locked; in a zippered gun case; or in a closed box or container which requires a lid or cover to be opened for access.
(18) "Sterile area" means the area of an airport to which access is controlled by the inspection of persons and property in accordance with federally approved airport security programs.

790.01 Carrying concealed weapons.

(1) Except as provided in subsection (4), a person who carries a concealed weapon or electric weapon or device on or about his or her person commits a misdemeanor of the first degree, punishable as provided in s. 775.082 or s. 775.083.
(2) A person who carries a concealed firearm on or about his or her person commits a felony of the third degree, punishable as provided in s. 775.082, s. 775.083, or s. 775.084.
(3) This section does not apply to a person licensed to carry a concealed weapon or a concealed firearm pursuant to the provisions of s. 790.06.
(4) It is not a violation of this section for a person to carry for purposes of lawful self-defense, in a concealed manner:
(a) A self-defense chemical spray.
(b) A nonlethal stun gun or remote stun gun or other nonlethal electric weapon or device which does not fire a dart or projectile and is designed solely for defensive purposes.
(5) This section does not preclude any prosecution for the use of an electric weapon or device or remote

stun gun or self-defense chemical spray during the commission of any criminal offense under s. 790.07, s. 790.10, s. 790.23, or s. 790.235, or for any other criminal offense.

790.02 Officer to arrest without warrant and upon probable cause.

The carrying of a concealed weapon is declared a breach of peace, and any officer authorized to make arrests under the laws of this state may make arrests without warrant of persons violating the provisions of s. 790.01 when said officer has reasonable grounds or probable cause to believe that the offense of carrying a concealed weapon is being committed.

790.051 Exemption from licensing requirements; law enforcement officers.

Law enforcement officers are exempt from the licensing and penal provisions of this chapter when acting at any time within the scope or course of their official duties or when acting at any time in the line of or performance of duty.

790.052 Carrying concealed firearms; off-duty law enforcement officers.

(1) All persons holding active certifications from the Criminal Justice Standards and Training Commission as law enforcement officers or correctional officers as defined in s. 943.10(1), (2), (6), (7), (8), or (9) shall have the right to carry, on or about their persons, concealed firearms, during off-duty hours, at the discretion of their superior officers, and may perform those law enforcement functions that they normally perform during duty hours, utilizing their weapons in a manner which is reasonably expected of on-duty officers in similar situations. However, nothing in this subsection shall be construed to limit the right of a law enforcement officer, or correctional officer, or correctional probation officer to carry a concealed firearm off duty as a private citizen under the exemption provided in s. 790.06 that allows a law enforcement officer, correctional officer, or correctional probation officer as defined in s. 943.10(1), (2), (6), (7), (8), or (9) to carry a concealed firearm without a concealed weapon or firearm license. The appointing or employing agency or department of an officer carrying a concealed firearm as a private citizen under s. 790.06 shall not be liable for the use of the firearm in such capacity. Nothing herein limits the authority of the appointing or employing agency or department from establishing policies limiting law enforcement officers or correctional officers from carrying concealed firearms during off-duty hours in their capacity as appointees or employees of the agency or department.
(2) The superior officer of any police department or sheriff's office or the Florida Highway Patrol, if he or she elects to direct the officers under his or her supervision to carry concealed firearms while off duty, shall file a statement with the governing body of such department of his or her instructions and requirements relating to the carrying of said firearms.

790.053 Open carrying of weapons.

(1) Except as otherwise provided by law and in subsection (2), it is unlawful for any person to openly carry on or about his or her person any firearm or electric weapon or device.
(2) A person may openly carry, for purposes of lawful self-defense:
(a) A self-defense chemical spray.
(b) A nonlethal stun gun or remote stun gun or other nonlethal electric weapon or device which does not fire a dart or projectile and is designed solely for defensive purposes.
(3) Any person violating this section commits a misdemeanor of the second degree, punishable as provided in s. 775.082 or s. 775.083.

790.054 Prohibited use of self-defense weapon or device against law enforcement officer; penalties.

A person who knowingly and willfully uses a self-defense chemical spray or a nonlethal stun gun or other nonlethal electric weapon or device or remote stun gun against a law enforcement officer engaged in the performance of his or her duties commits a felony of the third degree, punishable as provided in s. 775.082, s. 775.083, or s. 775.084.

790.06 License to carry concealed weapon or firearm.

(1) The Department of State is authorized to issue licenses to carry concealed weapons or concealed firearms to persons qualified as provided in this section. Each such license must bear a color photograph of the licensee. For the purposes of this section, concealed weapons or concealed firearms are defined as a handgun, electronic weapon or device, tear gas gun, knife, or billie, but the term does not include a machine gun as defined in s. 790.001(9). Such licenses shall be valid throughout the state for a period of 5 years from the date of issuance. Any person in compliance with the terms of such license may carry a concealed weapon or concealed firearm notwithstanding the provisions of s. 790.01. The licensee must carry the license, together with valid identification, at all times in which the licensee is in actual possession of a concealed weapon or firearm and must display both the license and proper identification upon demand by a law enforcement officer. Violations of the provisions of this subsection shall constitute a noncriminal violation with a penalty of $25, payable to the clerk of the court.

(2) The Department of State shall issue a license if the applicant:

(a) Is a resident of the United States or is a consular security official of a foreign government that maintains diplomatic relations and treaties of commerce, friendship, and navigation with the United States and is certified as such by the foreign government and by the appropriate embassy in this country;

(b) Is 21 years of age or older;

(c) Does not suffer from a physical infirmity which prevents the safe handling of a weapon or firearm;

(d) Is not ineligible to possess a firearm pursuant to s. 790.23 by virtue of having been convicted of a felony;

(e) Has not been committed for the abuse of a controlled substance or been found guilty of a crime under the provisions of chapter 893 or similar laws of any other state relating to controlled substances within a 3-year period immediately preceding the date on which the application is submitted;

(f) Does not chronically and habitually use alcoholic beverages or other substances to the extent that his or her normal faculties are impaired. It shall be presumed that an applicant chronically and habitually uses alcoholic beverages or other substances to the extent that his or her normal faculties are impaired if the applicant has been committed under chapter 397 or under the provisions of former chapter 396 or has been convicted under s. 790.151 or has been deemed a habitual offender under s. 856.011(3), or has had two or more convictions under s. 316.193 or similar laws of any other state, within the 3-year period immediately preceding the date on which the application is submitted;

(g) Desires a legal means to carry a concealed weapon or firearm for lawful self-defense;

(h) Demonstrates competence with a firearm by any one of the following:

1. Completion of any hunter education or hunter safety course approved by the Game and Fresh Water Fish Commission or a similar agency of another state;

2. Completion of any National Rifle Association firearms safety or training course;

3. Completion of any firearms safety or training course or class available to the general public offered by a law enforcement, junior college, or private or public institution or organization or firearms training school, utilizing instructors certified by the National Rifle Association, Criminal Justice Standards and Training Commission, or the Department of State;

4. Completion of any law enforcement firearms safety or training course or class offered for security guards, investigators, special deputies, or any division or subdivision of law enforcement or security enforcement;

5. Presents evidence of equivalent experience with a firearm through participation in organized shooting competition or military service;

6. Is licensed or has been licensed to carry a firearm in this state or a county or municipality of this state, unless such license has been revoked for cause; or

7. Completion of any firearms training or safety course or class conducted by a state-certified or National Rifle Association certified firearms instructor; any person who conducts a course pursuant to subparagraph 2., subparagraph 3., or subparagraph 7., or who, as an instructor, attests to the completion of such courses, must maintain records certifying that he or she observed the student safely handle and discharge the firearm;

A photocopy of a certificate of completion of any of the courses or classes; or an affidavit from the instructor, school, club, organization, or group that conducted or taught said course or class attesting to the completion of the course or class by the applicant; or a copy of any document which shows completion of the course or class or evidences participation in firearms competition shall constitute evidence of qualification under this paragraph;

(i) Has not been adjudicated an incapacitated person under s. 744.331, or similar laws of any other state, unless 5 years have elapsed since the applicant's restoration to capacity by court order;

(j) Has not been committed to a mental institution under chapter 394, or similar laws of any other state, unless the applicant produces a certificate from a licensed psychiatrist that he or she has not suffered from disability for at least 5 years prior to the date of submission of the application;

(k) Has not had adjudication of guilt withheld or imposition of sentence suspended on any felony or misdemeanor crime of domestic violence unless 3 years have elapsed since probation or any other conditions set by the court have been fulfilled, or the record has been sealed or expunged; and

(l) Has not been issued an injunction that is currently in force and effect and that restrains the applicant from committing acts of domestic violence or acts of repeat violence.

(3) The Department of State shall deny a license if the applicant has been found guilty of, had adjudication of guilt withheld for, or had imposition of sentence suspended for one or more crimes of violence constituting a misdemeanor, unless 3 years have elapsed since probation or any other conditions set by the court have been fulfilled or the record has been sealed or expunged. The Department of State shall revoke a license if the licensee has been found guilty of, had adjudication of guilt withheld for, or had imposition of sentence suspended for one or more crimes of violence within the preceding 3 years. The department shall, upon notification by a law enforcement agency, a court, or the Florida Department of Law Enforcement and subsequent written verification, suspend a license or the processing of an application for a license if the licensee or applicant is arrested or formally charged with a crime that would disqualify such person from having a license under this section, until final disposition of the case. The department shall suspend a license or the processing of an application for a license if the licensee or applicant is issued an injunction that restrains the licensee or applicant from committing acts of domestic violence or acts of repeat violence.

(4) The application shall be completed, under oath, on a form promulgated by the Department of State and shall include:

(a) The name, address, place and date of birth, race, and occupation of the applicant;

(b) A statement that the applicant is in compliance with criteria contained within subsections (2) and (3);

(c) A statement that the applicant has been furnished a copy of this chapter and is knowledgeable of its provisions;

(d) A conspicuous warning that the application is executed under oath and that a false answer to any question, or the submission of any false document by the applicant, subjects the applicant to criminal prosecution under s. 837.06; and

(e) A statement that the applicant desires a concealed weapon or firearms license as a means of lawful self-defense.

(5) The applicant shall submit to the Department of State:

(a) A completed application as described in subsection (4).

(b) A nonrefundable license fee not to exceed $85, if he or she has not previously been issued a statewide license, or a nonrefundable license fee not to exceed $70 for renewal of a statewide license. Costs for processing the set of fingerprints as required in paragraph (c) shall be borne by the applicant. However, an individual holding an active certification from the Criminal Justice Standards and Training Commission as a "law enforcement officer," "correctional officer," or "correctional probation officer" as defined in s. 943.10(1), (2), (3), (6), (7), (8), or (9) is exempt from the licensing requirements of this section. If any individual holding an active certification from the Criminal Justice Standards and Training Commission as a "law enforcement officer," "correctional officer," or "correctional probation officer" as defined in s. 943.10(1), (2), (3), (6), (7), (8), or (9) wishes to receive a concealed weapons or firearms license, such person is exempt from the background investigation and all background investigation fees, but shall pay the current license fees regularly required to be paid by nonexempt applicants. Further, a law enforcement officer, a correctional officer, or a correctional probation officer as defined in s. 943.10(1), (2), or (3) is exempt from the required fees and background investigation for a period of 1 year subsequent to the date of retirement of the said officer as a law enforcement officer, a correctional officer, or a correctional probation officer.

(c) A full set of fingerprints of the applicant administered by a law enforcement agency.

(d) A photocopy of a certificate or an affidavit or document as described in paragraph (2)(h).

(e) A full frontal view photograph of the applicant taken within the preceding 30 days, in which the head including hair, measures 7/8 of an inch wide and 1 1/8 inches high.

(6) (a) The Department of State, upon receipt of the items listed in subsection (5), shall forward the full set of fingerprints of the applicant to the Department of Law Enforcement for state and federal processing, provided the federal service is available, to be processed for any criminal justice information as defined in s. 943.045. The cost of processing such fingerprints shall be payable to the Department of Law Enforcement by the Department of State.

(b) The sheriff's office shall provide fingerprinting service if requested by the applicant and may charge a fee not to exceed $5 for this service.

(c) The Department of State shall, within 90 days after the date of receipt of the items listed in subsection (5):

1. Issue the license; or

2. Deny the application based solely on the ground that the applicant fails to qualify under the criteria listed in subsection (2) or subsection (3). If the Department of State denies the application, it shall notify the applicant in writing, stating the ground for denial and informing the applicant of any right to a hearing pursuant to chapter 120.

3. In the event the department receives criminal history information with no final disposition on a crime which may disqualify the applicant, the time limitation prescribed by this paragraph may be suspended until receipt of the final disposition or proof of restoration of civil and firearm rights.

(d) In the event a legible set of fingerprints, as determined by the Department of State or the Federal Bureau of Investigation, cannot be obtained after two attempts, the Department of State shall determine eligibility based upon the name checks conducted by the Florida Department of Law Enforcement.

(e) A consular security official of a foreign government that maintains diplomatic relations and treaties of commerce, friendship, and navigation with the United States and is certified as such by the foreign government and by the appropriate embassy in this country must be issued a license within 20 days after the date of the receipt of a completed application, certification document, color photograph as specified in paragraph (5)(e), and a nonrefundable license fee of $300. Consular security official licenses shall be valid for 1 year and may be renewed upon completion of the application process as provided in this section.

(7) The Department of State shall maintain an automated listing of license holders and pertinent information, and such information shall be available on-line, upon request, at all times to all law enforcement agencies through the Florida Crime Information Center.

(8) Within 30 days after the changing of a permanent address, or within 30 days after having a license lost or destroyed, the licensee shall notify the Department of State of such change. Failure to notify the Department of State pursuant to the provisions of this subsection shall constitute a noncriminal violation with a penalty of $25.

(9) In the event that a concealed weapon or firearm license is lost or destroyed, the license shall be automatically invalid, and the person to whom the same was issued may, upon payment of $15 to the Department of State, obtain a duplicate, or substitute thereof, upon furnishing a notarized statement to the Department of State that such license has been lost or destroyed.

(10) A license issued under this section shall be suspended or revoked pursuant to chapter 120 if the licensee:

(a) Is found to be ineligible under the criteria set forth in subsection (2);

(b) Develops or sustains a physical infirmity which prevents the safe handling of a weapon or firearm;

(c) Is convicted of a felony which would make the licensee ineligible to possess a firearm pursuant to s. 790.23;

(d) Is found guilty of a crime under the provisions of chapter 893, or similar laws of any other state, relating to controlled substances;

(e) Is committed as a substance abuser under chapter 397, or is deemed a habitual offender under s. 856.011(3), or similar laws of any other state;

(f) Is convicted of a second violation of s. 316.193, or a similar law of another state, within 3 years of a previous conviction of such section, or similar law of another state, even though the first violation may have occurred prior to the date on which the application was submitted;

(g) Is adjudicated an incapacitated person under s. 744.331, or similar laws of any other state; or

(h) Is committed to a mental institution under chapter 394, or similar laws of any other state.

(11) No less than 90 days prior to the expiration date of the license, the Department of State shall mail to each licensee a written notice of the expiration and a renewal form prescribed by the Department of State. The licensee must renew his or her license on or before the expiration date by filing with the Department of State the renewal form containing a notarized affidavit stating that the licensee remains qualified pursuant to the criteria specified in subsections (2) and (3), a color photograph as specified in paragraph (5)(e), and the required renewal fee. Out-of-state residents must also submit a completed fingerprint card and fingerprint processing fee. The license shall be renewed upon receipt of the completed renewal form, color photograph, appropriate payment of fees, and, if applicable, a completed fingerprint card. Additionally, a licensee who fails to file a renewal application on or before its expiration date must renew his or her license by paying a late fee of $15. No license shall be renewed 6 months or more after its expiration date, and such license shall be deemed to be

permanently expired. A person whose license has been permanently expired may reapply for licensure; however, an application for licensure and fees pursuant to subsection (5) must be submitted, and a background investigation shall be conducted pursuant to the provisions of this section. Persons who knowingly file false information pursuant to this subsection shall be subject to criminal prosecution under s. 837.06

(12) No license issued pursuant to this section shall authorize any person to carry a concealed weapon or firearm into any place of nuisance as defined in s. 823.05; any police, sheriff, or highway patrol station; any detention facility, prison, or jail; any courthouse; any courtroom, except that nothing in this section would preclude a judge from carrying a concealed weapon or determining who will carry a concealed weapon in his or her courtroom; any polling place; any meeting of the governing body of a county, public school district, municipality, or special district; any meeting of the Legislature or a committee thereof; any school, college, or professional athletic event not related to firearms; any school administration building; any portion of an establishment licensed to dispense alcoholic beverages for consumption on the premises, which portion of the establishment is primarily devoted to such purpose; any elementary or secondary school facility; any area technical center; any college or university facility unless the licensee is a registered student, employee, or faculty member of such college or university and the weapon is a stun gun or nonlethal electric weapon or device designed solely for defensive purposes and the weapon does not fire a dart or projectile; inside of the passenger terminal and the sterile area of any airport, provided that no person shall be prohibited from carrying any legal firearm into the terminal, which firearm is encased for shipment for purposes of checking such firearm as baggage to be lawfully transported on any aircraft; or any place where the carrying of firearms is prohibited by federal law. Any person who willfully violates any provision of this subsection commits a misdemeanor of the second degree, punishable as provided in s. 775.082 or s. 775.083.

(13)(a) All moneys collected by the department pursuant to this section shall be deposited in the Division of Licensing Trust Fund, and the Legislature shall appropriate from the fund those amounts deemed necessary to administer the provisions of this section. All revenues collected, less those costs determined by the Department of State to be nonrecurring or one-time costs, shall be deferred over the 3-year licensure period. Notwithstanding the provisions of s. 493.6117, all moneys collected pursuant to this section shall not revert to the General Revenue Fund; however, this shall not abrogate the requirement for payment of the service charge imposed pursuant to chapter 215.

(b) For the 1995-1996 fiscal year only, $1 million may be transferred from the Licensing Trust Fund administered by the Department of State to the Operating Trust Fund administered by the Department of Highway Safety and Motor Vehicles. This paragraph is repealed on July 1, 1996.

(14) All funds received by the sheriff pursuant to the provisions of this section shall be deposited into the general revenue fund of the county and shall be budgeted to the sheriff.

(15) The Legislature finds as a matter of public policy and fact that it is necessary to provide statewide uniform standards for issuing licenses to carry concealed weapons and firearms for self-defense and finds it necessary to occupy the field of regulation of the bearing of concealed weapons or firearms for self-defense to ensure that no honest, law-abiding person who qualifies under the provisions of this section is subjectively or arbitrarily denied his or her rights. The Department of State shall implement and administer the provisions of this section. The Legislature does not delegate to the Department of State the authority to regulate or restrict the issuing of licenses provided for in this section, beyond those provisions contained in this section. Subjective or arbitrary actions or rules which encumber the issuing process by placing burdens on the applicant beyond those sworn statements and specified documents detailed in this section or which create restrictions beyond those specified in this section are in conflict with the intent of this section and are prohibited. This section shall be liberally construed to carry out the constitutional right to bear arms for self-defense. This section is supplemental and additional to existing rights to bear arms, and nothing in this section shall impair or diminish such rights.

(16) The Department of State shall maintain statistical information on the number of licenses issued, revoked, suspended, and denied.

(17) As amended by chapter 87-24, Laws of Florida, this section shall be known and may be cited as the "Jack Hagler Self Defense Act."

790.061 Judges and justices; exceptions from licensure provisions.

A county court judge, circuit court judge, district court of appeal judge, justice of the supreme court, federal district court judge, or federal court of appeals judge serving in this state is not required to comply with the provisions of s. 790.06 in order to receive a license to carry a concealed weapon or firearm, except that any such justice or judge must comply with the provisions of s. 790.06(2)(h). The Department of State shall issue a license to carry a concealed weapon or firearm to any such justice or judge upon demonstration of competence of the justice or judge pursuant to s. 790.06(2)(h).

790.065 Sale and delivery of firearms.

(1) A licensed importer, licensed manufacturer, or licensed dealer may not sell or deliver from her or his inventory at her or his licensed premises any firearm to another person, other than a licensed importer, licensed manufacturer, licensed dealer, or licensed collector, until she or he has:

(a) Obtained a completed form from the potential buyer or transferee, which form shall have been promulgated by the Department of Law Enforcement and provided by the licensed importer, licensed manufacturer, or licensed dealer, which shall include the name, date of birth, gender, race, and social security number or other identification number of such potential buyer or transferee and has inspected proper identification including an identification containing a photograph of the potential buyer or transferee.

(b) Collected a fee from the potential buyer for processing the criminal history check of the potential buyer. The fee shall be $8. The Department of Law Enforcement shall, by rule, establish procedures for the fees to be transmitted by the licensee to the Department of Law Enforcement. All such fees shall be deposited into the Department of Law Enforcement Operating Trust Fund, but shall be segregated from all other funds deposited into such trust fund and must be accounted for separately. Such segregated funds must not be used for any purpose other than the operation of the criminal history checks required by this section. The Department of Law Enforcement, each year prior to February 1, shall make a full accounting of all receipts and expenditures of such funds to the President of the Senate, the Speaker of the House of Representatives, the majority and minority leaders of each house of the Legislature, and the chairs of the appropriations committees of each house of the Legislature. In the event that the cumulative amount of funds collected exceeds the cumulative amount of expenditures by more than $2.5 million, excess funds may be used for the purpose of purchasing soft body armor for law enforcement officers.

(c) Requested, by means of a toll-free telephone call, the Department of Law Enforcement to conduct a check of the information as reported and reflected in the Florida Crime Information Center and National Crime Information Center systems as of the date of the request.

(d) Received a unique approval number for that inquiry from the Department of Law Enforcement, and recorded the date and such number on the consent form. However, if the person purchasing, or receiving delivery of, the firearm is a holder of a valid concealed weapons or firearms license pursuant to the provisions of s. 790.06 or holds an active certification from the Criminal Justice Standards and Training Commission as a "law enforcement officer," a "correctional officer," or a "correctional probation officer" as defined in s. 943.10(1), (2), (3), (6), (7), (8), or (9), the provisions of this subsection do not apply.

(2) Upon receipt of a request for a criminal history record check, the Department of Law Enforcement shall, during the licensee's call or by return call, forthwith:

(a) Review criminal history records to determine if the potential buyer or transferee:

1. Has been convicted of a felony and is prohibited from receipt or possession of a firearm pursuant to s. 790.23;

2. Has been convicted of a misdemeanor crime of domestic violence, and therefore is prohibited from purchasing a firearm; or

3. Has had adjudication of guilt withheld or imposition of sentence suspended on any felony or misdemeanor crime of domestic violence unless 3 years have elapsed since probation or any other conditions set by the court have been fulfilled or expunction has occurred.

(b) Inform the licensee making the inquiry either that records demonstrate that the buyer or transferee is so prohibited and provide the licensee a nonapproval number, or provide the licensee with a unique approval number.

(c)1. Review any records available to it to determine whether the potential buyer or transferee has been indicted or has had an information filed against her or him for an offense that is a felony under either state or federal law, or, as mandated by federal law, has had an injunction for protection against domestic violence entered against the potential buyer or transferee under s. 741.30, has had an injunction for protection against repeat violence entered against the potential buyer or transferee under s. 784.046, or has been arrested for a dangerous crime as specified in s. 907.041(4)(a) or for any of the following enumerated offenses:

a. Criminal anarchy under ss. 876.01 and 876.02.

b. Extortion under s. 836.05.

c. Explosives violations under s. 552.22(1) and (2).

d. Controlled substances violations under chapter 893.

e. Resisting an officer with violence under s. 843.01.

f. Weapons and firearms violations under this chapter.

g. Treason under s. 876.32.

h. Assisting self-murder under s. 782.08.

i. Sabotage under s. 876.38.

j. Stalking or aggravated stalking under s. 784.048.

If the review indicates any such indictment, information, or arrest, the department shall provide to the licensee a conditional nonapproval number.

2. Within 24 working hours, the department shall determine the disposition of the indictment, information, or arrest and inform the licensee as to whether the potential buyer is prohibited from receiving or possessing a firearm. For purposes of this paragraph, "working hours" means the hours from 8 a.m. to 5 p.m. Monday through Friday, excluding legal holidays.

3. The office of the clerk of court, at no charge to the department, shall respond to any department request for data on the disposition of the indictment, information, or arrest as soon as possible, but in no event later than 8 working hours.

4. The department shall determine as quickly as possible within the allotted time period whether the potential buyer is prohibited from receiving or possessing a firearm.

5. If the potential buyer is not so prohibited, or if 30 the department cannot determine the disposition information within the allotted time period, the department shall provide the licensee with a conditional approval number.

6. If the buyer is so prohibited, the conditional nonapproval number shall become a nonapproval number.

7. The department shall continue its attempts to obtain the disposition information and may retain a record of all approval numbers granted without sufficient disposition information. If the department later obtains disposition information which indicates:

a. That the potential buyer is not prohibited from owning a firearm, it shall treat the record of the transaction in accordance with this section; or

b. That the potential buyer is prohibited from owning a firearm, it shall immediately revoke the conditional approval number and notify local law enforcement.

8. During the time that disposition of the indictment, information, or arrest is pending and until the department is notified by the potential buyer that there has been a final disposition of the indictment, information, or arrest, the conditional nonapproval number shall remain in effect.

(3) In the event of scheduled computer downtime, electronic failure, or similar emergency beyond the control of the Department of Law Enforcement, the department shall immediately notify the licensee of the reason for, and estimated length of, such delay. After such notification, the department shall forthwith, and in no event later than the end of the next business day of the licensee, either inform the requesting licensee if its records demonstrate that the buyer or transferee is prohibited from receipt or possession of a firearm pursuant to Florida and Federal law or provide the licensee with a unique approval number. Unless notified by the end of said next business day that the buyer or transferee is so prohibited, and without regard to whether she or he has received a unique approval number, the licensee may complete the sale or transfer and shall not be deemed in violation of this section with respect to such sale or transfer.

(4)(a) Any records containing any of the information set forth in subsection (1) pertaining to a buyer or transferee who is not found to be prohibited from receipt or transfer of a firearm by reason of Florida and Federal law which records are created by the Department of Law Enforcement to conduct the criminal history record check shall be confidential and exempt from the provisions of s. 119.07(1) and may not be disclosed by the Department of Law Enforcement or any officer or employee thereof to any person or to another agency. The Department of Law Enforcement shall destroy any such records forthwith after it communicates the approval and nonapproval numbers to the licensee and, in any event, such records shall be destroyed within 48 hours after the day of the response to the licensee's request. This exemption is subject to the Open Government Sunset Review Act in accordance with s. 119.14.

(b) Notwithstanding the provisions of this subsection, the Department of Law Enforcement may maintain records of NCIC transactions to the extent required by the Federal Government, and may maintain a log of dates of requests for criminal history records checks, unique approval and nonapproval numbers, license identification numbers, and transaction numbers corresponding to such dates for a period of not longer than 2 years or as otherwise required by law.

(c) Nothing in this chapter shall be construed to allow the State of Florida to maintain records containing the names of purchasers or transferees who receive unique approval numbers or to maintain records of firearm transactions.

(d) Any officer or employee, or former officer or employee of the Department of Law Enforcement or law enforcement agency who intentionally and maliciously violates the provisions of this subsection commits a felony of the third degree punishable as provided in s. 775.082 or s. 775.083.

(5) The Department of Law Enforcement shall establish a toll-free telephone number which shall be operational 7 days a week with the exception of Christmas Day and New Year's Day, for a period of 12 hours a day beginning at 9 a.m. and ending at 9 p.m., for purposes of responding to inquiries as described in this section from licensed manufacturers, licensed importers, and licensed dealers. The Department of Law Enforcement shall employ and train such personnel as are necessary expeditiously to administer the provisions of this section.

(6) Any person who is denied the right to receive or purchase a firearm as a result of the procedures established by this section may request a criminal history records review and correction in accordance with the rules promulgated by the Department of Law Enforcement.

(7) It shall be unlawful for any licensed dealer, licensed manufacturer, or licensed importer willfully and intentionally to request criminal history record information under false pretenses, or willfully and intentionally to disseminate criminal history record information to any person other than the subject of such information. Any person convicted of a violation of this subsection commits a felony of the third degree punishable as provided in s. 775.082 or s. 775.083.

(8) The Department of Law Enforcement shall promulgate regulations to ensure the identity, confidentiality, and security of all records and data provided pursuant to this section.

(9) This section shall become effective at such time as the Department of Law Enforcement has notified all licensed importers, licensed manufacturers, and licensed dealers in writing that the procedures and toll-free number described in this section are operational. This section shall remain in effect only during such times as the procedures described in subsection (2) remain operational.

(10) A licensed importer, licensed manufacturer, or licensed dealer is not required to comply with the requirements of this section in the event of:

(a) Unavailability of telephone service at the licensed premises due to the failure of the entity which provides telephone service in the state, region, or other geographical area in which the licensee is located to provide telephone service to the premises of the licensee due to the location of said premises; or the interruption of telephone services by reason of hurricane, tornado, flood, natural disaster, or other act of God, war, invasion, insurrection, riot, or other bona fide emergency, or other reason beyond the control of the licensee; or

(b) Failure of the Department of Law Enforcement to comply with the requirements of subsections (2) and (3).

(11) Compliance with the provisions of this chapter shall be a complete defense to any claim or cause of action under the laws of any state for liability for damages arising from the importation or manufacture, or the subsequent sale or transfer to any person who has been convicted in any court of a crime punishable by imprisonment for a term exceeding 1 year, of any firearm which has been shipped or transported in interstate or foreign commerce. The Department of Law Enforcement, its agents and employees shall not be liable for any claim or cause of action under the laws of any state for liability for damages arising from its actions in lawful compliance with this section.

(12)(a) Any potential buyer or transferee who willfully and knowingly provides false information or false or fraudulent identification commits a felony of the third degree punishable as provided in s. 775.082 or s. 775.083.

(b) Any licensed importer, licensed manufacturer, or licensed dealer who violates the provisions of subsection (1) commits a felony of the third degree punishable as provided in s. 775.082 or s. 775.083.

(c) Any employee or agency of a licensed importer, licensed manufacturer, or licensed dealer who violates the provisions of subsection (1) commits a felony of the third degree punishable as provided in s. 775.082 or s. 775.083.

(d) Any person who knowingly acquires a firearm through purchase or transfer intended for the use of a person who is prohibited by state or federal law from possessing or receiving a firearm commits a felony of the third degree, punishable as provided in s. 775.082 or s. 775.083.

(13) This section does not apply to employees of sheriff's offices, municipal police departments, correctional facilities or agencies, or other criminal justice or governmental agencies when the purchases or transfers are made on behalf of an employing agency for official law enforcement purposes.

<Note: "[t]his section expires on the effective date of federal law which provides access to national criminal history information and requires national criminal history checks on potential buyers or transferees on firearms." (State law Section 1, ch. 89-191)>

790.0655 Purchase and delivery of handguns; mandatory waiting period; exceptions; penalties. <enacted pursuant to constitutional amendment, see 790.33>

(1)(a) There shall be a mandatory 3-day waiting period, which shall be 3 days, excluding weekends and legal holidays, between the purchase and the delivery at retail of any handgun. "Purchase" means the transfer of money or other valuable consideration to the retailer. "Handgun" means a firearm capable of being carried and used by one hand, such as a pistol or revolver. "Retailer" means and includes every person engaged in the business of making sales at retail or for distribution, or use, or consumption, or storage to be used or consumed in this state, as defined in s. 212.02(14).

(b) Records of handgun sales must be available for inspection by any law enforcement agency, as defined in s. 934.02, during normal business hours.

(2) The 3-day waiting period shall not apply in the following circumstances:

(a) When a handgun is being purchased by a holder of a concealed weapons permit as defined in s. 790.06.

(b) To a trade-in of another handgun.

(3) It is a felony of the third degree, punishable as provided in s. 775.082, s. 775.083, or s. 775.084:

(a) For any retailer, or any employee or agent of a retailer, to deliver a handgun before the expiration of the 3-day waiting period, subject to the exceptions provided in subsection (2).

(b) For a purchaser to obtain delivery of a handgun by fraud, false pretense, or false representation.

790.07 Persons engaged in criminal offenses, having weapons.

(1) Whoever, while committing or attempting to commit any felony or while under indictment, displays, uses, threatens, or attempts to use any weapon or electric weapon or device or carries a concealed weapon is guilty of a felony of the third degree, punishable as provided in s. 775.082, s. 775.083, or s. 775.084.

(2) Whoever, while committing or attempting to commit any felony, displays, uses, threatens, or attempts to use any firearm or carries a concealed firearm is guilty of a felony of the second degree, punishable as provided in s. 775.082, s. 775.083, and s. 775.084.

(3) The following crimes are excluded from application of this section: Antitrust violations, unfair trade practices, restrains of trade, nonsupport of dependents, bigamy, or other similar offenses.

(4) Whoever, having previously been convicted of a violation of subsection (1) or subsection (2) and, subsequent to such conviction, displays, uses, threatens, or attempts to use any weapon, firearm, or electric weapon or device, carries a concealed weapon, or carries a concealed firearm while committing or attempting to commit any felony or while under indictment is guilty of a felony of the first degree, punishable as provided in s. 775.082, s. 775.083, or s. 775.084. Sentence shall not be suspended or deferred under the provisions of this subsection.

790.08 Taking possession of weapons and arms; reports; disposition; custody.

(1) Every officer making an arrest under the preceding section, or under any other law or municipal ordinance within the state, shall take possession of any weapons, electric weapons or devices, or arms mentioned in the preceding section found upon the person arrested and deliver them to the sheriff of the county, or the chief of police of the municipality wherein the arrest is made, who shall retain the same until after the trial of the person arrested.

(2) If the person arrested as aforesaid is convicted of violating s. 790.07, or of a similar offense under any municipal ordinance, or any other offense involving the use or attempted use of such weapons, electric weapons or devices, or arms, such weapons, electric weapons or devices, or arms shall become forfeited to the state, without any order of forfeiture being necessary, although the making of such an order shall be deemed proper, and such weapons, electric weapons or devices, or arms shall

be forthwith delivered to the sheriff by the chief of police or other person having custody thereof, and the sheriff is hereby made the custodian of such weapons, electric weapons or devices, and arms for the state.

(3) If the person arrested as aforesaid is acquitted of the offenses mentioned in subsection (2), the said weapons, electric weapons or devices, or arms taken from the person as aforesaid shall be returned to him or her; however, if he or she fails to call for or receive the same within 60 days from and after his or her acquittal or the dismissal of the charges against him or her, the same shall be delivered to the sheriff as aforesaid to be held by the sheriff as hereinafter provided. This subsection shall likewise apply to persons and their weapons, electric weapons or devices, or arms who have heretofore be acquitted or the charges against them dismissed.

(4) All such weapons, electric weapons or devices, and arms now in, or hereafter coming into, the hands of any peace officers of this state or any of its political subdivisions, which have been found abandoned or otherwise discarded, or left in their hands and not reclaimed by the owners shall, within 60 days, be delivered by such peace officers to the sheriff of the county aforesaid.

(5) Weapons, electric weapons or devices, and arms coming into the hands of the sheriff pursuant to subsections (3) and (4) aforesaid shall, unless reclaimed by the owner thereof within 6 months from the date the same come into the hands of the said sheriff, become forfeited to the state, and no action or proceeding for their recovery shall thereafter be maintained in this state.

(6) Weapons, electric weapons or devices, and arms coming into the hands of the sheriff as aforesaid shall be listed, kept, and held by him or her as custodian for the state. Any or all such weapons, electric weapons or devices, and arms suitable for use by the sheriff may be so used. All such weapons, electric weapons or devices, and arms not needed by the said sheriff may be loaned to any other department of the state or to any county or municipality having use for such weapons, electric weapons or devices, and arms. The sheriff shall take the receipt of such other department, county, or municipality for such weapons, electric weapons or devices, and arms loaned to them. All weapons, electric weapons or devices, and arms which are not needed or which are useless or unfit for use shall be destroyed or otherwise disposed of by the sheriff as provided in chapter 705 or as provided in the Florida Contraband Forfeiture Act. All sums received from the sale or other disposition of the said weapons, electric weapons or devices, or arms disposed of by the sheriff under chapter 705 as aforesaid shall be paid into the State Treasury for the benefit of the State School Fund and shall become a part thereof. All sums received from the sale or other disposition of any such weapons, electric weapons or devices, or arms disposed of by the sheriff under the Florida Contraband Forfeiture Act shall be disbursed as provided therein.

(7) This section does not apply to any municipality in any county having home rule under the State Constitution.

790.09 Manufacturing or selling slungshot.

Whoever manufactures or causes to be manufactured, or sells or exposes for sale any instrument or weapon of the kind usually known as slungshot, or metallic knuckles, shall be guilty of a misdemeanor of the second degree, punishable as provided in s. 775.082 or s. 775.083.

790.10 Improper exhibition of dangerous weapons or firearms.

If any person having or carrying any dirk, sword, sword cane, firearm, electric weapon or device, or other weapon shall, in the presence of one or more persons, exhibit the same in a rude, careless, angry, or threatening manner, not in necessary self-defense, the person so offending shall be guilty of a misdemeanor of the first degree, punishable as provided in s. 775.082 or s. 775.083.

790.11 Carrying firearms in national forests prohibited.

Except during the hunting season as established by law, no person shall carry, on or about his or her person, or in any vehicle in which such person may be riding, or on any animal which such person may be using, within the limits of a national forest area within the state, any gun or firearm of any description whatever, without first having obtained a permit as hereinafter prescribed except on state roads when securely locked within a vehicle.

790.115 Possessing or discharging weapons or firearms on school property prohibited; penalties; exceptions.

(1) A person who exhibits any sword, sword cane, firearm, electric weapon or device, destructive device, or other weapon, including a razor blade, box cutter, or knife, except as authorized in support of school-sanctioned activities, in the presence of one or more persons in a rude, careless, angry, or threatening manner and not in lawful self-defense, on the grounds or facilities of any school, school bus, or school bus stop, or within 1,000 feet of the real property that comprises a public or private elementary school, middle school, or secondary school, during school hours or during the time of a sanctioned school activity, commits a felony of the third degree, punishable as provided in s. 775.082, s. 775.083, or s. 775.084. This subsection does not apply to the exhibition of a firearm or weapon on private real property within 1,000 feet of a school by the owner of such property or by a person whose presence on such property has been authorized, licensed, or invited by the owner.

(2)(a) A person shall not possess any firearm, electric weapon or device, destructive device, or other weapon, including a razor blade, box cutter, or knife, except as authorized in support of school-sanctioned activities, on the property of any school, school bus, or school bus stop; however, a person may carry a firearm:

1. In a case to a firearms program, class or function which has been approved in advance by the principal or chief administrative officer of the school as a program or class to which firearms could be carried;

2. In a case to a vocational school having a firearms training range; or

3. In a vehicle pursuant to s. 790.25(5); except that school districts may adopt written and published policies that waive the exception in this subparagraph for purposes of student and campus parking privileges.

For the purposes of this section, "school" means any preschool, elementary school, middle school, junior high school, secondary school, vocational school, or postsecondary school, whether public or nonpublic.

(b) A person who willfully and knowingly possesses any electric weapon or device, destructive device, or other weapon, including a razor blade, box cutter, or knife, except as authorized in support of school-sanctioned activities, in violation of this subsection commits a felony of the third degree, punishable as provided in s. 775.082, s. 775.083, or s. 775.084.

(c)1. A person who willfully and knowingly possesses any firearm in violation of this subsection commits a felony of the third degree, punishable as provided in s. 775.082, s. 775.083, or s. 775.084.

2. A person who stores or leaves a loaded firearm within the reach or easy access of a minor who obtains the firearm and commits a violation of subparagraph 1 commits a misdemeanor of the second degree, punishable as provided in s. 775.082 or s. 775.083; except that this does not apply if the firearm was stored or left in a securely locked box or container or in a location which a reasonable person would have believed to be secure, or was securely locked with a firearm-mounted push-button combination lock or a trigger lock; if the minor obtains the firearm as a result of an unlawful entry by any person; or to members of the Armed Forces, National Guard, or State Militia, or to police or other law enforcement officers, with respect to firearm possession by a minor which occurs during or incidental to the performance of their official duties.

(d) A person who discharges any weapon or firearm while in violation of paragraph (a), unless discharged for lawful defense of himself or herself or another or for a lawful purpose, commits a felony of the second degree, punishable as provided in s. 775.082, s. 775.083, or s. 775.084.

(e) The penalties of this subsection shall not apply to persons licensed under s. 790.06. Persons licensed under s.790.06 shall be punished as provided in s. 790.06(12), except that a licenseholder who unlawfully discharges a weapon or firearm on school property as prohibited by this subsection commits a felony of the second degree, punishable as provided in s. 775.082, s. 775.083, or s. 775.084.

(3) This section does not apply to any law enforcement officer as defined in s. 943.10(1), (2), (3), (4), (6), (7), (8), (9), or (14).

790.12 Permit may be granted by county commissioners.

The board of county commissioners of the county, or counties, where such national forest area is located, may grant special permit for the carrying of firearms to be specifically described in such permit, when the granting of such permit shall have been recommended in writing by the officer or employee of the United States Government in charge of such national forest area; and, where such area lies in more than one county, such permit must be granted by the board of county commissioners of each of the several counties involved before the same shall be valid.

790.14 Penalty for violation of ss. 790.11 and 790.12

Any person violating the provisions of ss. 790.11 and 790.12 shall be guilty of a misdemeanor of the second degree, punishable as provided in s. 775.082 or s. 775.083.

790.145 Crimes in pharmacies; possession of weapons; penalties

(1) Unless otherwise provided by law, any person who is in possession of a concealed "firearm," as defined in s. 790.001(6), or a "destructive device," as defined in s. 790.001(4), within the premises of a "pharmacy," as defined in chapter 465, is guilty of a felony of the third degree, punishable as provided in s. 775.082, s. 775.083, or s. 775.084.
(2) The provisions of this section do not apply:
(a) To any law enforcement officer;
(b) To any person employed and authorized by the owner, operator, or manager of a pharmacy to carry a firearm or destructive device on such premises; or
(c) To any person licensed to carry a concealed weapon.

790.15 Discharging firearm in public

(1) Except as provided in subsection (2) or subsection (3), any person who knowingly discharges a firearm in any public place or on the right-of-way of any paved public road, highway, or street or whosoever knowingly discharges any firearm over the right-of-way of any paved public road, highway, or street or over any occupied premises is guilty of a misdemeanor of the first degree, punishable as provided in s. 775.082 or s. 775.083. This section does not apply to a person lawfully defending life or property or performing official duties requiring the discharge of a firearm or to a person discharging a firearm on public roads or properties expressly approved for hunting by the Game and Fresh Water Fish Commission or Division of Forestry.
(2) Any occupant of any vehicle who knowingly and wilfully discharges any firearm from the vehicle within 1,000 feet of any person commits a felony of the second degree, punishable as provided in s. 775.082, or s. 775.083, or s. 775.084.
(3) Any driver or owner of any vehicle, whether or not the owner of the vehicle is occupying the vehicle, who knowingly directs any other person to discharge any firearm from the vehicle commits a felony of the third degree, punishable as provided in s. 775.082, or s. 775.083, or s. 775.084.

790.151 Using firearm while under the influence of alcoholic beverages, chemical substances, or controlled substances; penalties

(1) As used in ss. 790.151-790.157, to "use a firearm" means to discharge a firearm or to have a firearm readily accessible for immediate discharge.
(2) For the purposes of this section, "readily accessible for immediate discharge" means loaded and in a person's hand.
(3) It is unlawful and punishable as provided in subsection (4) for any person who is under the influence of alcoholic beverages, any chemical substance set forth in s. 877.111, or any substance controlled under chapter 893, when affected to the extent that his or her normal faculties are impaired, to use a firearm in this state.
(4) Any person who violates subsection (3) commits a misdemeanor of the second degree, punishable as provided in s. 775.082 or s. 775.083.
(5) This section does not apply to persons exercising lawful self-defense or defense of one's property.

790.153 Test for impairment or intoxication; right to refuse

(1)(a) Any person who uses a firearm within this state shall submit to an approved chemical or physical breath test to determine the alcoholic content of the blood and to a urine test to detect the presence of controlled substances, if there is probable cause to believe that the person was using a firearm while under the influence of alcoholic beverages or controlled substances or that the person is lawfully arrested for any offense allegedly committed while he or she was using a firearm while under the influence of alcoholic beverages or controlled substances. The breath test shall be incidental to a lawful arrest and administered at the request of a law enforcement officer who has probable cause to believe such person was using the firearm within this state while under the influence of alcoholic beverages. The urine test shall be incidental to a lawful arrest and administered at a detention facility, mobile or otherwise, which is equipped to administer such tests at the request of a law enforcement officer who has probable cause to believe such person was using a firearm within this state while under the influence of controlled substances. The urine test shall be administered at a detention facility or any other facility, mobile or otherwise, which is equipped to administer such tests in a reasonable manner that will ensure the accuracy of the specimen and maintain the privacy of the individual involved. The administration of either test shall not preclude the administration of the other test. The refusal to submit to a chemical or physical breath or urine test upon the request of a law enforcement officer as provided in this section shall be admissible into evidence in any criminal proceeding. This section shall not hinder the taking of a mandatory blood test as outlined in s. 790.155.
(b) If the arresting officer does not request a chemical or physical test of the person arrested for any offense allegedly committed while the person was using a firearm while under the influence of alcoholic beverages or controlled substances, such person may request the arresting officer to have a chemical or physical test made of the arrested person's breath for the purpose of determining the alcoholic content of the person's blood or a chemical test of urine or blood for the purpose of determining the presence of controlled substances; and, if so requested, the arresting officer shall have the test performed.
(c) The provisions of s. 316.1932(1)(f), relating to administration of tests for determining the weight of alcohol in the defendant's blood, additional tests at the defendant's expense, availability of test information to the defendant or the defendant's attorney, and liability of medical institutions and persons administering such tests are incorporated into this act.
(2) The results of any test administered pursuant to this section for the purpose of detecting the presence of any controlled substance shall not be admissible as evidence in a criminal prosecution for the possession of a controlled substance.
(3) Notwithstanding any provision of law pertaining to the confidentiality of hospital records or other medical records, information obtained pursuant to this section shall be released to a court, prosecuting attorney, defense attorney, or law enforcement officer in connection with an alleged violation of s. 790.151 upon request for such information.

790.155 Blood test for impairment or intoxication in cases of death or serious bodily injury; right to use reasonable force

(1)(a) Notwithstanding any recognized ability to refuse to submit to the tests provided in s. 790.153, if a law enforcement officer has probable cause to believe that a firearm used by a person under the influence of alcoholic beverages or controlled substances has caused the death or serious bodily injury of a human being, such person shall submit, upon the request of a law enforcement officer, to a test of his or her blood for the purpose of determining the alcoholic content thereof or the presence of controlled substances therein. The law enforcement officer may use reasonable force if necessary to require such person to submit to the administration of the blood test. The blood test shall be performed in a reasonable manner.
(b) The term "serious bodily injury" means a physical condition which creates a substantial risk of death, serious personal disfigurement, or protracted loss or impairment of the function of any bodily member or organ.
(2) The provisions of s. 316.1933(2), relating to blood tests for impairment or intoxication, are incorporated into this act.
(3)(a) Any criminal charge resulting from the incident giving rise to the officer's demand for testing should be tried concurrently with a charge of any violation of s. 790.151. If such charges are tried separately, the fact that such person refused, resisted, obstructed, or opposed testing shall be admissible at the trial of the criminal offense which gave rise to the demand for testing.

(b) The results of any test administered pursuant to this section for the purpose of detecting the presence of any controlled substance shall not be admissible as evidence in a criminal prosecution for the possession of a controlled substance.

(4) Notwithstanding any provision of law pertaining to the confidentiality of hospital records or other medical records, information obtained pursuant to this section shall be released to a court, prosecuting attorney, defense attorney, or law enforcement officer in connection with an alleged violation of s. 790.151 upon request for such information.

790.157 Presumption of impairment; testing methods

(1) It is unlawful and punishable as provided in s. 790.151 for any person who is under the influence of alcoholic beverages or controlled substances, when affected to the extent that his or her normal faculties are impaired, to use a firearm in this state.

(2) Upon the trial of any civil or criminal action or proceeding arising out of acts alleged to have been committed by any person while using a firearm while under the influence of alcoholic beverages or controlled substances, when affected to the extent that his or her normal faculties were impaired or to the extent that the person was deprived of full possession of his or her normal faculties, the results of any test administered in accordance with s. 790.153 or s. 790.155 and this section shall be admissible into evidence when otherwise admissible, and the amount of alcohol in the person's blood at the time alleged, as shown by chemical analysis of the person's blood or chemical or physical analysis of the person's breath, shall give rise to the following presumptions:

(a) If there was at that time 0.05 percent or less by weight of alcohol in the person's blood, it shall be presumed that the person was not under the influence of alcoholic beverages to the extent that his or her normal faculties were impaired.

(b) If there was at that time in excess of 0.05 percent but less than 0.10 percent by weight of alcohol in the person's blood, such fact shall not give rise to any presumption that the person was or was not under the influence of alcoholic beverages to the extent that his or her normal faculties were impaired, but such fact may be considered with other competent evidence in determining whether the person was under the influence of alcoholic beverages to the extent that his or her normal faculties were impaired.

(c) If there was at that time 0.10 percent or more by weight of alcohol in the person's blood, that fact shall be prima facie evidence that the person was under the influence of alcoholic beverages to the extent that his or her normal faculties were impaired.

The percent by weight of alcohol in the blood shall be based upon grams of alcohol per 100 milliliters of blood. The foregoing provisions of this subsection shall not be construed as limiting the introduction of any other competent evidence bearing upon the question of whether the person was under the influence of alcoholic beverages to the extent that his or her normal faculties were impaired.

(3) A chemical analysis of a person's blood to determine its alcoholic content or a chemical or physical analysis of a person's breath, in order to be considered valid under the provisions of this section, must have been performed substantially in accordance with methods approved by the Department of Health and Rehabilitation Services and by an individual possessing a valid permit issued by the department for this purpose. Any insubstantial differences between approved techniques and actual testing procedures in an individual case shall not render the test or test results invalid. The Department of Health and Rehabilitative Services may approve satisfactory techniques or methods, ascertain the qualification and competence of individuals to conduct such analyses, and issue permits which shall be subject to termination or revocation in accordance with rules adopted by the department.

(4) Any person charged with using a firearm while under the influence of alcoholic beverages or controlled substances to the extent that his or her normal faculties were impaired, whether in a municipality or not, shall be entitled to trial by jury according to the Florida Rules of Criminal Procedure.

790.16 Discharging machine guns; penalty

(1) It is unlawful for any person to shoot or discharge any machine gun upon, across, or along any road, street, or highway in the state; upon or across any public park in the state; or in, upon, or across any public place where people are accustomed to assemble in the state. The discharge of such machine gun in, upon, or across such public street; in, upon, or across such public park; or in, upon, or across such public place, whether indoors or outdoors, including all theaters and athletic stadiums, with intent to do bodily harm to any person or with intent to do damage to property not resulting in the death of another person shall be a felony of the first degree, punishable as provided in s. 775.082. A sentence not exceeding life imprisonment is specifically authorized when great bodily harm to another or serious disruption of governmental operations results.

(2) This section shall not apply to the use of such machine guns by any United States or state militia or by any law enforcement office while in the discharge of his or her lawful duty in suppressing riots and disorderly conduct and in preserving and protecting the public peace or in the preservation of public property, or when said use is authorized by law.

790.161 Making, possessing, throwing, projecting, placing, or discharging any destructive device or attempts so to do, felony; penalties

A person who willfully and unlawfully makes, possesses, throws, projects, places, discharges, or attempts to make, possess, throw, project, place, or discharge any destructive device:

(1) Commits a felony of the third degree, punishable as provided in s. 775.082 or s. 775.084.
(2) If the act is perpetrated with the intent to do bodily harm to any person, or with the intent to do property damage, or if the act results in a disruption of governmental operations, commerce, or the private affairs of another person, commits a felony of the second degree, punishable as provided in s. 775.082 or s. 775.084.
(3) If the act results in bodily harm to another person or in property damage, commits a felony of the first degree, punishable as provided in s. 775.082 or s. 775.084.
(4) If the act results in the death of another person, commits a capital felony, punishable as provided in s. 775.082. In the event the death penalty in a capital felony is held to be unconstitutional by the Florida Supreme Court or the United States Supreme Court, the court having jurisdiction over a person previously sentenced to death for a capital felony shall cause such person to be brought before the court, and the court shall sentence such person to life imprisonment if convicted of murder in the first degree or of a capital felony under this subsection, and such person shall be ineligible for parole. No sentence of death shall be reduced as a result of a determination that a method of execution is held to be unconstitutional under the State Constitution or the Constitution of the United States.

790.1612 Authorization for governmental manufacture, possession, and use of destructive devices.

The governing body of any municipality or county and the Division of State Fire Marshal of the Department of Insurance have the power to authorize the manufacture, possession, and use of destructive devices as defined in s. 790.001(4).

790.1615 Unlawful throwing, projecting, placing, or discharging of destructive device or bomb that results in injury to another; penalty.

(1) A person who perpetrates any unlawful throwing, projecting, placing, or discharging of a destructive device or bomb that results in any bodily harm to a firefighter or any other person, regardless of intent or lack of intent to cause such harm, commits a misdemeanor of the first degree, punishable as provided in s. 775.082 or s. 775.083.
(2) A person who perpetrates any unlawful throwing, projecting, placing, or discharging of a destructive device or bomb that results in great bodily harm, permanent disability, or permanent disfigurement to a firefighter or any other person, regardless of intent or lack of intent to cause such harm, commits a felony of the second degree, punishable as provided in s. 775.082, s. 775.083, or s. 775.084.
(3) Upon conviction and adjudication of guilt, a person may be sentenced separately, pursuant to s. 775.021(4), for any violation of this section and for any unlawful throwing, projecting, placing, or discharging of a destructive device or bomb committed during the same criminal episode. A conviction for any unlawful throwing, projecting, placing, or discharging of a destructive device or bomb, however, is not necessary for a conviction under this section.

790.162 Threat to throw, project, place, or discharge any destructive device, felony; penalty.

It is unlawful for any person to threaten to throw, project, place, or discharge any destructive device with intent to do bodily harm to any person or with intent to do damage to any property of any person, and any person convicted thereof commits a felony of the second degree, punishable as provided in s. 775.082, s. 775.083, or s. 775.084.

790.163 False report about planting bomb or explosive; penalty.

It is unlawful for any person to make a false report, with intent to deceive, mislead, or otherwise misinform any person, concerning the placing or planting of any bomb, dynamite, or other deadly explosive; and any person convicted thereof is guilty of a felony of the second degree, punishable as provided in s. 775.082, s. 775.083, or s. 775.084.

790.164 False reports of bombing or arson against state-owned property; penalty; reward.

(1) It is unlawful for any person to make a false report, with intent to deceive, mislead, or otherwise misinform any person, concerning the placing or planning of any bomb, dynamite, or other deadly explosive, or concerning any act of arson or other violence to property owned by the state or any political subdivision. Any person violating the provisions of this subsection is guilty of a felony of the second degree, punishable as provided in s. 775.082, s. 775.083, or s. 775.084.

(2)(a) There shall be a $5,000 reward for the giving of information to any law enforcement agency in the state, which information leads to the arrest and conviction of any person violating the provisions of this section. Any person claiming such reward shall apply to the law enforcement agency developing the case and be paid by the Department of Law Enforcement from the deficiency fund.

(b) There shall be only one reward given for each case, regardless of how many persons are arrested and convicted in connection with the case and regardless of how many persons submit claims for the reward.

(c) The Department of Law Enforcement shall establish procedures to be used by all reward applicants, and the circuit judge in whose jurisdiction the action occurs shall review all such applications and make final determination as to those applicants entitled to receive an award.

790.165 Planting of "hoax bomb" prohibited; penalties.

(1) For the purposes of this section, "hoax bomb" means any device or object that by its design, construction, content, or characteristics appears to be, or to contain, or is represented to be or to contain, a destructive device or explosive as defined in this chapter, but is, in fact, an inoperative facsimile or imitation of such a destructive device or explosive, or contains no destructive device or explosive as was represented.

(2) Any person who manufactures, possesses, sells, or delivers a hoax bomb or mails or sends a hoax bomb to another person commits a felony of the third degree, punishable as provided in s. 775.082, s. 775.083, or s. 775.084.

(3) Any person who, while committing or attempting to commit any felony, possesses, displays, or threatens to use any hoax bomb commits a felony of the second degree, punishable as provided in s. 775.082, s. 775.083, or s. 775.084. Notwithstanding the provisions of s. 948.01, adjudication of guilt or imposition of sentence shall not be suspended, deferred, or withheld. However, the state attorney or defense attorney may move the sentencing court to reduce or suspend the sentence of any person who is convicted of a violation of this section and who provides substantial assistance in the identification, arrest, or conviction of any of his or her accomplices, accessories, coconspirators, or principals.

(4) The provisions of subsection (2) shall not apply to any law enforcement officer, firefighter, person, or corporation licensed pursuant to chapter 493, or member of the armed forces of the United States while engaged in training or other lawful activity within the scope of his or her employment, or to any person properly authorized to test a security system, or to any security personnel, while operating within the scope of their employment, including, but not limited to, security personnel in airports and other controlled access areas, or to any member of a theatrical company or production utilizing a hoax bomb as property during the course of a rehearsal or performance.

790.169 Juvenile offenders; release of names and addresses.

A law enforcement agency may release for publication the name and address of a child who has been convicted of any offense involving the possession or use of a firearm.

790.17 Furnishing weapons to minors under 18 years of age or persons of unsound mind and furnishing firearms to minors under 18 years of age prohibited.

(1) A person who sells, hires, barters, lends, transfers, or gives any minor under 18 years of age any dirk, electronic weapon or device, or other weapon, other than an ordinary pocketknife, without permission of the minor's parent or guardian, or sells, hires, barters, lends, transfers, or gives to any person of unsound mind an electric weapon or device or any dangerous weapon, other than an ordinary pocketknife, commits a misdemeanor of the first degree, punishable as provided in s. 775.082 or s. 775.083.

(2)(a) A person may not knowingly or willfully sell or transfer a firearm to a minor under 18 years of age, except that a person may transfer ownership of a firearm to a minor with permission of the parent or guardian. A person who violates this paragraph commits a felony of the third degree, punishable as provided in s. 775.082, s. 775.083, or s. 775.084.

(b) The parent or guardian must maintain possession of the firearm except pursuant to s. 790.22.

790.173 Legislative findings and intent.

(1) The Legislature finds that a tragically large number of Florida children have been accidentally killed or seriously injured by negligently stored firearms; that placing firearms within the reach or easy access of children is irresponsible, encourages such accidents, and should be prohibited; and that legislative action is necessary to protect the safety of our children.

(2) It is the intent of the Legislature that adult citizens of the state retain their constitutional right to keep and bear firearms for hunting and sporting activities and for defense of self, family, home, and business and as collectibles. Nothing in this act shall be construed to reduce or limit any existing right to purchase and own firearms, or to provide authority to any state or local agency to infringe upon the privacy of any family, home, or business except by lawful warrant.

790.174 Safe storage of firearms required.

(1) A person who stores or leaves, on a premise under his or her control, a loaded firearm, as defined in s. 790.001, and who knows or reasonably should know that a minor is likely to gain access to the firearm without the lawful permission of the minor's parent or the person having charge of the minor, or without the supervision required by law, shall keep the firearm in a securely locked box or container or in a location which a reasonable person would believe to be secure or shall secure it with a trigger lock, except when the person is carrying the firearm on his or her body or within such close proximity thereto that he or she can retrieve and use it as easily and quickly as if he or she carried it on his or her body.

(2) It is a misdemeanor of the second degree, punishable as provided in s. 775.082 or s. 775.083, if a person violates subsection (1) by failing to store or leave a firearm in the required manner and as a result thereof a minor gains access to the firearm, without the lawful permission of the minor's parent or the person having charge of the minor, and possesses or exhibits it, without the supervision required by law:

(a) In a public place; or

(b) In a rude, careless, angry, or threatening manner in violation of s. 790.10.

This subsection does not apply if the minor obtains the firearm as a result of an unlawful entry by any person.

(3) As used in this act, the term "minor" means any person under the age of 16.

790.175 Transfer or sale of firearms; required warnings; penalties.

(1) Upon the retail commercial sale or retail transfer of any firearm, the seller or transferor shall deliver a written warning to the purchaser or transferee, which warning states, in block letters not less than 1/4 inch in height:

"IT IS UNLAWFUL, AND PUNISHABLE BY IMPRISONMENT AND FINE, FOR ANY ADULT TO STORE OR LEAVE A FIREARM IN ANY PLACE WITHIN THE REACH OR EASY ACCESS OF A MINOR UNDER 18 YEARS OF AGE OR TO KNOWINGLY SELL OR OTHERWISE TRANSFER OWNERSHIP OR POSSESSION OF A FIREARM TO A MINOR OR A PERSON OF UNSOUND MIND."

(2) Any retail or wholesale store, shop, or sales outlet which sells firearms must conspicuously post at each purchase counter the following warning in block letters not less than 1 inch in height:

"IT IS UNLAWFUL TO STORE OR LEAVE A FIREARM IN ANY PLACE WITHIN THE REACH OR EASY ACCESS OF A MINOR UNDER 18 YEARS OF AGE OR TO KNOWINGLY SELL OR OTHERWISE TRANSFER OWNERSHIP OR POSSESSION OF A FIREARM TO A MINOR OR A PERSON OF UNSOUND MIND."

(3) Any person or business knowingly violating a requirement to provide warning under this section commits a misdemeanor of the second degree, punishable as provided in s. 775.082 or s. 775.083.

790.18 Sale or transfer of arms to minors by dealers.

It is unlawful for any dealer in arms to sell or transfer to a minor any firearm, pistol, Springfield rifle or other repeating rifle, Bowie knife or dirk knife, brass knuckles, slungshot, or electric weapon or device. A person who violates this section commits a felony of the second degree, punishable as provided in s. 775.082, s. 775.083, or s. 775.084.

790.19 Shooting into or throwing deadly missiles into dwellings, public or private buildings, occupied or not occupied; vessels, aircraft, buses, railroad cars, streetcars, or other vehicles.

Whoever, wantonly or maliciously, shoots at, within, or into, or throws any missile or hurls or projects a stone or other hard substance which would produce death or great bodily harm, at, within, or in any public or private building, occupied or unoccupied, or public or private bus or any train, locomotive, railway car, caboose, cable railway car, street railway car, monorail car, or vehicle of any kind which is being used or occupied by any person, or any boat, vessel, ship, or barge lying in or plying the waters of this state, or aircraft flying through the airspace of this state shall be guilty of a felony of the second degree, punishable as provided in s. 775.082, s. 775.083, or s. 775.084.

790.22 Use of BB guns, air or gas-operated guns, or electric weapons or devices by minor under 16; limitation; possession of firearms by minor under 18 prohibited; penalties.

(1) The use for any purpose whatsoever of BB guns, air or gas-operated guns, or electric weapons or devices, by any minor under the age of 16 years is prohibited unless such use is under the supervision and in the presence of an adult who is acting with the consent of the minor's parent.

(2) Any adult responsible for the welfare of any child under the age of 16 years who knowingly permits such child to use or have in his or her possession any BB gun, air or gas-operated gun, electric weapon or device, or firearm in violation of the provisions of subsection (1) of this section commits a misdemeanor of the second degree, punishable as provided in s. 775.082 or s. 775.083.

(3) A minor under 18 years of age may not possess, a firearm, other than an unloaded firearm at his or her home, unless:

(a) The minor is engaged in a lawful hunting activity and is:

1. At least 16 years of age; or

2. Under 16 years of age and supervised by an adult.

(b) The minor is engaged in a lawful marksmanship competition or practice or other lawful recreational shooting activity and is:

1. At least 16 years of age; or

2. Under 16 years of age and supervised by an adult who is acting with the consent of the minor's parent or guardian.

(c) The firearm is unloaded and is being transported by the minor directly to or from an event authorized in paragraph (a) or paragraph (b).

(4)(a) Any parent or guardian of a minor, or other adult responsible for the welfare of a minor, who knowingly and willfully permits the minor to possess a firearm in violation of subsection (3) commits a felony of the third degree, punishable as provided in s. 775.082, s. 775.083, or s. 775.084.

(b) Any natural parent or adoptive parent, whether custodial or noncustodial, or any legal guardian or legal custodian of a minor, if that minor possesses a firearm in violation of subsection (3) may, if the court finds it appropriate, be required to participate in classes on parenting education which are approved by the Department of Juvenile Justice, upon the first conviction of the minor. Upon any subsequent conviction of the minor, the court may, if the court finds it appropriate, require the parent to attend further parent education classes or render community service hours together with the child.

(c) No later than July 1, 1994, the district juvenile justice boards or county juvenile justice councils or the Department of Juvenile Justice shall establish appropriate community service programs to be available to the alternative sanctions coordinators of the circuit courts in implementing this subsection. The boards or councils or department shall propose the implementation of a community service program in each circuit, and may submit a circuit plan, to be implemented upon approval of the circuit alternative sanctions coordinator.

(d) For the purposes of this section, community service may be provided on public property as well as on private property with the expressed permission of the property owner. Any community service provided on private property is limited to such things as removal of graffiti and restoration of vandalized property.

(5)(a) A minor who violates subsection (3) commits a misdemeanor of the first degree, and, in addition to any other penalty provided by law, shall be required to perform 100 hours of community services, and:

1. If the minor is eligible by reason of age for a driver license or driving privilege, the court shall direct the Department of Highway Safety and Motor Vehicles to revoke or to withhold issuance of the minor's driver license or driving privilege for up to 1 year.

2. If the minor's driver license or driving privilege is under suspension or revocation for any reason, the court shall direct the Department of Highway Safety and Motor Vehicles to extend the period of suspension or revocation by an additional period of up to 1 year.

3. If the minor is ineligible by reason of age for a driver license or driving privilege, the court shall direct the Department of Highway Safety and Motor Vehicles to withhold issuance of the minor's driver license or driving privilege for up to 1 year after the date on which the minor would otherwise have become eligible.

(b) For a second or subsequent offense, the minor shall be required to perform not less than 100 nor more than 250 hours of community service, and:

1. If the minor is eligible by reason of age for a driver license or driving privilege, the court shall direct the Department of Highway Safety and Motor Vehicles to revoke or to withhold issuance of the minor's driver license or driving privilege for up to 2 years.

2. If the minor's driver license or driving privilege is under suspension or revocation for any reason, the court shall direct the Department of Highway Safety and Motor Vehicles to extend the period of suspension or revocation by an additional period of up to 2 years.

3. If the minor is ineligible by reason of age for a driver license or driving privilege, the court shall direct the Department of Highway Safety and Motor Vehicles to withhold issuance of the minor's driver license or driving privilege for up to 2 years after the date on which the minor would otherwise have become eligible.

(6) Any firearm that is possessed or used by a minor in violation of this section shall be promptly seized by a law enforcement officer and disposed of in accordance with s. 790.08(1)-(6).

(7) The provisions of this section are supplemental to all other provisions of law relating to the possession, use, or exhibition of a firearm.

(8) Notwithstanding s. 985.213 or s. 985.215(1), if a minor under 18 years of age is charged with an offense that involves the use or possession of a firearm, as defined in s. 790.001, other than a violation of subsection (3), or is charged for any offense during the commission of which the minor possessed a firearm, the minor shall be detained in secure detention, unless the state attorney authorizes the release of the minor, and shall be given a hearing within 24 hours after being taken into custody. At the hearing, the court may order that the minor continue to be held in secure detention in accordance with the applicable time periods specified in s. 985.215(5), if the court finds that the minor meets the criteria specified in s. 985.215(2), or if the court finds by clear and convincing evidence that the minor is a clear and present danger to himself or herself or the community. The Department of Juvenile Justice shall prepare a form for all minors charged under this subsection that states the period of detention and the relevant demographic information, including, but not limited to, the sex, age, and race of the minor; whether or not the minor was represented by private counsel or a public defender; the current offense; and the minor's complete prior record, including any pending cases. The form shall be provided to the judge to be considered when determining whether the minor should be continued in secure detention under this subsection. An order placing a minor in secure detention because the minor is a clear and present danger to himself or herself or the community must be in writing, must specify the need for detention and the benefits derived by the minor or the community by placing the minor in secure detention, and must include a copy of the form provided by the department. The Department of Juvenile Justice must send the form, including a copy of any order, without client-identifying information, to the Division of Economic and Demographic Research of the Joint Legislative Management Committee.

(9) Notwithstanding s. 985.214, if the minor is found to have committed an offense that involves the use or possession of a firearm, as defined in s. 790.001, other than a violation of subsection (3), or an offense during the commission of which the minor possessed a firearm, and the minor is not committed to a residential commitment program of the Department of Juvenile Justice, in addition to any other punishment provided by law, the court shall order:

(a) For a first offense, that the minor serve a mandatory period of detention of 5 days in a secure detention facility and perform 100 hours of community service.

(b) For a second or subsequent offense, that the minor serve a mandatory period of detention of 10 days in a secure detention facility and perform not less than 100 nor more than 250 hours of community service.

The minor shall receive credit for time served before adjudication.

(10) If a minor is found to have committed an offense under subsection (9), the court shall impose the following penalties in addition to any penalty imposed under paragraph (9)(a) or paragraph (9)(b):

(a) For a first offense:

1. If the minor is eligible by reason of age for a driver license or driving privilege, the court shall direct the Department of Highway Safety and Motor Vehicles to revoke or to withhold issuance of the minor's driver license or driving privilege for up to 1 year.

2. If the minor's driver license or driving privilege is under suspension or revocation for any reason, the court shall direct the Department of Highway Safety and Motor Vehicles to extend the period of suspension or revocation by an additional period for up to 1 year.

3. If the minor is ineligible by reason of age for a driver license or driving privilege, the court shall direct the Department of Highway Safety and Motor Vehicles to withhold issuance of the minor's driver license or driving privilege for up to 1 year after the date on which the minor would otherwise have become eligible.

(b) For a second or subsequent offense:

1. If the minor is eligible by reason of age for a driver license or driving privilege, the court shall direct the Department of Highway Safety and Motor Vehicles to revoke or to withhold issuance of the minor's driver license or driving privilege for up to 2 years.

2. If the minor's driver license or driving privilege is under suspension or revocation for any reason, the court shall direct the Department of Highway Safety and Motor Vehicles to extend the period of suspension or revocation by an additional period for up to 2 years.

3. If the minor is ineligible by reason of age for a driver license or driving privilege, the court shall direct the Department of Highway Safety and Motor Vehicles to withhold issuance of the minor's driver license or driving privilege for up to 2 years after the date on which the minor would otherwise have become eligible.

790.221 Possession of short-barreled rifle, short-barreled shotgun, or machine gun; penalty.

(1) It is unlawful for any person to own or to have in his or her care, custody, possession, or control any short-barreled rifle, short-barreled shotgun, or machine gun which is, or may readily be made, operable; but this section shall not apply to antique firearms.

(2) A person who violates this section commits a felony of the second degree, punishable as provided in s. 775.082, s. 775.083, or s. 775.084.

(3) Firearms in violation hereof which are lawfully owned and possessed under provisions of federal law are excepted.

790.225 Self-propelled knives; unlawful to manufacture, sell, or possess; forfeiture; penalty.

(1) It is unlawful for any person to manufacture, display, sell, own, possess, or use a self-propelled knife which is a device that propels a knifelike blade as a projectile by means of a coil spring, elastic material, or compressed gas. A self-propelled knife is declared to be a dangerous or deadly weapon and a contraband item. It shall be subject to seizure and shall be disposed of as provided in s. 790.08(1) and (6).

(2) This section shall not apply to any device which propels an arrow, a bolt, or a dart by means of any common bow, compound bow, crossbow, or underwater spear gun.

(3) Any person violating the provisions of subsection (1) is guilty of a misdemeanor of the first degree, punishable as provided in s. 775.082 or s. 775.083.

790.23 Felons and delinquents; possession of firearms or electric weapons or devices unlawful.

(1) It is unlawful for any person to own or to have in his or her care, custody, possession, or control any firearm or electric weapon or device, or to carry a concealed weapon, including a tear gas gun or chemical weapon or device, if that person has been:

(a) convicted of a felony or found to have committed a delinquent act that would be a felony if committed by an adult in the courts of this state;

(b) convicted of or found to have committed a crime against the United States which is designated as a felony;

(c) found to have committed a delinquent act in another state, territory, or country that would be a felony if committed by an adult and which was punishable by imprisonment for a term exceeding 1 year; or

(d) found guilty of an offense which is a felony in another state, territory, or country and which was punishable by imprisonment for a term exceeding 1 year.

(2) This section shall not apply to a person convicted of a felony whose civil rights and firearm authority have been restored, or to a person found to have committed a delinquent act that would be a felony if committed by an adult with respect to which the jurisdiction of the court pursuant to chapter 985 has expired.

(3) Any person who violates this section commits a felony of the second degree, punishable as provided in s. 775.082, s. 775.083, or s. 775.084.

790.233 Possession of firearm or ammunition prohibited when person is subject to an injunction against committing acts of domestic violence; penalties.

(1) A person may not have in his or her care, custody, possession, or control any firearm or ammunition if the person has been issued a final injunction that is currently in force and effect, restraining that person from committing acts of domestic violence, and that has been issued under s. 741.30.

(2) A person who violates subsection (1) commits a misdemeanor of the first degree, punishable as provided in s. 775.082 or s. 775.083.

(3) It is the intent of the Legislature that the disabilities regarding possession of firearms and ammunition are consistent with federal law. Accordingly, this section shall not apply to a state or local officer as defined in s. 943.10(14), holding an active certification, who receives or possesses a firearm or ammunition for use in performing official duties on behalf of the officer's employing agency, unless otherwise prohibited by the employing agency.

790.235 Possession of firearm by violent career criminal unlawful; penalty.

(1) Any person who meets the violent career criminal criteria under s. 775.084(1)(c), regardless of whether such person is or has previously been sentenced as a violent career criminal, who owns or has in his or her care, custody, possession, or control any firearm or electric weapon or device, or carries a concealed weapon, including a tear gas gun or chemical weapon or device, commits a felony of the first degree, punishable as provided in s. 775.082, s. 775.083, or s. 775.084. A person convicted of a violation of this section shall be sentenced to a mandatory minimum of 15 years' imprisonment; however, if the person would be sentenced to a longer term of imprisonment under s. 775.084(4)(c), the person must be sentenced under that provision. A person convicted of a violation of this section is not eligible for any form of discretionary early release, other than pardon, executive clemency, or conditional medical release under s. 947.149.

(2) For purposes of this section, the previous felony convictions necessary to meet the violent career criminal criteria under s. 775.084(1)(c) may be convictions for felonies committed as an adult or adjudications of delinquency for felonies committed as a juvenile. In order to be counted as a prior felony for purposes of this section, the felony must have resulted in a conviction sentenced separately, or an adjudication of delinquency entered separately, prior to the current offense, and sentenced or adjudicated separately from any other felony that is to be counted as a prior felony.

(3) This section shall not apply to a person whose civil rights and firearm authority have been restored.

790.24 Report of medical treatment of gunshot wounds; penalty for failure to report.

Any physician, nurse, or employee thereof and any employee of a hospital, sanitarium, clinic, or nursing home knowingly treating any person suffering from a gunshot wound or other wound indicating violence, or receiving a request for such treatment, shall report the same immediately to the sheriff's department of the county in which said treatment is administered or requested therefor received. Any such person willfully failing to report such treatment or request therefor is guilty of a misdemeanor of the first degree, punishable as provided in s. 775.082 or s. 775.083.

790.25 Lawful ownership, possession, and use of firearms and other weapons.

(1) DECLARATION OF POLICY.--The Legislature finds as a matter of public policy and fact that it is necessary to promote firearms safety and to curb and prevent the use of firearms and other weapons in crime and by incompetent persons without prohibiting the lawful use in defense of life, home, and property, and the use by United States or state military organizations, and as otherwise now authorized by law, including the right to use and own firearms for target practice and marksmanship on target practice ranges or other lawful places, and lawful hunting and other lawful purposes.

(2) USES NOT AUTHORIZED.--

(a) This section does not authorize carrying a concealed weapon without a permit, as prohibited by ss. 790.01 and 790.02.

(b) The protections of this section do not apply to the following:

1. A person who has been adjudged mentally incompetent, who is addicted to the use of narcotics or any similar drug, or who is a habitual or chronic alcoholic, or a person using weapons or firearms in violation of ss. 790.07-790.12, 790.14-790.19, 790.22-790.24;

2. Vagrants and other undesirable persons as defined in s. 856.02;

3. A person in or about a place of nuisance as defined in s. 823.05, unless such person is there for law enforcement or some other lawful purpose.

(3) LAWFUL USES.--The provisions of ss. 790.053 and 790.06 do not apply in the following instances, and, despite such sections, it is lawful for the following persons to own, possess, and lawfully use firearms and other weapons, ammunition, and supplies for lawful purposes:

(a) Members of the Militia, National Guard, Florida State Defense Force, Army, Navy, Air Force, Marine Corps, Coast Guard, organized reserves, and other armed forces of the state and of the United States, when on duty, when training or preparing themselves for military duty, or while subject to recall or mobilization;

(b) Citizens of this state subject to duty in the Armed Forces under s. 2, Art. X of the State Constitution, under chapters 250 and 251, and under federal laws, when on duty or when training or preparing themselves for military duty;

(c) Persons carrying out or training for emergency management duties under chapter 252;

(d) Sheriffs, marshals, prison or jail wardens, police officers, Florida highway patrol officers, game wardens, revenue officers, forest officials, special officers appointed under the provisions of chapter 354, and other peace and law enforcement officers and their deputies and assistants and full-time paid peace officers of other states and of the Federal Government who are carrying out official duties while in this state;

(e) Officers or employees of the state or United States duly authorized to carry a concealed weapon;

(f) Guards or messengers of common carriers, express companies, armored car carriers, mail carriers, banks, and other financial institutions, while actually employed in and about the shipment, transportation, or delivery of any money, treasure, bullion, bonds, or other thing of value within this state;

(g) Regularly enrolled members of any organization duly authorized to purchase or receive weapons from the United States or from this state, or regularly enrolled members of clubs organized for target, skeet, or trap shooting, while at or going to or from shooting practice; or regularly enrolled members of clubs organized for modern or antique firearms collecting, while such members are at or going to or from their collectors' gun shows, conventions, or exhibits;

(h) A person engaged in fishing, camping, or lawful hunting or going to or returning from a fishing, camping, or lawful hunting expedition;

(i) A person engaged in the business of manufacturing, repairing, or dealing in firearms, or the agent or representative of any such person while engaged in the lawful course of such business;

(j) A person firing weapons for testing or target practice under safe conditions and in a safe place not prohibited by law or going to or from such place;

(k) A person firing weapons in a safe and secure indoor range for testing and target practice;

(l) A person traveling by private conveyance when the weapon is securely encased or in a public conveyance when the weapon is securely encased and not in the person's manual possession;

(m) A person while carrying a pistol unloaded and in a secure wrapper, concealed or otherwise, from the place of purchase to his or her home or place of business or to a place of repair or back to his or her home or place of business;

(n) A person possessing arms at his or her home or place of business;

(o) Investigators employed by the several public defenders of the state, while actually carrying out official duties, provided such investigators:

1. Are employed full time;

2. Meet the official training standards for firearms established by the Criminal Justice Standards and Training Commission as provided in s. 943.12(5) and the requirements of ss. 493.6108(1)(a) and 943.13(1)-(4); and

3. Are individually designated by an affidavit of consent signed by the employing public defender and filed with the clerk of the circuit court in the county in which the employing public defender resides.

(p) Investigators employed by the capital collateral representative, while actually carrying out the official duties, provided such investigators:

1. Are employed full time;

2. Meet the official training standards for firearms as established by the Criminal Justice Standards and Training Commission as provided in s. 943.12(1) and the requirements of ss. 493.6108(1)(a) and 943.13(1)-(4); and

3. Are individually designated by an affidavit of consent signed by the capital collateral representative and filed with the clerk of the circuit court in the county in which the investigator is headquartered.

(4) CONSTRUCTION.--This act shall be liberally construed to carry out the declaration of policy herein and in favor of the constitutional right to keep and bear arms for lawful purposes. This act is supplemental and additional to existing rights to bear arms now guaranteed by law and decisions of the courts of Florida, and nothing herein shall impair or diminish any of such rights. This act shall supersede any law, ordinance, or regulation in conflict herewith.

(5) POSSESSION IN PRIVATE CONVEYANCE.-- Notwithstanding subsection (2), it is lawful and is not a violation of s. 790.01 for a person 18 years of age or older to possess a concealed firearm or other weapon for self-defense or other lawful purpose within the interior of a private conveyance, without a license, if the firearm or other weapon is securely encased or is otherwise not readily accessible for immediate use. Nothing herein contained prohibits the carrying of a legal firearm other than a handgun anywhere in a private conveyance when such firearm is being carried for a lawful use. Nothing herein contained shall be construed to authorize the carrying of a concealed firearm or other weapon on the person. This subsection shall be liberally construed in favor of the lawful use, ownership, and possession of firearms and other weapons, including lawful self-defense as provided in s. 776.012.

790.256 Public service announcements.

The Department of Health and Rehabilitative Services shall prepare public service announcements for dissemination to parents throughout the state, of the provisions of chapter 93-416, Laws of Florida.

790.27 Alteration or removal of firearm serial number or possession, sale, or delivery of firearm with serial number altered or removed prohibited; penalties.

(1)(a) It is unlawful for any person to knowingly alter or remove the manufacturer's or importer's serial number from a firearm with intent to disguise the true identity thereof.

(b) Any person violating paragraph (a) is guilty of a felony of the third degree, punishable as provided in s. 775.082, s. 775.083, or s. 775.084.

(2)(a) It is unlawful for any person to knowingly sell, deliver, or possess any firearm on which the manufacturer's or importer's serial number has been unlawfully altered or removed.

(b) Any person violating paragraph (a) is guilty of a misdemeanor of the first degree, punishable as provided in s. 775.082 or s. 775.083.

(3) This section shall not apply to antique firearms.

790.28 Purchase of rifles and shotguns in contiguous states.

A resident of this state may purchase a rifle or shotgun in any state contiguous to this state if he or she conforms to applicable laws and regulations of the United States, of the state where the purchase is made, and of this state.

790.29 Paramilitary training; teaching or participation prohibited.

(1) This act shall be known and may be cited as the "State Antiparamilitary Training Act."

(2) As used in this section, the term "civil disorder" means a public disturbance involving acts of violence by an assemblage of three or more persons, which disturbance causes an immediate danger of, or results in, damage or injury to the property or person of any other individual within the United States.

(3)(a) Whoever teaches or demonstrates to any other person the use, application, or making of any firearm, destructive device, or technique capable of causing injury or death to persons, knowing or having reason to know or intending that the same will be unlawfully employed for use in, or in furtherance of, a civil disorder within the United States, is guilty of a felony of the third degree, punishable as provided in s. 775.082, s. 775.083, or s. 775.084.

(b) Whoever assembles with one or more persons for the purpose of training with, practicing with, or being instructed in the use of any firearm, destructive device, or technique capable of causing injury of death to persons, intending to unlawfully employ the same for use in, or in furtherance of, a civil disorder within the United States, is guilty of a felony of the third degree, punishable as provided in s. 775.082, s. 775.083, or s. 775.084.

(4) Nothing contained in this section shall be construed to prohibit any act of a law enforcement officer which is performed in connection with the lawful performance of his or her official duties or to prohibit the training or teaching of the use of weapons to be used for hunting, recreation, competition, self-defense or the protection of one's person or property, or other lawful use.

790.31 Armor-piercing or exploding ammunition or dragon's breath shotgun shells, bolo shells, or flechette shells prohibited.

(1) As used in this section, the term:

(a) "Armor-piercing bullet" means any bullet which has a steel inner core or core of equivalent hardness and a truncated cone and which is designed for use in a handgun as an armor-piercing or metal-piercing bullet.

(b) "Exploding bullet" means any bullet that can be fired from any firearm, if such bullet is designed or altered so as to detonate or forcibly break up through the use of an explosive or deflagrant contained wholly or partially within or attached to such bullet. The term does not include any bullet designed to expand or break up through the mechanical forces of impact alone or any signaling device or pest control device not designed to impact on any target.

(c) "Handgun" means a firearm capable of being carried and used by one hand, such as a pistol or revolver.

(d) "Dragon's breath shotgun shell" means any shotgun shell that contains exothermic pyrophoric misch metal as the projectile and that is designed for the sole purpose of throwing or spewing a flame or fireball to simulate a flamethrower.

(e) "Bolo shell" means any shell that can be fired in a firearm and that expels as projectiles two or more metal balls connected by solid metal wire.

(f) "Flechette shell" means any shell that can be fired in a firearm and that expels two or more pieces of fin-stabilized solid metal wire or two or more solid dart-type projectiles.

(2)(a) Any person who manufactures, sells, offers for sale, or delivers any armor-piercing bullet or exploding bullet, or dragon's breath shotgun shell, bolo shell, or flechette shell is guilty of a felony of the third degree, punishable as provided in s. 775.082, s. 775.083, or s. 775.084.

(b) Any person who possesses an armor-piercing bullet or exploding bullet with knowledge of its armor-piercing or exploding capabilities loaded in a handgun, or who possesses a dragon's breath shotgun shell, bolo shell, or flechette shell with knowledge of its capabilities loaded in a firearm, is guilty of a felony of the third degree, punishable as provided in s. 775.082, s. 775.083, or s. 775.084.

(c) Any person who possesses with intent to use an armor-piercing bullet or exploding bullet or dragon's breath shotgun shell, bole shell, or flechette shell to assist in the commission of a criminal act is guilty of a felony of the second degree, punishable as provided in s. 775.082, s. 775.083, or s. 775.084.

(3) This section does not apply to:

(a) The possession of any item described in subsection (1) by any law enforcement officer, when possessed in connection with the performance of his or her duty as a law enforcement officer, or law enforcement agency.

(b) The manufacture of items described in subsection (1) exclusively for sale or delivery to law enforcement agencies.

(c) The sale or delivery of items described in subsection (1) to law enforcement agencies.

790.33 Field of regulation of firearms and ammunition preempted. <subsection (2)(d) superseded by constitutional amendment passed in 1990, see 790.0655>

(1) PREEMPTION.--Except as expressly provided by general law, the Legislature hereby declares that it is occupying the whole field of regulation of firearms and ammunition, including the purchase, sale, transfer, taxation, manufacture, ownership, possession, and transportation thereof, to the exclusion of all existing and future county, city, town, or municipal ordinances or regulations relating thereto. Any such existing ordinances are hereby declared null and void. This subsection shall not affect zoning ordinances which encompass firearms businesses along with other businesses. Zoning ordinances which are designed for the purpose of restricting or prohibiting the sale, purchase, transfer, or manufacture of firearms or ammunition as a method of regulating firearms or ammunition are in conflict with this subsection and are prohibited.

(2) LIMITED EXCEPTION; COUNTY WAITING-PERIOD ORDINANCES.

a) Any county may have the option to adopt a waiting-period ordinance requiring a waiting period of up to, but not to exceed, 3 working days between the purchase and delivery of a handgun. For purposes of this subsection, "purchase" means payment of deposit, payment in full, or notification of intent to purchase. Adoption of a waiting-period ordinance, by any county, shall require a majority vote of the county commission on votes on waiting-period ordinances. This exception is limited solely to individual counties and is limited to the provisions and restrictions contained in this subsection.

b) Ordinances authorized by this subsection shall apply to all sales of handguns to individuals by a retail establishment except those sales to individuals exempted in this subsection. For purposes of this subsection, "retail establishment" means a gun shop, sporting goods store, pawn shop, hardware store, department store, discount store, bait or tackle shop, or any other store or shop that offers handguns for walk-in retail sale but does not include gun collectors shows or exhibits, or gun shows.

c) Ordinances authorized by this subsection shall not require any reporting or notification to any source outside the retail establishment, but records of handgun sales must be available for inspection, during normal business hours, by any law enforcement agency as defined in s. 934.02.

d) The following shall be exempt from any waiting period:

. Individuals who are licensed to carry concealed firearms under the provisions of s. 790.06 or who are licensed to carry concealed firearms under any other provision of state law and who show a valid license;

. Individuals who already lawfully own another firearm and who show a sales receipt for another firearm; who are known to own another firearm through a prior purchase from the retail establishment; or who have another firearm for trade-in;

. A law enforcement or correctional officer as defined in s. 943.10;

. A law enforcement agency as defined in s. 934.02;

. Sales or transactions between dealers or between distributors or between dealers and distributors who have current federal firearms licenses; or

. Any individual who has been threatened or whose family has been threatened with death or bodily injury, provided the individual may lawfully possess a firearm and provided such threat has been duly reported to local law enforcement.

3) POLICY AND INTENT.

a) It is the intent of this section to provide uniform firearms laws in the state; to declare all ordinances and regulations null and void which have been enacted by any jurisdictions other than state and federal, which regulate firearms, ammunition, or components thereof; to prohibit the enactment of any future ordinances or regulations relating to firearms, ammunition, or components thereof unless specifically authorized by this section or general law; and to require local jurisdictions to enforce state firearms laws.

) As created by chapter 87-23, Laws of Florida, this section shall be known and may be cited as the "Joe Carlucci Uniform Firearms Act."

CHAPTER 794
SEXUAL BATTERY

794.011 Sexual battery.

(1) Definitions:

(a) The term "consent" means intelligent, knowing, and voluntary consent and shall not be construed to include coerced submission.

(h) The term "sexual battery" means oral, anal, or vaginal penetration by, or union with, the sexual organ of another or the anal or vaginal penetration of another by any other object; however, sexual battery does not include an act done for a bona fide medical purpose.

(3) A person who commits sexual battery upon a person 12 years of age or older, without that person's consent, and in the process thereof uses or threatens to use a deadly weapon or uses actual physical force likely to cause serious personal injury is guilty of a life felony, punishable as provided in s. 775.082, or s. 775.083, or s. 775.084.

CHAPTER 806
ARSON AND CRIMINAL MISCHIEF

806.01 Arson

(1) Any person who wilfully and unlawfully, or while in the commission of any felony, by fire or explosion, damages or causes to be damaged:

(a) Any dwelling, whether occupied or not, or its contents;

(b) Any structure, or contents thereof, where persons are normally present, such as: jails, prisons, or detention centers; hospitals, nursing homes, or other health care facilities; department stores, office buildings, business establishments, churches, or educational institutions during normal hours of occupancy; or other similar structures; or

(c) Any other structure that he or she knew or had reasonable grounds to believe was occupied by a human being,

is guilty of arson in the first degree, which constitutes a felony of the first degree, punishable as provided in s. 775.082, or s. 775.083, or s. 775.084.

(2) Any person who wilfully and unlawfully, or while in the commission of any felony, by fire or explosion, damages or causes to be damaged any structure, whether the property of himself or herself or another, under any circumstances not referred to in subsection (1), is guilty of arson in the second degree, which constitutes a felony of the second degree, punishable as provided in s. 775.082, s. 775.083, or s. 775.084.

(3) As used in this chapter, "structure" means any building of any kind, any enclosed area with a roof over it, any real property and appurtenances thereto, any tent or other portable building, and any vehicle, vessel, watercraft, or aircraft.

CHAPTER 810
BURGLARY AND TRESPASS

810.011 Definitions.

As used in this chapter:

(1) "Structure" means a building of any kind, either temporary or permanent, which has a roof over it, together with the curtilage thereof.

(2) "Dwelling" means a building or conveyance of any kind, including any attached porch, whether such building or conveyance is temporary or permanent, mobile or immobile, which has a roof over it and is designed to be occupied by people lodging therein at night, together with the curtilage thereof. However, during the time of a state of emergency declared by executive order or proclamation of the Governor under chapter 252 and within the area covered by such executive order or proclamation and for purposes of ss. 810.02 and 810.08 only, the term includes such portions or remnants thereof as exist at the original site, regardless of absence of a wall or roof.

(3) "Conveyance" means any motor vehicle, ship, vessel, railroad car, trailer, aircraft, or sleeping car; and "to enter a conveyance" includes taking apart any portion of the conveyance.

(5)(a) "Posted land" is that land upon which signs are placed not more than 500 feet apart along, and at each corner of, the boundaries of the land, upon which signs there appears prominently, in letters of not less than 2 inches in height, the words "no trespassing" and in addition thereto the name of the owner, lessee, or occupant of said land. Said signs shall be placed along the boundary line of posted land in a manner and in such position as to be clearly noticeable from outside the boundary line.

(b) It shall not be necessary to give notice by posting on any enclosed land or place not exceeding 5 acres in area on which there is a dwelling house in order to obtain the benefits of ss. 810.09 and 810.12 pertaining to trespass on enclosed lands.

(6) "Cultivated land" is that land which has been cleared of its natural vegetation and is presently planted with a crop, orchard, grove, pasture, or trees or is fallow land as part of a crop rotation.

(7) "Fenced land" is that land which has been enclosed by a fence of substantial construction, whether with rails, logs, post and railing, iron, steel, barbed wire, other wire, or other material, which stands at least 3 feet in height. For the purpose of this chapter, it shall not be necessary to fence any boundary or part of a boundary of any land which is formed by water.

(8) Where lands are posted, cultivated, or fenced as described herein, then said lands, for the purpose of this chapter, shall be considered as enclosed and posted.

810.02 Burglary

(1) "Burglary" means entering or remaining in a dwelling, a structure, or a conveyance with the intent to commit an offense therein, unless the premises are at the time open to the public or the defendant is licensed or invited to enter or remain.

(2) Burglary is a felony of the first degree, punishable by imprisonment for a term of years not exceeding life imprisonment or as provided in s. 775.082, s. 775.083, or s. 775.084, if, in the course of committing the offense, the offender:

(a) Makes an assault or battery upon any persons; or

(b) Is or becomes armed within such dwelling, structure, or conveyance, with explosives or a dangerous weapon.

(3) Burglary is a felony of the second degree, punishable as provided in s. 775.082, s. 775.083, or s. 775.084, if, in the course of committing the offense the offender does not make an assault or battery and is not or does not become armed with a dangerous weapon or explosive, ...

810.08 Trespass in structure or conveyance.

(1) Whoever, without being authorized, licensed, or invited, willfully enters or remains in any structure or conveyance, or, having been authorized, licensed, or invited, is warned by the owner or lessee of the premises, or by a person authorized by the owner or lessee, to depart and refuses to do so, commits the offense of trespass in a structure or conveyance.

(2)(c) If the offender is armed with a firearm or other dangerous weapon, or arms himself or herself with such while in the structure or conveyance, the trespass in a structure or conveyance is a felony of the third degree, punishable as provided in s. 775.082, s. 775.083, or s. 775.084. Any owner or person authorized by the owner may, for prosecution purposes, take into custody and detain, in a reasonable manner, for a reasonable length of time, any person when he or she reasonably believes that a violation of this paragraph has been or is being committed, and he or she reasonably believes that the person to be taken into custody and detained has committed or is committing such violation, In the event a person is taken into custody, a law enforcement officer shall be called as soon as is practicable after the person has been taken into custody. The taking into custody and detention by such person, if done in compliance with the requirements of this paragraph, shall not render such person criminally or civilly liable for false arrest, false imprisonment, or unlawful detention.

810.09 Trespass on property other than structure or conveyance.

(1) (a) A person who, without being authorized, licensed, or invited, willfully enters upon or remains in any property other than a structure or conveyance:

1. as to which notice against entering or remaining is given, either by actual communication to the offender or by posting, fencing, or cultivation as described in s. 810.011; or

2. if the property is the unenclosed curtilage of a dwelling and the offender enters or remains with the intent to commit an offense thereon, other than the offense of trespass, commits the offense of trespass on property other than a structure or conveyance.

(2) (a) Except as provided in this subsection, trespass on property other than structure or conveyance is a misdemeanor of the first degree, punishable as provided in s. 775.082 or s. 775.083.

(b) If the offender defies an order to leave, personally communicated to the offender by the owner of the premises or by an authorized person, or if the offender wilfully opens any door, fence, or gate or does any act that exposes animals, crops, or other property to waste, destruction, or freedom, unlawfully dumps litter on property, or trespasses on property other than a structure or conveyance, the offender commits a misdemeanor of the first degree, punishable as provided in s. 775.082 or s. 775.083.

(c) If the offender is armed with a firearm or other dangerous weapon during the commission of the offense of trespass on property other than a structure or conveyance, he or she is guilty of a felony of the third degree, punishable as provided in s. 775.082, s. 775.083, or s. 775.084. Any owner or person authorized by the owner may, for prosecution purposes, take into custody and detain, in a reasonable manner, for a reasonable length of time, any person when he or she reasonably believes that a violation of this paragraph has been or is being committed, and that the person to be taken into custody and detained has committed or is committing such violation. In the event a person is taken into custody, a law enforcement officer shall be called as soon as is practicable after the person has been taken into custody. The taking into custody and detention in compliance with the requirements of this paragraph, does not result in criminal or civil liability for false arrest, false imprisonment, or unlawful detention.

(d) The offender shall be guilty of a felony of the third degree, punishable as provided in s. 775.082, s. 775.083, or s. 775.084, if the property trespassed is a construction site that is legally posted and identified in substantially the following manner: This area is a designated construction site, and anyone trespassing on this property shall, upon conviction, be guilty of a felony.

(e) The offender commits a felony of the third degree, punishable as provided in s. 775.082, s. 775.083, or s. 775.084, if the property trespassed upon is commercial horticulture property and the property is legally posted and identified in substantially the following manner: "THIS AREA IS DESIGNATED COMMERCIAL PROPERTY FOR HORTICULTURE PRODUCTS, AND ANYONE WHO TRESPASSES ON THIS PROPERTY COMMITS A FELONY."

810.095 Trespass on school property with firearm or other weapon prohibited.

(1) It is a felony of the third degree, punishable as provided in s. 775.082, s. 775.083, or s. 775.084, for a person who is trespassing upon school property to bring onto, or to possess on, such school property, and weapon or firearm.

(2) As used in this section, "school property" means the grounds or facility of any kindergarten, elementary school, middle school, junior high school, secondary school, vocational school, or post-secondary school, whether public or nonpublic.

CHAPTER 812
THEFT, ROBBERY, AND RELATED CRIMES

812.014 Theft

(1) A person commits theft if he or she knowingly obtains or uses, or endeavors to obtain or to use, the property of another with intent to, either temporarily or permanently:
(a) Deprive the other person of a right to the property or a benefit from the property.
(b) Appropriate the property to his or her own use or to the use of any person not entitled to the use of the property.
(2)(c) It is grand theft of the third degree and a felony of the third degree, punishable as provided in s. 775.082, s. 775.083, or s. 775.084, if the property stolen is:
5. A firearm.

812.13 Robbery

(1) "Robbery" means the taking of money or other property which may be the subject of larceny from the person or custody of another, with intent to either permanently or temporarily deprive the person or the owner of the money or other property, when in the course of the taking there is the use of force, violence, assault, or putting in fear.
(2)(a) If in the course of committing the robbery the offender carried a firearm or other deadly weapon, then the robbery is a felony of the first degree, punishable by imprisonment for a term of years not exceeding life imprisonment or as provided in s. 775.082, or s. 775.083, or s. 775.084.
(b) If in the course of committing the robbery the offender carried a weapon, then the robbery is a felony of the first degree, punishable as provided in s. 775.082, or s. 775.083, or s. 775.084.
(c) If in the course of committing the robbery the offender carried no firearm, deadly weapon, or other weapon, then the robbery is a felony of the second degree, punishable as provided in s. 775.082, or s. 775.083, or s. 775.084.

812.133

(1) "Carjacking" means the taking of a motor vehicle which may be the subject of larceny from the person or custody of another, with intent to either permanently or temporarily deprive the person or the owner of the motor vehicle, when in the course of the taking there is the use of force, violence, assault, or putting in fear.
(2) (a) If in the course of committing the carjacking the offender carried a firearm or other deadly weapon, then the carjacking is a felony of the first degree, punishable by imprisonment for a term of years not exceeding life imprisonment or as provided in s. 775.082, s. 775.083, or s. 775.084.
(b) If in the course of committing the carjacking the offender carried no firearm, deadly weapon, or other weapon, then the carjacking is a felony of the first degree, punishable as provided in 775.082, s. 775.083, or s. 775.084.
(3)(a) An act shall be deemed "in the course of committing the carjacking" if it occurs in an attempt to commit carjacking or in flight after the attempt or commission.
(b) An act shall be deemed "in the course of the taking" if it occurs either prior to, contemporaneous with, or subsequent to the taking of the property and if it and the act of taking constitute a continuous series of acts or events.

812.135 Home-invasion robbery.

(1) "Home-invasion robbery" means any robbery that occurs when the offender enters a dwelling with the intent to commit a robbery, and does commit a robbery of the occupants therein.
(2) A person who commits a home-invasion robbery is guilty of a felony of the first degree, punishable as provided in 775.082, s. 775.083, or s. 775.084.

CHAPTER 823
PUBLIC NUISANCES

823.05 Places declared a nuisance

Whoever shall erect, establish, continue, or maintain, own or lease any building, booth, tent or place which tends to annoy the community or injure the health of the community, or become manifestly injurious to the morals or manners of the people as described in s. 823.01, or shall be frequented by the class of persons mentioned in s. 856.02, or any house or place of prostitution, assignation, lewdness or place or building where games of chance are engaged in violation of law or any place where any law of the state is violated, shall be deemed guilty of maintaining a nuisance, and the building, erection, place, tent or booth and the furniture, fixtures and contents are declared a nuisance. All such places or persons shall be abated or enjoined as provided in ss. 60.05 and 60.06.

CHAPTER 828
ANIMALS: CRUELTY; SALES; ANIMAL ENTERPRISE PROTECTION

828.05 Killing an injured or diseased domestic animal.

(1) The purpose of this section is to provide a swift and merciful means whereby domestic animals which are suffering from an incurable or untreatable condition or are imminently near death from injury or disease may be destroyed without unconscionable delay and in a humane and proficient manner.

(2) As used in this section, the term "officer" means

(a) Any law enforcement officer;

(b) Any veterinarian; and

(c) Any officer or agent of any municipal or county animal control unit or of any society or association for the prevention of cruelty to animals, or the designee of such an officer or agent.

(3) Whenever any domestic animal is so injured or diseased as to appear useless and is suffering, and it reasonably appears to an officer that such animal is imminently near death or cannot be cured or rendered fit for service and the officer has made a reasonable and concerted, but unsuccessful, effort to locate the owner, the owner's agent, or a veterinarian, then such officer, acting in good faith and upon reasonable belief, may immediately destroy such animal by shooting the animal or injecting it with a barbiturate drug. If the officer locates the owner or the owner's agent, the officer shall notify him or her of the animal's location and condition. If the officer locates only a veterinarian, the officer shall destroy the animal only upon the advice of the veterinarian. However, this section does not prohibit any owner from destroying his or her own domestic animal in a humane and proficient manner when the conditions described in this section exist.

(4) No officer or veterinarian acting in good faith and with due care pursuant to this section will be liable either criminally or civilly for such act, nor will any civil or criminal liability attach to the employer of the officer or veterinarian.

(5) A court order is not necessary to carry out the provisions of this section.

828.27 Local animal control or cruelty ordinances; penalty.

(1)(b) "Animal control officer: means any person employed or appointed by a county or municipality who is authorized to investigate, on public or private property, civil infractions relating to animal control or cruelty and to issues citations as provided in this section. An animal control officer is not authorized to bear arms or make arrests; however, such officer may carry a device to chemically subdue and tranquilize an animal, provided that such officer has successfully completed a minimum of 16 hours of training in marksmanship, equipment handling, safety and animal care, and can demonstrate proficiency in chemical immobilization of animals in accordance with guidelines prescribed in the Chemical Immobilization Operational Guide of the American Humane Association.

CHAPTER 836
DEFAMATION; LIBEL; THREATENING LETTERS AND SIMILAR OFFENSES

836.05 Threats; extortion.

Whoever, either verbally or by a written or printed communication, maliciously threatens to accuse another of any crime or offense, or by such communication maliciously threatens an injury to the person, property or reputation of another, or maliciously threatens to expose another to disgrace, or to expose any secret affecting another, or to impute any deformity or lack of chastity to another, with intent thereby to extort money or any pecuniary advantage whatsoever, or with intent to compel the person so threatened, or any other person, to do any act or refrain from doing any act against his or her will, shall be guilty of a felony of the second degree, punishable as provided in s. 775.082, s. 775.083, or s. 775.084.

CHAPTER 843
OBSTRUCTING JUSTICE

843.01 Resisting officer with violence to his or her person.

Whoever knowingly and willfully resists, obstructs, or opposes any officer as defined in s. 943.10(1), (2), (3), (6), (7), (8), or (9); member of the Parole Commission or any administrative aide or supervisor employed by the commission; parole and probation supervisor; county probation officer; personnel or representative of the Department of Law Enforcement; or other person legally authorized to execute process in the execution of legal process or in the lawful execution of any legal duty, by offering or doing violence to the person of such officer or legally authorized person, is guilty of a felony of the third degree, punishable as provided in s. 775.082, s. 775.083, or s. 775.084.

843.025 Depriving officer of means of protection or communication

It is unlawful for any person to deprive a law enforcement officer as defined in s. 943.10(1), a correctional officer as defined in s. 943.10(2), or a correctional probation officer as defined in s. 943.10(3) of her or his weapon or radio or to otherwise deprive the officer of the means to defend herself or himself or summon assistance. Any person who violates this section is guilty of a felony of the third degree, punishable as provided in s. 775.082, s. 775.083, or s. 775.084.

843.04 Refusing to assist prison officers in arresting escaped convicts.

(1) All prison officers and correctional officers shall immediately arrest any convict, held under the provisions of law, who may have escaped. Any such officer or guard may call upon the sheriff or other officer of the state, or of any county or municipal corporation, or any citizen, to make search and arrest such convict.

(2) Any officer or citizen refusing to assist shall be guilty of a misdemeanor of the first degree, punishable as provided in s. 775.082 or s. 775.083.

843.06 Neglect or refusal to aid peace officers.

Whoever, being required in the name of the state by any officer of the Florida Highway Patrol, police officer, beverage enforcement agent, or watchman, neglects or refuses to assist him or her in the execution of his or her office in a criminal case, or in the preservation of the peace, or the apprehending or securing of any person for a breach of the peace, or in case of the rescue or escape of a person arrested upon civil process, shall be guilty of a misdemeanor of the second degree, punishable as provided in s. 775.082 or s. 775.083.

843.11 Conveying tools into jail to aid escape; forcible rescue

Whoever conveys into a jail or other like place of confinement, any disguise, instrument, tool, weapon, or other thing adapted or useful to aid a prisoner in making his or her escape, with intent to facilitate the escape of any prisoner there lawfully committed or detained, or, by any means whatever, aids or assists such prisoner in his or her endeavors to escape therefrom, whether such escape is effected or attempted or not; and whoever forcibly rescues any prisoner held in custody upon any conviction or charge of an offense, shall be guilty of a felony of the second degree, punishable as provided in s. 775.082, s. 775.083, or s. 775.084; or if the person whose escape or rescue was effected or intended was charged with an offense not capital nor punishable by imprisonment in the state prison, then a person who assists a prisoner as described in this section shall be guilty of a misdemeanor of the first degree, punishable as provided in s. 775.082 or s. 775.083; or if the prisoner while his or her escape or rescue is being effected or attempted commits any crime with the weapon, tool, or instrument conveyed to him or her, the person conveying the weapon, tool, or instrument to the prisoner shall be subject to whatever fine, imprisonment, or other punishment the law imposes for the crime committed, as an accessory before the fact.

CHAPTER 860
OFFENSES CONCERNING AIRCRAFT, MOTOR VEHICLES, VESSELS, AND RAILROADS

860.121 Crimes against railroad vehicles; penalties.

(1) It shall be unlawful for any person to shoot at, throw any object capable of causing death or great bodily harm at, or place any object capable of causing death or great bodily harm in the path of any railroad train, locomotive, car, caboose, or other railroad vehicle.

(2)(a) Any person who violates subsection (1) with respect to an unoccupied railroad vehicle is guilty of a felony of the third degree, punishable as provided in s. 775.082, s. 775.083, or s. 775.084.

(b) Any person who violates subsection (1) with respect to any unoccupied railroad vehicle or a railroad vehicle connected thereto is guilty of a felony of the section degree, punishable as provided in s. 775.082, s. 775.083, or s. 775.084.

(c) Any person who violates subsection (1), if such violation results in great bodily harm, is guilty of a felony of the first degree, punishable as provided in s. 775.082, s. 775.083, or s. 775.084.

(d) Any person who violates subsection (1), if such violation results in death, is guilty of homicide as defined in chapter 782, punishable as provided in s. 775.082.

860.16 Aircraft piracy

Whoever without lawful authority seizes or exercises control, by force or violence and with wrongful intent, of any aircraft containing a nonconsenting person or persons within this state is guilty of the crime of aircraft piracy, a felony of the first degree, punishable as provided in s. 775.082, or s. 775.083, or s. 775.084.

CHAPTER 870
AFFRAYS; RIOTS; ROUTS; UNLAWFUL ASSEMBLIES

870.043 Declaration of emergency

Whenever the sheriff or designated city official determines that there has been an act of violence or a flagrant and substantial defiance of, or resistance to, a lawful exercise of public authority and that, on account thereof, there is reason to believe that there exists a clear and present danger of a riot or other general public disorder, widespread disobedience of the law, and substantial injury to persons or to property, all of which constitute an imminent threat to public peace or order and to the general welfare of the jurisdiction affected or a part or parts thereof, he or she may declare that a state of emergency exists within that jurisdiction or any part or parts thereof.

870.044 Automatic emergency measures

Whenever the public official declares that a state of emergency exists, pursuant to s. 870.043, the following acts shall be prohibited during the period of said emergency throughout the jurisdiction:
(1) The sale of, or offer to sell, with or without consideration, any ammunition or gun or other firearm of any size or description.
(2) The intentional display, after the emergency is declared, by or in any store or shop of any ammunition or gun or other firearm of any size or description.
(3) The intentional possession in a public place of a firearm by any person, except a duly authorized law enforcement official or person in military service acting in the official performance of her or his duty.

870.05 When killing excused.

If, by reason of the efforts made by any of said officers or by their direction to disperse such assembly, or to seize and secure the persons composing the same, who have refused to disperse, any such person or other person present is killed or wounded, the said officers and all persons acting by their order or under their direction, shall be held guiltless and fully justified in law; and if any of said officers or any person acting under or by their direction is killed or wounded, all persons so assembled and all other persons present who when commanded refused to aid and assist said officer shall be held answerable therefor.

870.06 Unauthorized military organizations

No body of men, other than the regularly organized land and naval militia of this state, the troops of the United States, and the students of regularly chartered educational institutions where military science is a prescribed part of the course of instruction, shall associate themselves together as a military organization for drill or parade in public with firearms, in this state, without special license from the Governor for each occasion, and application for such license must be approved by the mayor and aldermen of the cities and towns where such organizations may propose to parade. Each person unlawfully engaging in the formation of such military organization, or participating in such drill or parade, shall be guilty of a misdemeanor of the second degree, punishable as provided in s. 775.082 or s. 775.083.

CHAPTER 876
CRIMINAL ANARCHY, TREASON, AND OTHER CRIMES AGAINST PUBLIC ORDER

876.01 Criminal anarchy, Communism, and other specified doctrines; advocacy prohibited.

"Criminal anarchy," "criminal Communism," "criminal Naziism," or "criminal Fascism" are doctrines that existing form of constitutional government should be overthrown by force or violence or by any other unlawful means, or by assassination of officials of the Government of the United States or of the several states. The advocacy of such doctrines either by word of mouth or writing or the promotion of such doctrines independently or in collaboration with or under the guidance of officials of a foreign state or an international revolutionary party or group is unlawful.

876.02 Criminal anarchy, Communism, and other specified doctrines; prohibitions.

Any person who:
(1) By word of mouth or writing advocates, advises, or teaches the duty, necessity, or propriety of overthrowing or overturning existing forms of constitutional government by force or violence; of disobeying or sabotaging or hindering the carrying out of the laws, orders, or decrees of duly constituted civil, naval, or military authorities; or by the assassination of officials of the Government of the United States or of the state, or by any unlawful means or under the guidance of, or in collaboration with, officials, agents, or representatives of a foreign state or an international revolutionary party or group; or

(2) Prints, publishes, edits, issues, or knowingly circulates, sells, distributes, or publicly displays any book, paper, document, or written or printed matter in any form, containing or advocating, advising, or teaching the doctrine that constitutional government should be overthrown by force, violence, or any unlawful means; or

(3) Openly, willfully and deliberately urges, advocates, or justifies by word of mouth or writing the assassination or unlawful killing or assaulting of any official of the Government of the United States or of this state because of his or her official character, or any other crime, with intent to teach, spread, or advocate the propriety of the doctrines of criminal anarchy, criminal Communism, criminal Naziism, or criminal Fascism; or

(4) Organizes or helps to organize or becomes a member of any society, group, or assembly of persons formed to teach or advocate such doctrines; or

(5) Becomes a member of, associated with or promotes the interest of any criminal anarchistic, Communistic, Naziistic or Fascistic organization, or helps to organize or becomes a member of or affiliated with any subsidiary organization or associated group of persons who advocates, teaches, or advises the principles of criminal anarchy, criminal Communism, criminal Naziism or criminal Fascism; shall be guilty of a felony of the second degree, punishable as provided in s. 775.082, s. 775.083, or s. 775.084.

876.32 Treason

Treason against the state shall consist only in levying war against the same, or in adhering to the enemies thereof, or giving them aid and comfort. Whoever commits treason against this state shall be guilty of a felony of the first degree, punishable as provided in s. 775.082, or s. 775.083, or s. 775.084.

876.38 Intentional injury to or interference with property.

Whoever intentionally destroys, impairs, or injures, or interferes or tampers with, real or personal property and such act hinders, delays, or interferes with the preparation of the United States, any country with which the United States shall then maintain friendly relations, or any of the states for defense or for war, or with the prosecution of war by the United States, is guilty of a life felony, punishable as provided in s. 775.082.

CHAPTER 895
OFFENSES CONCERNING RACKETEERING AND ILLEGAL DEBTS

895.02 Definitions.

As used in ss. 895.01-895.08, the term:

(1) "Racketeering activity" means to commit, to attempt to commit, to conspire to commit, or to solicit, coerce, or intimidate another person to commit:

(a) Any crime which is chargeable by indictment or information under the following provisions of the Florida Statutes:

19. Chapter 790, relating to weapons and firearms.

CHAPTER 901
ARRESTS

901.1505 Federal law enforcement officers; powers

(1) As used in this section, the term "federal law enforcement officer" means a person who is employed by the Federal Government as a full-time law enforcement officer as defined by the applicable provisions of the United States Code, who is empowered to effect an arrest for violations of the United States Code, who is authorized to carry firearms in the performance of her or his duties, and who has received law enforcement training equivalent to that prescribed in s. 943.13.(2) Every federal law enforcement officer has the following authority:

(d) To possess firearms; and to seize weapons in order to protect herself or himself from attack, prevent the escape of an arrested person, or assure the subsequent lawful custody of the fruits of a crime or the articles used in the commission of a crime, as provided in s. 901.21.

901.151 Stop and Frisk Law.

(1) This section may be known and cited as the "Florida Stop and Frisk Law."

(2) Whenever any law enforcement officer of this state encounters any person under circumstances which reasonably indicate that such person has committed, is committing, or is about to commit a violation of the criminal laws of this state or the criminal ordinances of any municipality or county, the officer may temporarily detain such person for the purpose of ascertaining the identity of the person temporarily detained and the circumstances surrounding the person's presence abroad which led the officer to believe that the person had committed, was committing, or was about to commit a criminal offense.

(3) No person shall be temporarily detained under the provisions of subsection (2) longer than is reasonably necessary to effect the purposes of that subsection. Such temporary detention shall not extend beyond the place where it was first effected or the immediate vicinity thereof.

(4) If at any time after the onset of the temporary detention authorized by subsection (2), probable cause for arrest of person shall appear, the person shall be arrested. If, after an inquiry into the circumstances which prompted the temporary detention, no probable cause for the arrest of the person shall appear, the person shall be released.

(5) Whenever any law enforcement officer authorized to detain temporarily any person under the provisions of subsection (2) has probable cause to believe that any person whom the officer has temporarily detained, or is about to detain temporarily, is armed with a dangerous weapon and therefore offers a threat to the safety of the officer or any other person, the officer may search such person so temporarily detained only to the extent necessary to disclose, and for the purpose of disclosing, the presence of such weapon. If such a search discloses such a weapon or any evidence of a criminal offense it may be seized.

(6) No evidence seized by a law enforcement officer in any search under this section shall be admissible against any person in any court of this state or political subdivision thereof unless the search which disclosed its existence was authorized by and conducted in compliance with the provisions of subsections (2)-(5).

901.18 Officer may summon assistance.

A peace officer making a lawful arrest may command the aid of persons she or he deems necessary to make the arrest. A person commanded to aid shall render assistance as directed by the officer. A person commanded to aid a peace officer shall have the same authority to arrest as that peace officer and shall not be civilly liable for any reasonable conduct in rendering assistance to that officer.

CHAPTER 916
MENTALLY DEFICIENT AND MENTALLY ILL DEFENDANTS

916.106 Definitions

For the purposes of this chapter:

(1) "Chemical weapon" means any shell, cartridge, bomb, gun, or other device capable of emitting chloroacetophenone (CN), chlorobenzalmalononitrile (CS) or any derivatives thereof in any form, or any other agent with lacrimatory properties, and shall include products such as that commonly known as "mace."

916.178 Introduction or removal of certain articles unlawful; penalty.

(1)(a) Except as authorized by law or as specifically authorized by the person in charge of a forensic facility, it is unlawful to introduce into or upon the grounds of any forensic facility under the supervision or control of the department, or to take or attempt to take or send therefrom, any of the following articles, which are hereby declared to be contraband for the purposes of this section:

3. Any firearm or deadly weapon;

(2)(a) All individuals or vehicles entering upon the grounds of any forensic facility under the supervision or control of the department shall be subject to reasonable search and seizure of any contraband materials introduced thereon, for purpose of enforcement of this chapter.

916.19 Duties, functions, and powers of institutional security personnel.

In case of emergency, and when necessary to provide protection and security to any patient, to the personnel, equipment, buildings, or grounds of a department facility, or to citizens in the surrounding community, institutional security personnel may, when authorized by the administrator of the facility or her or his designee when the administrator is not present, use a chemical weapon against a patient housed in a forensic facility. However, such weapon shall be used only to the extent necessary to provide such protection and security. Under no circumstances shall any such officer carry a chemical weapon on her or his person except during the period of the emergency for which its use was authorized. All chemical weapons shall be placed in secure storage when their use is not authorized as provided in this section.

CHAPTER 933
SEARCH AND INSPECTION WARRANTS

933.14 Return of property taken under search warrant.

(3) No pistol or firearm taken by any officer with a search warrant or without a search warrant upon a view by the officer of a breach of the peace shall be returned except pursuant to an order of a circuit judge or a county court judge.

CHAPTER 943
DEPARTMENT OF LAW ENFORCEMENT

943.051 Criminal justice information; collection and storage; fingerprinting.

(3)(b) A minor who is charged with or found to have committed the following misdemeanors shall be fingerprinted and the fingerprints shall be submitted to the department:

3. Carrying a concealed weapon, as defined in s. 790.01(1).

7. Open carrying of a weapon, as defined in s. 790.053.

9. Unlawful possession of a firearm, as defined in s. 790.22(5).

CHAPTER 944
STATE CORRECTIONAL SYSTEM

944.105 Contractual arrangements with private entities for operation and maintenance of correctional facilities and supervision of inmates.

(4) A private correctional officer may use force only while on the grounds of a facility, while transporting inmates, and while pursuing escapees from a facility. A private correctional officer may use nondeadly force in the following situations:

(a) To prevent the commission of a felony or a misdemeanor, including escape.

(b) To defend oneself or others against physical assault.

(c) To prevent serious damage to property.

(d) To enforce institutional regulations and orders.

(e) To prevent or quell a riot.

Private correctional officers may carry and use firearms and may use deadly force only as a last resort, and then only to prevent an act that could result in death or serious bodily injury to oneself or to another person.

(5) Private correctional officers shall be trained in the use of force and the use of firearms and shall be trained at the private firm's expense, at the facilities that train correctional officers employed by the department.

(8) As used in this section, the term:

(a) "Nondeadly force" means force that normally would neither cause death nor serious bodily injury.

(b) "Deadly force" means force which would likely cause death or serious bodily injury.

944.47 Introduction, removal, or possession of certain articles unlawful; penalty.

(1)(a) Except through regular channels as authorized by the officer in charge of the correctional institution, it is unlawful to introduce into or upon the grounds of any state correctional institution, or to take or attempt to take or send or attempt to send therefrom, any of the following articles which are hereby declared to be contraband for the purposes of this section, to wit:

5. Any firearm or weapon of any kind or any explosive substance.

CHAPTER 947
PAROLE COMMISSION

947.146 Control Release Authority

(3) A panel of no fewer than two members of the authority shall establish a control release date for each parole ineligible inmate committed to the department and incarcerated within the state, within 90 days following notification by the department of receipt of the inmate or within 90 days following the completion of proceedings revoking an offender's release and notification by the department of receipt of the inmate, except an inmate who:

(l) Is serving a sentence for an offense committed on or after January 1, 1994, for possession of a firearm, semiautomatic firearm, or machine gun in which additional points are added to the subtotal of the offender's sentence points pursuant to former s. 921.0014 or s. 921.0024;

947.16 Eligibility for parole; initial parole interviews; powers and duties of commission.

(4) A person who has become eligible for an initial parole interview and who may, according to the objective parole guidelines of the commission, be granted parole shall be placed on parole in accordance with the provisions of this law; except that, in any case of a person convicted of murder, robbery, burglary of a dwelling or burglary of a structure or conveyance in which a human being is present, aggravated assault, aggravated battery, kidnapping, sexual battery or attempted sexual battery, incest or attempted incest, an unnatural and lascivious act or an attempted unnatural and lascivious act. lewd and lascivious behavior, assault or aggravated assault when a sexual act is

completed or attempted, battery or aggravated battery when a sexual act is completed or attempted, arson, or any felony involving the use of a firearm or other deadly weapon or the use of intentional violence, at the time of sentencing the judge may enter an order retaining jurisdiction over the offender for review of a commission release order. This jurisdiction of the trial court judge is limited to the first one-third of the maximum sentence imposed. When any person is convicted of two or more felonies and concurrent sentences are imposed, then the jurisdiction of the trial court judge as provided herein applies to the first one-third of the maximum sentence imposed for the highest felony of which the person was convicted. When any person is convicted of two or more felonies and consecutive sentences are imposed, then the jurisdiction of the trial court judge as provided herein applies to one-third of the total consecutive sentences imposed.

CHAPTER 948
PROBATION AND COMMUNITY CONTROL

948.03 Terms and conditions of probation or community control.

(1) The court shall determine the terms and conditions of probation or community control. Conditions specified in paragraphs (a) through and including (m) do not require oral pronouncement at the time of sentencing and may be considered standard conditions of probation. Conditions specified in paragraphs (a) through and including (m) and (2)(a) do not require oral pronouncement at sentencing and may be considered standard conditions of community control. These conditions may include among them the following, that the probationer or offender in community control shall:

(l) Be prohibited from possessing, carrying, or owning any firearm unless authorized by the court and consented to by the probation officer.

948.09 Payment for cost of supervision and rehabilitation.

(1)(a)2. In addition to any other contribution or surcharge imposed by this section, each felony offender assessed under this paragraph shall pay a $2-per-month surcharge to the department. The surcharge shall be deemed to be paid only after the full amount of the contribution required by subparagraph 1. has been collected by the department. These funds shall be used by the department to pay for correctional probation officers' training and equipment, including radios, and firearms training, firearms, and attendant equipment necessary to train and equip officers who choose to carry a concealed firearm while on duty. Nothing in this subparagraph shall be construed to limit the department's authority to determine who shall be authorized to carry a concealed firearm while on duty, or to limit the right of a correctional probation officer to carry a personal firearm approved by the department.

CHAPTER 951
COUNTY AND MUNICIPAL PRISONERS

951.22 County detention facilities; contraband articles

(1) It is unlawful, except through regular channels as duly authorized by the sheriff or officer in charge, to introduce into or possess upon the grounds of any county detention facility as defined in s. 951.23 or to give to or receive from any inmate of any such facility wherever said inmate is located at the time or to take or to attempt to take or send therefrom any of the following articles which are hereby declared to be contraband for the purposes of this act, to with: Any written or recorded communication; any currency or coin; any article of food or clothing; an tobacco products as defined in s. 210.25(11); any cigarette as defined in s. 210.01(1); any cigar; any intoxicating beverage or beverage which causes or may cause an intoxicating effect; any narcotic, hypnotic, or excitative drug or drug of any kind or nature, including nasal inhalators, sleeping pills, barbiturates, and controlled substances as defined in s. 893.02(4); any firearm or any instrumentality customarily used or which is intended to be used as a dangerous weapon; and any instrumentality of any nature that may be or is intended to be used as an aid in effecting or attempting to effect an escape from a county facility.

(2) Whoever violates subsection (1) shall be guilty of a felony of the third degree, punishable as provided in s. 775.082, s. 775.083, or s. 775.084.

CHAPTER 985
DELINQUENCY;
INTERSTATE COMPACT ON JUVENILES

985.08 Information systems. <formerly s. 39.0585>

(1)(c) As used in this section, "a juvenile who is at risk of becoming a serious habitual juvenile offender" means a juvenile who has been adjudicated delinquent and who meets one or more of the following criteria:

1. Is arrested for a capital, life, or first degree felony offense or sexual battery.
2. Has five or more arrests, at least three of which are for felony offenses. Three of such arrests must have occurred within the preceding 12-month period.
3. Has 10 or more arrests, at least 2 of which are for felony offenses. Three of such arrests must have occurred within the preceding 12-month period.
4. Has four or more arrests, at least one of which is for a felony offense and occurred within the preceding 12-month period.
5. Has 10 or more arrests, at least 8 of which are for any of the following offenses:
a. Petit theft;
b. Misdemeanor assault;
c. Possession of a controlled substance;
d. Weapon or firearm violation; or
e. Substance abuse.
Four of such arrests must have occurred within the preceding 12-month period.
6. Meets at least one of the criteria for youth and street gang membership.

985.212 Fingerprinting and photographing. <formerly s. 39.039>

(1)(b) A child who is charged with or found to have committed one of the following misdemeanors shall be fingerprinted and the fingerprints shall be submitted to the Department of Law Enforcement as provided in s. 943.051(3)(b):
1. Assault, as defined in s. 784.011.
2. Battery, as defined in s. 784.03.
3. Carrying a concealed weapon, as defined in s. 790.01(1).
4. Unlawful use of destructive devices or bombs, as defined in s. 790.1615(1).
5. Negligent treatment of children, as defined in former s. 827.05.
6. Assault on a law enforcement officer, a firefighter, or other specified officers, as defined in s. 784.07(2)(a).
7. Open carrying of a weapon, as defined in s. 790.053.
8. Exposure of sexual organs, as defined in s. 800.03.
9. Unlawful possession of a firearm, as defined in s. 790.22(5).
10. Petit theft, as defined in s. 812.014.
11. Cruelty to animals, as defined in s. 828.12(1).
12. Arson, resulting in bodily harm to a firefighter, as defined in s. 806.031(1).

985.213 Use of detention. <formerly s. 39.043>

(2)(a) All determinations and court orders regarding placement of a child into detention care shall comply with all requirements and criteria provided in this part and shall be based on a risk assessment of the child, unless the child is placed into detention care as provided in subparagraph (b)3.
(b)1. The risk assessment instrument for detention care placement determinations and orders shall be developed by the Department of Juvenile Justice in agreement with representatives appointed by the following associations: the Conference of Circuit Judges of Florida, the Prosecuting Attorneys Association, and the Public Defenders Association. Each association shall appoint two individuals, one representing an urban area and one representing a rural area. The parties involved shall evaluate and revise the risk assessment instrument as is considered necessary using the method for revision as agreed by the parties. The risk assessment instrument shall take into consideration, but need not be

limited to, prior history of failure to appear, prior offenses, offenses committed pending adjudication, any unlawful possession of a firearm, theft of a motor vehicle or possession of a stolen motor vehicle, and community control status at the time the child is taken into custody. The risk assessment instrument shall also take into consideration appropriate aggravating and mitigating circumstances, and shall be designed to target a narrower population of children than s. 985.215(2). The risk assessment instrument shall also include any information concerning the child's history of abuse and neglect. The risk assessment shall indicate whether detention care is warranted, and, if detention care is warranted, whether the child should be placed into secure, nonsecure, or home detention care.

2. If, at the detention hearing, the court finds a material error in the scoring of the risk assessment instrument, the court may amend the score to reflect factual accuracy.

3. A child who is charged with committing an offense of domestic violence as defined in s. 741.28(1) and who does not meet detention criteria may be held in secure detention if the court makes specific written findings that:

a. The offense of domestic violence which the child is charged with committing caused physical injury to the victim;

b. Respite care for the child is not available; and

c. It is necessary to place the child in secure detention in order to protect the victim from further injury.

The child may not be held in secure detention under this subparagraph for more than 48 hours unless ordered by the court. After 48 hours, the court shall hold a hearing if the state attorney or victim requests that secure detention be continued. The child may continue to be held in secure detention if the court makes a specific, written finding that secure detention is necessary to protect the victim from further injury. However, the child may not be held in secure detention beyond the time limits set forth in s. 39.044 <now 985.215>.

985.214 Prohibited uses of detention. <formerly s. 39.043>

(1) A child alleged to have committed a delinquent act or violation of law may not be placed into secure, nonsecure, or home detention care for any of the following reasons:

(a) To allow a parent to avoid his or her legal responsibility.

(b) To permit more convenient administrative access to the child.

(c) To facilitate further interrogation or investigation.

(d) Due to a lack of more appropriate facilities.

(2) A child alleged to be dependent under part III of this chapter <the reference is to former part III of chapter 39, redesignated as part II to conform to the repeal and transfer of the provisions of former part II of chapter 39 by ch. 97-238.> may not, under any circumstances, be placed into secure detention care.

985.215 Detention. <formerly s. 39.044>

(2) Subject to the provisions of subsection (1), a child taken into custody and placed into nonsecure or home detention care or detained in secure detention care prior to a detention hearing may continue to be detained by the court if:

(e) The child is charged with a capital felony, a life felony, a felony of the first degree, a felony of the second degree that does not involve a violation of chapter 893, or a felony of the third degree that is also a crime of violence, including any such offense involving the use or possession of a firearm.

(f) The child is charged with any second degree or third degree felony involving a violation of chapter 893 or any third degree felony that is not also a crime of violence, and the child:

5. Is found to have been in possession of a firearm.

985.227 Prosecution of juveniles as adults by the direct filing of an information in the criminal division of the circuit court; discretionary criteria; mandatory criteria.

(1) DISCRETIONARY DIRECT FILE; CRITERIA.

(a) With respect to any child who was 14 or 15 years of age at the time the alleged offense was committed, the state attorney may file an information when in the state attorney's judgment and discretion the public interest requires that adult sanctions be considered or imposed and when the offense charged is:

10. Unlawful throwing, placing, or discharging of a destructive device or bomb;

11. Armed burglary in violation of s. 810.02(2)(b) or specified burglary of a dwelling or structure in violation of s. 810.02(2)(c);

14. Carrying, displaying, using, threatening, or attempting to use a weapon or firearm during the commission of a felony; or

(2) MANDATORY DIRECT FILE.

(a) With respect to any child who was 16 or 17 years of age at the time the alleged offense was committed, the state attorney shall file an information if the child has been previously adjudicated delinquent for murder, sexual battery, armed or strong-armed robbery, carjacking, home-invasion robbery, aggravated battery, or aggravated assault, and is currently charged with a second or subsequent violent crime against a person.

CRC-167
Proposed Constitutional Amendment
To be voted on in November 1998:

Article VII
Local Government
Section 5. Local Option.--

(b) Each county shall have the authority to require a criminal records check and a waiting period of not less than 3 days, nor more than 5 days, excluding weekends and legal holidays, in connection with the sale of any firearm occurring within such county. For purposes of this subsection, the term "sale" means the transfer of money or other valuable consideration for any firearm when any part of the transaction is conducted on property to which the public has the right of access. Holders of a concealed weapons permit as prescribed in Florida law shall not be subject to the provisions of this subsection when purchasing a firearm.

(The above has been proposed by the 1998 legislature
and only becomes law if confirmed by public vote.)

In Nov. 1998, Florida voters will decide whether to adopt CRC-167, a constitutional amendment that grants new law-making authority to each county in the state, instead of leaving it where it is now, at the state legislature. The proposal, if enacted, creates a number of questionable conditions.

Certain felony gun crimes would be forced down to misdemeanors under county control, reducing the penalties. It's hard to see what is gained by having counties institute their own waiting period and background checks, on top of identical activity at the state level.

Uniform application of the laws statewide would end, with no practical mechanism for knowing which county has adopted what policy. Just try to imagine *The Okeechobee Gun Owner's Guide*. The dangerously ambiguous phrase "property to which the public has the right of access" replaces the concise language of "retailer."

The taxing aspect of the proposal is not immediately evident but is a basic element of the plan. National Instant Checks (NICS) go into effect in Florida, under Part 2 of the Brady law, also in Nov.

1998. The FBI's proposed NICS tax will be at a tax rate of $13–$16 for every background check they conduct. This includes all handgun and long gun sales by dealers.

Dealers currently rely on the state's central facility run by FDLE when doing their mandatory background checks. When Brady Part 2 takes effect, FDLE will have an FBI hotline to NICS with no per-inquiry charges, and the NICS process will be transparent to dealers. But the FBI has made it clear that all other users would have to pay the tax, a price that would be passed on to retail customers. Additional delays might also apply to non-central facilities, such as county offices.

Counties will be compelled to use the same database systems as the state, or else do an inferior job of checking, and no gun sale from a dealer would be legal without including the FBI's NICS system. In other words, counties that decide to conduct their own checks would be in addition to, not instead of, the existing state and upcoming federal NICS requirements. Customers will wait while dealers make two calls, to conduct essentially the same process twice. The value of such redundancy is unclear, though the FBI will raise an estimated revenue of $1 million per week from the NICS system.

Visit our website or send us a self-addressed stamped envelope for updates on the results of this proposed new delegation of power.

APPENDIX E
LIST OF CASE

This is a list of court cases mentioned in *The Florida Gun Owner's Guide*. It is provided so any reader who wants to read the full text of the case can find it easily in a law library. Librarians can locate the cases for you from the official designations, called *citations*, provided below.

This list and the citations in this book are not all of the cases on firearms in Florida. These are only selected cases that have been chosen to illustrate how courts in the past have enforced or interpreted various sections of the laws relating to firearms. Readers should be aware that some of these cases may have been followed or reversed by later court decisions.

How to Read Case Citations

Legal citations may look like Latin to many people (and occasionally contain Latin just for effect) but they are actually quite easy to read, once you know how. Cases are named after the parties involved, with the name of the defendant first and the state department or official complainant second.

Cases are bound in sets of books called *Reports*, or sometimes *Reporters*. The first number in the citation is the volume number of the set of books.

The letters that follow (usually "So." for the Florida cases we've been looking at) are an abbreviation of the name of the set, and may reflect the region of the country where the court is located, the level of the court in the judiciary, or both. *So.* is the abbreviation for the first series of *Southern Reports*. *So.2d* refers to the second set of *Southern Reports*. Publishers periodically start publishing new sets of reports, starting at volume one again for the second (or third etc.) series, and continuing the cases from where the previous set leaves off.

The next element is the page number in the printed edition.

The number in parenthesis is the year the case was reported. This is usually the same as the year it was decided but may be the following year depending on the publishing date. The reporting process, and the decision on whether to publish a case or not—thereby affecting the official set of precedents—would make an interesting book on its own. A case can be known by different dates because the start, finish, decision and publication dates can sometimes be spread across many years. The decision date is the most key, since that is when the case begins affecting other business.

To find a case listed here ask a reference librarian where the report series is shelved. Then choose the volume number and turn to the page. What could be easier. Most cases are only a few pages long. Some read better than a good novel.

Selected List of Florida Court Cases Related to Firearms

Ammons v. State, 102 So. 642 (1924)
Bacom v. State, 317 So.2d 148 (1975)
Barnhill v. State, 48 So. 251 (1908)
Brown v. State, 94 So. 874 (1922)
Brant v. State, 349 So.2d 674 (1977)
Cleveland v. State, 673 So.2d 983 (1996)
Cockin v. State, 43 So.2d 189 (1984)
Collins v. State, 102 So. 880 (1925)
Collins v. State, 475 So.2d 968 (1985)
Crane v. Department of State, 547 So.2d 266 (1989)
Crockett v. State, 188 So. 214 (1939)
Deeb v. State, 179 So. 894 (1938)
Facion v. State, 290 So.2d 75 (1974)
Falco v. State, 407 So.2d 203 (1981)
French v. State, 279 So.2d 317 (1973)
Gaff v. State, 138 So. 48 (1931)
Gainer v. State, 327 So.2d 873 (1991)
Garner v. State, 9 So. 835 (1991)
Gonzales v. Liberty Mutual Insurance, 634 So.2d 178 (1994)
Hamilton v. State, 11 So. 523 (1892)

Harris v. State, 104 So.2d 739 (1958)
Howell v. State, 63 So. 421 (1913)
Huntley v. State, 66 So.2d 504 (1958)
Lightbourn v. State, 175 So. 857 (1937)
McCray v. State, 102 So. 831 (1925)
McCullers v. State, 206 So.2d 30 (1968)
McKinney v. State, 260 So.2d 239 (1972)
Miller v. State, 613 So.2d 530 (
Padgett v. State, 24 So. 145 (1898)
Peele v. State, 20 So.2d 120 (1944)
Pell v. State, 122 So. 110 (1929)
Peoples v. State, 287 So.2d 63 (1973)
Perkins v. State, 576 So.2d 1310 (1991)
Pinder v. State, 8 So. 837 (1891)
Pressley v. State, 395 So.2d 1175 (1981)
Price v. Gray's Guard Service, Inc. 298 So.2d 461 (1974)
Prudential Ins. Co. of America v. Marullo, 774 F.Supp. 631
Raneri v. State, 255 So.2d 291 (1971)
Reimel v. State, 532 So.2d 16 (1988)
Rinzler v. Carson, 262 So.2d 661 (1972)
Rippie v. State, 404 So.2d 160 (1981)
Roberts v. State, 425 So.2d 70 (1983)
Sanders v. State, 359 So.2d 899 (1978)
Scholl v. State, 115 So. 43 (1927)
Sherrod v. State, 484 So.2d 1279 (1986)
Skinner v. State, 450 So.2d 595 (1984)
Smith v. State, 463 So.2d 542 (1985)
    affirmed 487 So.2d 1088 (1986)
State v. Coles, 91 So. 2d 200 (1956)
State v. Smith, 376 So.2d 261 (1979)
Stewart v. State, 672 So.2d 865 (1996)
Toledo v. State, 452 So.2d 661 (1984)

About Donna Lea Hawley

Donna Lea Hawley possesses a rare combination of skills and credentials. She has a law degree and more than 20 years of legal research and practice experience, has authored 15 books, is a highly certified firearms instructor who has trained more than one thousand students, contributes regularly to national magazines, and is a competitive shooter. She found Bloomfield Press while searching for a publisher to do a book on Florida gun laws. It was a perfect match.

Donna Lea has been a firearms enthusiast since the age of nine, when she got her first BB gun as a Christmas present. At the age of 11, encouraged by her parents, she started shooting a .22 rifle. She started competitive shooting in high school where she joined the school smallbore rifle team. Since then she has competed in pistol, smallbore rifle, and is now an IPSC practical-shooting competitor.

Ms. Hawley teaches firearms safety and concealed-weapons classes through Paramount Defense Academy in Florida. She is a graduate of the Florida Dept. of Law Enforcement Firearms Instructor Course, Massad Ayoob's Lethal Force Institute, and the National Range Officer's Institute. Donna Lea holds six NRA Instructor certifications and is certified by the State of Florida as a Hunter Education Instructor. Her teaching skills have been honed as an instructor in the Dept. of Criminology at Simon Fraser University, and by teaching legal seminars on sports liability and self defense for the past 15 years.

Donna Lea Hawley holds a Master's Degree in Physical Education and uses this background in her shooting instruction. She conducts research in various aspects of shooting skills including reaction time, aspects of vision related to shooting, and the application of kinesiology to shooting positions. She has published more than 200 articles on shooting, training for physical skill development, self defense, unarmed defensive skills, legal issues and other topics.

About Alan Korwin

Alan Korwin is a professional writer and management consultant with a twenty-year track record in news, business, technical, and promotional communication. He is a founder and two-term past president of the Arizona Book Publishing Association, has won national awards for his publicity work as a member of the Society for Technical Communication, and is a past board member of the Arizona chapter of the Society of Professional Journalists.

In an executive-level strategic plan, Mr. Korwin helped American Express define its worldwide telecommunications strategy for the 1990s; he wrote the business plan which raised $5 million in venture capital and launched SkyMall; he did the publicity for Pulitzer Prize cartoonist Steve Benson's fourth book; he helped forge the largest enclave of technologists in the state, as steering committee chair for the Arizona Coalition for Computer Technologies; and he had a hand in developing ASPED, Arizona's economic strategic plan. Korwin's writing appears regularly in local and national publications, and he serves an extensive business client base. This is his ninth book.

In 1990 Mr. Korwin introduced a unique seminar entitled, *Instant Expertise—How To Find Out Practically Anything, Fast.* The four-hour course reveals the trade secrets he uses to gather any information short of espionage—and this is not about databases. He also teaches writing (How To Get Yourself Published At Last), publishing (The Secret of Self-Publishing), phone power (How to Supercharge Your Telephones) and publicity (The Secret of Free Publicity), at colleges, for businesses and privately. His talk on Constitutional issues (The Pen and The Sword, Constitutional Rights Under Attack) is a real powerhouse.

Alan Korwin is originally from New York City, where his clients included IBM, AT&T, NYNEX and others, many with real names. In 1986, finally married, he moved to the Valley of the Sun. It was a joyful and successful move.

Order these books about firearms and personal safety from
BLOOMFIELD PRESS

"It doesn't make sense to own a gun and not know the rules." This is an ongoing theme at Bloomfield Press. These books are for concerned and responsible private individuals. Know your rights and obligations. Help protect yourself and your family from firearms accidents and crime. Order your copies of these classic books today. **Wholesale orders are welcome!**

IN THE GRAVEST EXTREME
by Masaad Ayoob $9.95
Widely recognized as the definitive work on the use of deadly force. This former law enforcement officer describes what you actually face in a lethal confrontation, the criminal mindset, gun-fighting tactics, the judicial system's view on self-defense cases and more. Dispels the myths, truly excellent—a must for any armed household & especially CCW permit holders.

ARMED AND FEMALE
by Paxton Quigley $5.95
Read about the tough decisions of a former activist in the anti-gun movement, who finally chose the victor over victim psychology. Features lessons she learned through extensive study, research and personal experience. Compelling reading, packed with thought-provoking ideas and advice.

GUN-PROOF YOUR CHILDREN
by Masaad Ayoob $4.95
One of the world's leading experts on lethal force issues, this father of two shares his thoughts and very practical ideas on gun safety for kids in a classic short booklet. Includes a good primer on handguns for the novice.

SAFE NOT SORRY
by Tanya Metaksa $22.95
The chief lobbyist of the NRA explains what it takes to keep yourself safe in a violent world. Packed with statistics, sage advice and anecdotes from assault victims (including Luby's survivor Suzanna Gratia Hupp), the book features three supplements on federal, state and self-defense gun law by Alan Korwin. Hardcover, published by HarperCollins.

THAT EVERY MAN BE ARMED
by Stephen P. Halbrook, $16.95
Put to rest any questions you have about the intent behind the 2nd Amendment. With 1,300 annotations, Halbrook looks at, reports on, and quotes sheaves of actual original documents of the founding fathers. There may be confusion on this issue in America today, but as you'll see, there wasn't any back then. The title is from a quote by Patrick Henry, "The whole object is that every man be armed. Everyone who is able may have a gun." Henry's peers make similarly unambiguous remarks, removing all doubt.

THE TRUTH ABOUT SELF-PROTECTION
by Masaad Ayoob $7.95
Get the facts on every aspect of personal safety, from evasive driving to planting cactus by your windows. Lifesaving techniques will help keep you, your family and your possessions safe, prepare you for defense if it becomes necessary, and guide you in buying lethal and less-than-lethal goods, from locks to firearms.

STRESSFIRE—Gunfighting Tactics for Police
by Massad Ayoob $9.95
Heavy-duty reading for advanced students and those citizens who want the deepest understanding of lethal confrontations and how to survive in a deadly encounter. Master lethal-force specialist Ayoob pours out the experience and techniques which make him a sought-after world-class expert, in a page-turning style you won't forget. Not for the faint of heart, this book will make you think.

NO SECOND PLACE WINNER
by Bill Jordan $14.95
An absolutely unique discussion of armed response by a man who literally made it his trade. Author Jordan worked the U.S. Border Patrol of the old days, for 30 years, and lived to tell about it. In the process, he became one of the deadliest shots of modern times. In an easy and unassuming way he describes with chilling clarity what it takes to come out on top of gun battles. "Be first or be dead... there are no second place winners." Packed with his personal tips on draw-and-shoot techniques, with wonderful stop-action photos.

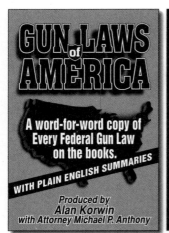

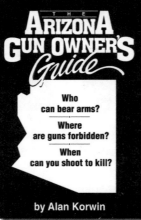

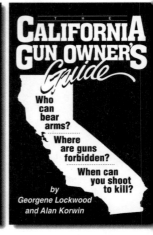

Published by

BLOOMFIELD PRESS

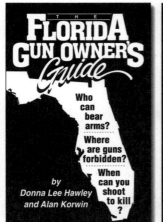

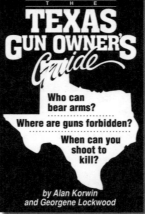

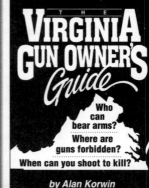